Everyman, I will go with thee,
and be thy guide

Benito Pérez Galdós

THAT BRINGAS
WOMAN

Translated and Edited by
CATHERINE JAGOE
Northern Illinois University

Consultant Editor for this Volume
MELVINA MCKENDRICK
University of Cambridge

EVERYMAN
J. M. DENT · LONDON
CHARLES E. TUTTLE
VERMONT

J. M. Dent
Orion Publishing Group
Orion House
5 Upper St Martin's Lane
London WC2H 9EA
and
Charles E. Tuttle Co. Inc.
28 South Main Street
Rutland, Vermont 05701, USA

Typeset by CentraCet Ltd, Cambridge
Printed in Great Britain by
The Guernsey Press Co. Ltd, Guernsey, C. I.

British Library Cataloguing-in-Publication Data
is available upon request.

ISBN 0 460 87636 8

CONTENTS

*For Charlotte, Liz, Vicky, Becca and Bob,
who love to read*

NOTE ON THE AUTHOR
AND TRANSLATOR

BENITO PÉREZ GALDÓS was born on 10 May 1843 in Las Palmas in the Canary Islands. At nineteen, he left the Canaries, ostensibly to study law in Madrid, but devoted himself instead to experimenting with creative writing and becoming a journalist and editor. In 1867 he travelled to Paris, where he discovered the work of Balzac. The following year, which saw the overthrow of the monarchy in Spain, he translated Dickens's *Pickwick Papers*. Inspired by his reading of the great masters of European Realism, he decided that Spain needed Realist novels of its own, and devoted the rest of his life to creating them. Galdós's writing bears witness to the tumultuous events of the 1868 revolution, the rise and fall of the First Republic, and the Restoration of the Bourbon Monarchy. He displayed amazing tenacity and productivity as a writer, publishing a total of seventy-eight novels, twenty-four plays and numerous articles and essays. He is famous for two panoramic series: the *National Episodes*, which trace Spain's history through the nineteenth century, and the *Contemporary Novels*, which centred on Madrid in his own time. His signature works date mostly from the 1880s and 1890s, including *The Disinherited* (1881), which marks his appropriation of Naturalism, after an intense encounter with Zola's work in 1878; *Torment* and *That Bringas Woman* (1884), and his masterpiece novel of adultery, *Fortunata and Jacinta* (1887).

From 1910 on, he had to dictate his work, and had become functionally blind by 1912. In that year, tragically, he was denied a nomination for the Nobel Prize for political reasons. His finances were in such a dire state that a national subscription fund was launched to help him out. He died on 4 January 1920.

CATHERINE JAGOE is Associate Professor of Spanish at Northern Illinois University. She has a PhD from Cambridge University and is the author of a book on Galdós.

CHRONOLOGY OF GALDÓS'S LIFE

Year   *Age*   *Life*

1843   Galdós born May 10

CHRONOLOGY OF HIS TIMES

Year	Literary Context	Historical Events
1843		British annex Natal and conquer Sind in India; Queen Isabel II comes to throne in Spain
1844	Dumas, *The Three Musketeers*	Creation of Spanish Civil Guard
1845		US–Mexican war
1846		Isabel II marries Francisco de Asís; Great Famine starts in Ireland
1847	Emily Brontë, *Wuthering Heights* Balzac, *Cousin Bette*	
1848		Marx and Engels, *Communist Manifesto*; Spanish Democratic Party formed; revolutionary uprisings in Europe; gold rush in California; Mormons settle in Utah; British North American colonies achieve self-government
1850	Dickens, *David Copperfield* Hawthorne, *The Scarlet Letter*	
1851		Universal Exposition, London; boom years begin in Melbourne, Australia
1852		Napoleon III declares himself Emperor of France
1853–6		Crimean War
1854		Revolution in Spain led by General O'Donnell; Boers found Republic of the Orange Free State in South Africa

Year   Age   Life

1862	19	Moves to Madrid to study law at the Central University
1865	22	Participates in student uprising in Madrid. Becomes reporter for *La Nación*. Joins Atheneum Club
1866	23	Witnesses mutiny and execution of the sergeants of the San Gil barracks
1867	24	Goes to Paris for first time and discovers Balzac. Starts writing novels
1868	25	Returns to Madrid in time to witness revolutionaries' triumphal welcome. Translates Dickens's *Pickwick Papers* from the French
1869	26	Becomes political correspondent for *Las Cortes* and begins to criticise the progress of the revolution

Year	Literary Context	Historical Events
1855		Spanish Liberal government sells Church properties
1856		Bank of Spain founded and Conservatives return to power; invention of the Bessemer process for making steel and of first synthetic fabric dyes
1857	Flaubert, *Madame Bovary*	Spain legislates mandatory attendance of primary school for first time, to little avail
1857-8		Indian Mutiny
1858		Charles Frederick Worth sets up his couture salon in Paris
1859	Darwin, *On the Origin of Species* Kingsley, *The Recollections of Geoffrey Hamlyn*	
1859-60		Spain at war with Morocco
1860	George Eliot, *The Mill on the Floss*	
1861	Dickens, *Great Expectations* Wagner, *Tristan and Isolde*	American Civil War begins
1864	Verne, *A Journey to the Centre of the Earth*	Socialists found The International in London
1865		Abolition of slavery in USA
1865-9	Tolstoy, *War and Peace*	
1867		Marx, *Capital*; Alfred Nobel invents dynamite; creation of the Dominion of Canada
1868		September Revolution in Spain; Isabel II goes into exile in France; Cuban separatist war starts
1869		Inauguration of the Suez Canal; new constitution promulgated in Spain

Year	Age	Life
1870	27	Becomes editor of *El Debate* and correspondent for *La Revista de España*. Publishes his landmark essay, 'Observations on the Contemporary Novel in Spain', and his first novella, *The Shadow*
1871	28	Publication of *The Golden Fountain Café* and *The Bold*, his first full-length novels. Father dies
1872	29	Becomes editor of *La Revista de España*
1873	30	Starts first series of *National Episodes*
1875	32	Starts second series of *National Episodes*
1876	33	*Doña Perfecta*
1877	34	*Gloria*
1878	35	Discovers Zola. *León Roch's Family*
1881	38	*The Disinherited*
1882	39	*Our Friend Manso*
1883	40	Makes first of many summer trips to England. Becomes correspondent for *La Prensa* of Buenos Aires. *Doctor Centeno* and *Marianela*
1884	41	*Torment, That Bringas Woman* and vol. 1 of *The Forbidden*
1885	42	Vol. 2 of *The Forbidden*
1886	43	Becomes Liberal member of parliament for a district in Puerto Rico that he has never visited
1887	44	*Fortunata and Jacinta* published in four volumes. Mother dies

Year	Literary Context	Historical Events
1870		Franco–Prussian war; first Riel rebellion in West Canada; Amadeo of Savoy made King of Spain
1871	George Eliot, *Middlemarch*	March–May, Paris Commune; fall of Third Empire in France, replaced by Third Republic; Great Fire of Chicago
1872		Carlist Civil War breaks out in Spain
1873		King Amadeo abdicates and First Republic proclaimed
1874	Valera, *Pepita Jiménez*	Porfirio Díaz insurrection in Mexico; General Pavía stages military coup in Spain
1875	Bizet, *Carmen*	Restoration of Bourbon Monarchy in Spain
1875–7	Tolstoy, *Anna Karenin*	
1876		Alexander Bell invents the telephone
1877		Thomas Edison makes first recording machine, a prototype of the gramophone
1878		Balkan War
1879	Ibsen, *A Doll's House*	
1879–80	Dostoyevsky, *The Brothers Karamazov*	Spanish Socialist Party formed
1880	Zola, *Nana*	
1881	James, *The Portrait of a Lady*	
1884	Twain, *The Adventures of Huckleberry Finn*	
1884–5	Clarín, *La Regenta*	
1885	Zola, *Germinal*	English found Nigeria
1885–7		Gottlieb Daimler and Karl Benz, working independently, make automobiles
1886	Pardo Bazán, *The House of Ulloa*	

Year	Age	Life
1889–90	46–7	Clandestine affair with writer Emilia Pardo Bazan. *The Unknown, Reality* and *Torquemada in the Fire*
1890–1	47–8	*Angel Guerra*
1891	48	Galdós's illegitimate daughter María born in January, to Lorenza Cobián, a peasant woman
1892	49	First play, *Reality*, performed. *Tristana*
1893	50	*Torquemada on the Cross*
1894	51	*Torquemada in Purgatory*
1895	52	*Nazarín, Halma* and *Torquemada and St Peter*
1897	54	Galdós becomes member of Spanish Royal Academy. Sues his publisher and takes on publication of his own works. *Compassion*
1898	55	Starts third series of *National Episodes*
1901	58	Performance of Galdós's play *Electra* causes anticlerical rioting
1902	59	Starts fourth series of *National Episodes*
1906	63	Suicide of Galdós's mistress Lorenza Cobián
1907	64	Elected Republican member of parliament for Madrid. Eyesight begins to fail and he hires a private secretary. Starts fifth series of *National Episodes*

Year	Literary Context	Historical Events
1890	Wilde, *The Picture of Dorian Gray*	Fall of Otto von Bismarck, Chancellor of the German Empire
1893	Tchaikovsky, Symphony no. 6 in B minor	
1895		Wilhelm Conrad Röntgen discovers X-rays; separatist war in Cuba revives
1896		Henri Becquerel discovers radioactivity; beginning of Klondike gold rush in Canada; Philippine separatist war
1897		Spanish prime minister Cánovas assassinated
1898		Spanish–American War; Spain loses Cuba, Puerto Rico and the Philippines
1899	Joplin, *Maple Leaf Rag*	
1900		Max Planck lays the groundwork for Quantum theory
1901		Death of Queen Victoria; end of Boxer rebellion in China; assassination of US President McKinley; commonwealth of Australia proclaimed
1902		US buys French rights to Panama Canal
1903		Wright brothers' first flight; Henry Ford founds the Ford Motor Company in USA
1904		Russo–Japanese War
1905	Freud, *Three Essays on the Theory of Sexuality*	Red Sunday in St Petersburg; Albert Einstein's special Theory of Relativity
1907		Dominican Republic taken over by America

Year	Age	Life
1910	67	Begins dictating novels because of increasing blindness. Becomes Co-president of the Republican–Socialist alliance; re-elected Republican member of parliament for Madrid
1912	69	Galdós sues his business manager but agrees to an out-of-court settlement. His nomination for Nobel Prize thwarted by right-wing opposition. Second cataract operation fails; now functionally blind. Publishes *Cánovas*, last of the unfinished fifth series of *National Episodes*
1914	71	National subscription fund started to help Galdós's finances but never reaches projected goal
1915	72	Last novel *The Reason of Unreason* published
1919	76	Statue of Galdós unveiled in Retiro Park, Madrid
1920	76	Dies in Madrid on 4 January. Funeral attended by huge crowds of mourners

Year	Literary Context	Historical Events
1909		Popular opposition to military campaign in Morocco sparks strikes throughout Spain and Tragic Week in Barcelona; execution of the anarchist leader Francisco Ferrer; start of Mexican Revolution
1912		Sinking of Titanic; Amundsen and Scott expeditions reach South Pole; assassination of Spanish President Canalejas
1913	Lawrence, *Sons and Lovers* Proust, *Swann's Way* Unamuno, *Del sentimiento trágico de la vida*	First boat goes through Panama Canal
1914		Outbreak of First World War
1915	Woolf, *The Voyage Out*	
1916	Joyce, *Portrait of the Artist as a Young Man*	Battle of the Somme, over a million dead. Bolsheviks stage October Revolution in Russia; Republican Easter Rising in Ireland; Margaret Sanger opens first birth control clinic in New York
1917		USA declares war on Germany
1918		End of First World War; start of influenza pandemic across Europe that kills millions
1919		Eight-hour working day in Spain legislated
1920	Wharton, *The Age of Innocence*	League of Nations begins work in Geneva; Nazi Party founded in Germany; Mahatma Gandhi leads non-violent resistance campaigns against British rule in India

INTRODUCTION

Galdós and Realism

Benito Pérez Galdós is Spain's best-kept literary secret. The greatest novelist since Cervantes, he remains inexplicably unknown to many English-speaking readers who are familiar with his European contemporaries, such as Balzac, Dickens, Zola, Flaubert, Tolstoy, Eliot and Hardy. A writer of prodigious output, Galdós produced a vast collection of novels, articles and plays. He is generally regarded as the creator of the modern Realist novel in Spain, pioneering a movement that was shortly to include other major authors such as Emilia Pardo Bazán and Leopoldo Alas (Clarín).

That Bringas Woman was written and published in 1884 as part of Galdós's panoramic series about Madrid social life, entitled the *Contemporary Novels*. Although it can be read independently, it forms a sequel to *Torment*; in *That Bringas Woman* the Bringas family move centre-stage, replacing the protagonists of the earlier novel, who have left Spain. It is a novel of adultery that is a sustained meditation on the precarious situation of the middle class in Madrid. It offers a shrewd and none-too-flattering analysis of feminine psychology and a curiously intimate portrait of a marriage, all the more so since its author never married. It is also, indirectly, a novel about the revolution in Spain. Galdós benefited from the window of opportunity for progress and innovation in education and the arts that came with the revolution of 1868, when the rigid censorship of the previous regime was revoked and Church power relaxed. He strongly supported the revolution but, as his political articles show, became disillusioned with its failure to overcome political chaos and produce a programme for real social change, a disillusionment that registers strongly both in the subject matter and ironic style of *That Bringas Woman*.

Realism, the literary movement that seeks to capture the elusive essence of character and situation via the prose description of ordinary, everyday events, speech and objects, came to Spain late. Galdós wrote his manifesto calling for a Spanish Realist novel in 1870, decades after Realism had taken hold in England and elsewhere on the continent. Yet the very lateness of its entry meant that it was a very sophisticated form of Realism that he introduced, one that questioned many of the initial, simplistic premises of its earlier practitioners, that was highly self-conscious and ironic. There was considerable resistance to Realism in Spain when Galdós began writing. It was seen as a toxic foreign import, one that was both ethically and artistically unworthy. Galdós's great achievement was to transform public and critical opinion on both counts, the moral and the aesthetic. His apparently banal choice of subject matter – daily life and conversations between family members and friends, where the main action is psychological – as well as his treatment of it, which consisted of using ordinary, colloquial language and not elevated diction, came to be valued for their brilliant powers of observation. He often dealt with 'immoral' issues such as adultery, but he succeeded in educating his reading public not to equate a moral stance on the part of the author with exemplary punitive endings for characters who sinned. His novels do all deal with moral issues, but in a far more subtle and indirect way than had previously been the custom.

The Novel as Historical Allegory

That Bringas Woman is indisputably a critique of contemporary Spanish society and history. It contains a carefully structured web of allusions to current affairs in the late 1860s. The characters as well as the temporal and spatial montage function as microcosmic doubles of national figures and events. Via the Bringas family and their entourage, Galdós undertakes a critique of the Royal Family and the circumstances that led up to the 1868 revolution, although he never mentions the larger ghostly doubles behind his characters, presumably for political as well as literary reasons, since he was writing in 1884, nine years after the restoration of the Bourbon Monarchy.[1]

That Bringas Woman is set largely in Madrid's Royal Palace, in an apartment on the second floor, above the royal household, after whose famous salons its own rooms are named. At the end of the novel, both families leave the Palace, made redundant by the revolution. Many of the characters are fictional mirrors of the Queen and her Royal Consort, Francisco de Asís. Rosalía is plump, pretty, generous, ignorant, and extravagant, as well as unfaithful to her husband, like Isabel II. She is married to a puny, unprepossessing character who physically recalls his royal namesake. Yet the parallelism between Rosalía and Isabel II is not a hermetic one. For one thing, three other female characters, Cándida, Milagros and Refugio, also evoke resonances of the Queen. Furthermore, the representation of Rosalía tends to 'outgrow her identification with the Queen',[2] and spill out (as she does out of her corset and as her materials spill out all over her sewing room) into a wider critique of middle-class Spain itself, with its social pretensions and lack of taste, its reckless overspending and its perilously low Treasury funds; its dangerous fascination with the aristocracy and its attraction to revolutionary upheaval. The Rosalía who is excited at the prospect of revolution is not simply doubling for the monarch. Her eventual lover, Manuel Pez, is explicitly presented as a likeness of the nation also: of its laziness, empty religiosity, favouritism and corruption, disguised by an attractive but superficial bonhomie.

The Hair Picture and Disorder

The novel begins with an extraordinary passage of description that anticipates all the themes in the work. Francisco's hair picture, like Charles Bovary's hat, serves as a *tour de force* of Realist technique. Indeed, Galdós may have got the idea for his opening from a detail in Flaubert's novel *Madame Bovary* (1856), in which the heroine, inflamed with schoolgirl romanticism, has a mourning picture made out of her dead mother's hair. But Francisco Bringas's memento of the Pez's daughter breaks all records for its astounding complexity. Hair pictures, which date from the early eighteenth century on, typically depicted a simple tomb or urn in the countryside, with a weeping woman on one side and a weeping willow above. Usually, only the background and parts of the picture were done in human hair.[3] The absurdly ambitious scale of Francisco Bringas's enterprise can be measured against the two tiny hair pictures in the Romantic Museum in Madrid, depicting merely a spray of pansies and an elaborate curlicue respectively. Bringas decides to do a lavish composition, using every symbol of death known to romantic iconography, all of which, as well as the background, he resolves to represent in human hair.

The cenotaph chapter lends itself to multiple interpretations. On one level, the picture functions as a Realist's parody of Romanticism, with the pastiche of the tomb of Napoleon, the Romantic hero *par excellence*, the scornful reference to Lamartine, and the ironising at the expense of sentimental excess. The fact that the picture represents a cenotaph, a monument commemorating a death, is significant, too, for it is a fitting symbol of the approaching demise of the Isabelline era.[4] The minute attention to detail in the hair picture has been read as a sign of the smallness of Bringas's character and his obsession with the trivial.[5] On yet another level, the hair picture betrays its maker's humble social origins in its ludicrously lachrymose depiction of the angel and its unwitting mix of Gothic, Plateresque, Tyrolean, Greco-Roman and oriental architectural styles, revealing that the artist aspires to a culture he does not altogether possess, just as Rosalía aspires to become a great lady by wearing the clothes of a class to which she does not belong by birth or wealth.

A cenotaph is, we should remember, a sepulchral monument that contains no body, a tomb that is not a tomb, which brings us to another layer of meaning: the appearance/reality dichotomy so apparent throughout the novel. Michael Nimetz interprets the hair picture as a symbol of the mendacious ostentation of the doomed monarchy:

> Like the Royal Palace, the cenotaph is grandiose in conception . . . But Bringas fills in the monumental outline with microscopic wisps of hair of the utmost fragility, and the total sum which he can afford to spend on its execution is a paltry twenty-eight to thirty reals. This corresponds exactly to the apparent strength and real weakness, the outward pomp and the inner poverty, of the royal household.[6]

The hair picture brings up the appearance/reality antithesis in another way, too, for its own status fluctuates repeatedly, like a trick of perspective. Is it a frame for the novel or a framed object in the novel, a finished work or one in progress? The hair picture provides a false start, since it does not give us the information we need about characters or plot; furthermore, it is presented at the beginning as finished when we learn at the end of the novel that in fact it was never completed, because Bringas's eyesight does not permit further work on the project. The 'real' start of the novel does not occur until chapter 17, and even that is not a beginning but a continuation of the previous novel, *Torment*. Thus Galdós succeeds in subtly unsettling any notion of a 'real' beginning, middle and end, a clear delineation of the boundaries of the Realist fiction, by his disturbing use of the hair picture as 'concealed flashback'.[7]

The readers' first encounter with the hair picture is disorienting and bewildering. We are at a loss, initially, to interpret the mass of details laid before us, because we are not told that the passage we are reading is a description of a hair work until the last sentence of the first chapter. Before that, the narrator slyly claims not to know what genre it is and throws out various suggestions – a woodcut, an engraving, a pencil line drawing, a pen and ink sketch, an engraving or an etching. Even when we are told what it is, the scene appears to make little sense. It seems a wild confusion of incompatible architectural styles, made out of different people's hair, a macabre object that is also funny. Ricardo Gullón links the confusing, labyrinthine description of the hair work, in which the first-time reader gets hopelessly lost, to the labyrinth of the Royal Palace, in which the narrator himself promptly gets lost in the novel's second beginning in chapter 3.[8] Although Gullón speaks of chaos and the labyrinth as if they were interchangeable, the labyrinth is not simply chaos, but *planned* chaos: the point of its design is precisely for the user to get lost. The cenotaph thus acts as a *mise-en-abîme* of the novel, precisely because it involves disorientation and loss of control.

There is an important parallel between the chaos of styles in the hair picture, crammed with incongruous objects which seem to have come to life, and the chaos of dress materials in the novel, which also seem to have a life of their own. Women's dress styles of the 1860s were at their most complicated and extravagant ever. They required combinations of materials and a degree of detail in trimmings that later came to seem hideously elaborate. The fact that Francisco Bringas is losing control of his materials prefigures the way that Rosalía will lose control of hers,[9] when the dress material she is working on metaphorically comes to life and crawls round the room. The memorable images of Rosalía's materials as alive or liquid recall those of the hair picture objects clambering over one another and battling for space, and the letters on the tomb that metamorphose into tears drooling down the marble. The aquatic imagery so lurkingly insistent in the novel relates, as Labanyi shows, to the nineteenth-century preoccupation with keeping things under control and defining safe boundaries.[10]

The chaotic mix of architectural styles and incongruous objects in the first chapter will reoccur in many different forms during the rest of the novel. Like the hair work, the Palace too is a hotchpotch of styles from different eras. The disorder of the cenotaph, full of things and styles in the wrong places and conjunctions, is followed by a succession of people out of their allotted place, both in class and patriarchal terms. Francisco Bringas's loss of control of his materials prefigures the government's loss of control of the working classes, who will spill into the Palace by the end of the novel, displacing the Queen. The concern with improper mixing of people and things extends to marriage too. The disorder of Francisco Bringas's materials is reflected in the disorder of Rosalía's materials, and *that* disorder leads to another, greater one: her decision to use adultery to finance her desire to buy expensive new dress fabrics.

Clothes and Luxury

That Bringas Woman offers an arresting exposé of one of the great preoccupations of nineteenth-century Spain: luxury. The topic is not a familiar one to Anglophone readers, but it was the watchword of Spanish social commentators from the eighteenth century on, who inveighed against aristocratic habits of conspicuous consumption, and urged the up-and-coming middle classes not to imitate them, but to cultivate the virtues of thrift and moderation instead. Writers of many different kinds described luxury as a drug or a contagious disease, a cancer eating into the moral fabric of their society.[11]

The rise of the bourgeoisie was dependent upon the transition to a consumer society based on the use of credit and investment; yet the repeated denouncements of luxury point to the fact that there was considerable residual anxiety about the shift away from an older, agrarian economy in which money was static (Milagros calls Bringas a peasant for hoarding his money instead of investing it) to an economy where capital was fluid, where large sums of money changed hands rapidly, and where debts were constantly circulating by being refinanced. This anxiety centred on women as consumers, since in the new capitalist societies, middle-class women were excluded from any role as producers and were allotted instead the role of biological and cultural reproducers and displayers of their husbands' wealth. It was bourgeois women who chose, acquired, managed and displayed the clothes, food, entertainment and furnishings that advertised their families' social standing and values. In a class which both imitated the aristocracy and sought to distinguish itself from it on moral grounds, the question of how to define proper spending became an important one. There was much criticism in the popular and domestic fiction of women who sought to imitate aristocrats.

The problem depicted in *That Bringas Woman* is that appearance is no longer a safe indicator of income and status; clothes can be used to disguise and deceive, a practice which is presented as dangerous and potentially contagious. We can detect here an ambivalence about the democratisation of the system which had so profited the middle classes: there is a kind of nostalgia for a clearer, more hierarchised world, with clearly differentiated class boundaries, the kind of world that disappeared with the demise of the feudal sumptuary laws, which decreed the kind of attire that could be worn by members of the various social classes.

Throughout the novel Rosalía's passion for clothes and finery is trivialised by the narrator, who often uses the term *trapos* (rags), a dismissiveness which contrasts oddly with the fact that this passion was important enough to motivate the writing of a novel. The disparaging masculine voice which mocks Rosalía's desire is clearly motivated by anxiety, however. For even though he would have us believe that women's love of clothes is unworthy of attention, he also presents it variously as a fetish, a drug, an intoxicant, that leads to a compulsive disease reminiscent of alcoholism. This creates a curious current of explicit negation that is undercut by imagery that presents the considerable power of Rosalía's actions.

The narrative further disseminates a deceptive notion of Rosalía's loss of control. The narrator himself declares that she 'could no longer control herself'. Yet, objectively, Rosalía's passion costs less than Francisco's: her final debt at Torquemada's is six thousand reals, whereas Bringas's bill from the eye doctor is for eight thousand reals, a third of his savings. While Bringas's behaviour is ridiculed as absurd, it is not portrayed as particularly threatening. It involves his active withdrawal from family and conjugal life, his attention utterly absorbed by the hairs he is sticking on to the glass pane bounded by an oval frame. Rosalía's passion for new dresses is portrayed as invasive, undermining the family structure and finances, even though capitalist society depended on women such as her buying the fabrics and dresses and becoming clients of the new department stores portrayed in the novel. Rosalía's financial difficulties are caused not so much by her own overspending (although this certainly compounds her problems), but by the substantial loan she agrees to make to Milagros, at interest. The problem, then, is not simply that Rosalía's spending is out of control. She is remarkably calculated in her indiscretions, although the novel's rhetoric of her being irremediably fallen might lead us to believe otherwise. The change that takes place during the novel is that Rosalía moves irrevocably out of Bringas's control. She begins to make her own financial decisions and act upon them. She discreetly uses her body as merchandise, again in a calculated way, for although clearly attracted to Pez, she does not commit adultery with him for love, but because she needs money. She is not possessed with passion, like Emma Bovary or Anna Karenin. Neither is her overspending that of a flighty, impractical child-bride such as David Copperfield's wife or Rosamond Vincy. There is a hard-headed determination about her that the narrator would have us believe is much more morally reprehensible. Perhaps it is the very fact that Rosalía is *not* out of control, that she is so clearly not sexually but financially dependent on men, that mobilises a stratum of male anxiety as well as the class questions we have already discussed.

The Characters and their Names

Galdós adopts Balzac's technique from the *Comédie Humaine* of making his characters reappear in various novels, thereby increasing our sense of them as real, autonomous beings, as we see them from different perspectives – protagonists of one novel, minor characters in another – and at different points in their lives. In *That Bringas Woman* there are a record number of reappearing personages: virtually all the peripheral characters we meet have appeared in some capacity in a previous novel.[12] Galdós further refines the technique by playing with the linear development of his characters; many of the minor figures in *That Bringas Woman* such as Cándida, Milagros, Gloria, María Egipcíaca, León Roch, and Alejandro Sánchez Botín, have appeared in earlier novels at a later point in their life. As Bly points out, these novels 'describe events that occurred *after La de Bringas* but yet they were published *before* ... [The reader] is told to think of a future condition of which he is already aware.' This technique creates a sense of shared omniscience, since, like the narrator, the reader already knows the future destiny of almost all the characters in the novel. Yet this sense of omniscience is deceptive, for we lack crucial information about a central character, the narrator himself, which he chooses not to reveal until the end. Furthermore, our 'knowledge' of Rosalía from the preceding novel *Torment* is misleading; the Rosalía of *Torment* is in some vital ways not the Rosalía of *That Bringas Woman*, since the narrative presentation is so different; thus our prior acquaintance with the character tends to bias us against her, making us unwilling to accept the more sympathetic, human side of her that is presented here via the interior monologues and free indirect style.[13]

Names in Galdós's work tend to be freighted with literary or social significance, and *That Bringas Woman* is one of the best examples of this practice. Rosalía's self-awarded aristocratic-sounding maiden name, Pipaón de la Barca, recalls that of the illustrious Spanish dramatist Pedro Calderón de la Barca. The unusual family surname, Bringas, evokes a sense of instability thanks to its similarity to the Spanish verb *brincar* (to jump or skip around), perhaps alluding to the couple's would-be upward social mobility.[14] Their children are named after the monarchs and their heir (Francisco de Asís, Isabel and Alfonso). It is no accident that little Alfonso is the child who most resembles Rosalía, for the prince of that name was to succeed his deposed mother after the Restoration as Alfonso XII.[15] Galdós's mocking nickname for Francisco Bringas, 'our dear Thiers', is an ironic reference to the great French statesman and economist whose treatise defending the vital importance of hard work and private property was the Bible of nineteenth-century economic liberalism. Thiers was a fierce defender of the French monarch before the 1848 revolution, just as Bringas staunchly defends the Spanish Queen twenty years later.[16]

We can expect Torquemada, the moneylender to whom Rosalía unwisely turns in her hour of need, to be as cruel as his namesake, the first head of the Spanish Inquisition. Milagros does indeed perform miracles, managing to come up with thousands of reals one day where she had nothing the day before. Cándida is anything but candid. Refugio's maid and companion in the demi-monde which the two of them inhabit is called Celestina, the name of a famous Spanish novel featuring a procuress. Refugio's own name ironically recalls the words of the litany to the Virgin Mary, in which she is addressed as *refugium peccatorum*, the refuge of sinners.[17] Refugio is clearly not a virgin, nor is she religious, but she is indeed the refuge of sinners, both sexually for her numerous gentlemen friends and financially for Rosalía, who comes to implore a loan after having deceived her husband.

Finally, there is the figure of Manuel Pez, whose name has both religious and animal connotations. As Juaristi points out, Manuel is the Spanish version of Christ's title, Emmanuel, a sardonic comment on his omnipotent nature in the Administration. His full name is Manuel María José, like the Holy Family, an ironic allusion since Pez's family life is far from beatific harmony. Furthermore, 'Pez' means 'fish' in Spanish, not only an ancient Christian symbol,[18] but reminiscent of the miracle of the infinite multiplication of the loaves and fishes. The notion of infinite multiplication takes us to the biological terrain: Pez comes from a clan of seemingly infinite relations. He is a cold and slippery customer, who swims easily through the teeming and turbulent social sea of Madrid. However, he is not, in the end, a big enough fish for Rosalía's extra-matrimonial plans; she resolves to throw him back in favour of the high financiers and industrial barons, sharks and whales who make a more substantial 'catch'.

Irony and Inversion

Although binary logic is characteristic of nineteenth-century thought and Galdós's writing in particular, in *That Bringas Woman* it reaches truly manic proportions. A bewildering string of characters, motifs, scenes and events are echoed later in inverted form, a technique we could call ironic reprise. The use of the younger Bringas children as cross-sex miniature portraits of their parents is symptomatic of the rampant double vision so prevalent in this novel. All this doubling could be simply the effect of one standing too close (we are forced to view the hair picture close up without a distanced perspective, and as a result are unable to make sense of it at first),[19] rather than the view of the practised eye that can pick out patterns from a distance. *That Bringas Woman* is indeed, as Bly has pointed out, a 'novel about perspective and vision',[20] a novel about how we perceive things, and its conclusion is highly modern. It radically unsettles any notion that there can be a single, proper way of seeing.

This novel is replete with opposing categories: rich and poor; light and dark; blindness and vision; appearance versus reality; high and low; Romanticism and Realism; nature and culture; chastity and promiscuity; dirt and purity; monarchy and revolution; fullness and emptiness; master and slave; hoarders and spendthrifts. Yet the striking thing is that none of these pairs is fixed or static: far from being stable, polar opposites, they are all in the process of becoming each other, of switching places. Galdós's novel is one of unsettled boundaries, of a society in flux. In a novel about upward and downward social mobility, the poor can become rich (as occurs with Refugio and later Rosalía) and the rich – such as Cándida and Milagros – are eating their way through fortunes and becoming poor. The Pauper's Feast at the Palace on Maundy Thursday, where Isabel II's entourage serve the homeless, is farcically inverted later when the supposedly wealthy Rosalía serves her 'poor relation', Refugio, as a maid, doing her hair and lacing her corset; a ritual humiliation just like the feast, except that this time Rosalía, for all her courtly airs and graces, is there to beg for money. The power dynamic between the two has been inverted, to Refugio's great satisfaction. Likewise, the master–slave dialectic characteristic of Francisco and Rosalía's relationship in the early stages of the novel and in their past life is voluntarily reversed by Bringas when he becomes blind.

The meditation on upward and downward social movement is also seen in the inversion of high and low: in nineteenth-century Madrid, the higher up one lived in a building, the poorer one was. The lower the rank of the Palace staff, the higher up they live in the Palace. As a result, there is a contradictory downward–upward dynamic set into motion, as characters like Cándida move higher up in the Palace accommodations as their fortunes dwindle. The Bringas family move up in the world and then down again after the revolution, as we see from Rosalía's complaint in the final chapter that Bringas has chosen to move the family to the highest apartment in Madrid. In similarly confusing fashion, the narrator describes his first visit to the Palace as a descent into Hades, the underworld, but then proceeds to go *up* into the darkness.

Light is often shown in the process of metamorphosing into

dark, as in the various scenes of setting suns and daylight dying
out in the palace passageways. Likewise, Francisco's eagle eyes
go temporarily blind but then recover their vision. The Monarchy is in the process of being supplanted by revolutionary
democracy, but when this finally arrives, it looks just like the
same system under another name, with new characters. Nature
and culture are not clearly demarcated as opposites, either: the
Retiro Park is a manicured form of nature, and the Palace, that
monument to civilisation, is likened to a living colossus inhabited by parasites, the 'republic' of wild pigeons who nest on its
roofs and ledges. The full can be empty, as we see in the case of
the hair picture, packed with details but void of value, just as
the tomb it depicts is an empty one. It uses all the icons of
Romanticism in a representation that is actually Realist.

Another series of parallels involves adultery and adulteration
of the pure. The clean air from the mountains that Rosalía
enjoys up on the walkway of the Palace terrace later becomes
the fetid, suffocating miasma of the city centre in August.
Likewise the beneficent effect of fresh water from the Fountain
of Health, which does Manuel Pez so much good, is later
substituted by a vision of the brackish, polluted waters of the
Manzanares in August. The cool, refreshing water from the
hoses that the cleaners spray on the streets soon settles into
grimy puddles from which stray dogs lap thirstily. The formerly
faithful wife commits adultery with Pez and embarks with no
remorse upon a profitable career as mistress of the rich and
powerful. We foresee that she will acquire as many 'gentleman
friends' as Refugio, whose artfully careless reference to Pez
shows that they have already shared one lover. Yet the disturbing thing is that this moral change is not even remotely obvious:
afterwards, Rosalía looks even more the respectable wife.

Language and the Narrator

Galdós's writing is famous for the value it assigns to the notion
of voice: it is dominated by the spoken word of the day, in its
multiple varieties and registers. One of the hallmarks of his
achievement as a novelist was the creation of much more
realistic-sounding dialogue than was previously considered per-
missible or desirable; his championing of linguistic realism,
though it met with resistance at first, ultimately succeeded in
changing the course of literary history. It is not just that there is

a great deal of authentic-sounding dialogue in *That Bringas Woman*; the author has carefully created distinctively different voices for his characters, and their speech occupies a disproportionately large amount of the novel in one form or another. As well as novelistic dialogue, there is also dramatic dialogue (with stage directions),[21] reported speech, interior monologue, and a great deal of free indirect style, in which the narrator reproduces the character's voice directly, without framing it with an announcement to that effect.

That Bringas Woman deploys the Realist technique of eschewing moral judgements on the part of the narrator, but in a comically distorted way, for the narrator is far from being either invisible or rigorously objective, an ideal to which much earlier Realist writing aspired. He is a shadowy, sardonic presence whose pronouncements are always either questionable or tongue-in-cheek. The aim is to simulate a real-life encounter; there are no authoritative statements meted out by the narrator, so readers must make their own possibly faulty assessments of the characters based on their speech, appearance and behaviour. The narrator's frequent intrusions to remark on the characters cannot be taken at face value. He often claims to believe only the best of the characters, to take them at their own word, while mercilessly showing them to us at their worst. He too is part of what we must assess: his behaviour shows that there is no such thing as a stable viewpoint, that the vision of the Realist novel as a simple mirror of life is an illusion, and underlines the fact that 'all knowledge is intersubjective.'[22]

Nowhere is this intersubjectivity clearer than at the points where the narrator's cultured, courtly voice becomes 'infected' with the epithets and verbal tics of his own characters,[23] as when he keeps using Rosalía's secret insults for her husband or referring to the 'so-called revolution', a disparaging term of Francisco's. This is not exactly free indirect style, since it is still discernibly the narrator speaking, but with interference from a lower frequency. The narrator is such a protean character, whose discourse is so easily coloured by other people's speech habits, that his own identity and allegiances are an enigma. Yet solving this riddle is a vital part of the novel's message about current events. From the beginning the narrator addresses the reader with suspiciously jocular familiarity, dispensing with proper introductions as if he were already a close friend. Just as he presented the hair picture in such a way as to make it initially incomprehensible, he places himself too close for the reader to be able to make out who he is, although he does drop hints and clues, apparently inadvertently. He is a friend of Manuel Pez, but seems to be the more influential of the two because Pez is more indebted to him than vice versa. He is duplicitous, because despite his friendship with Pez and the Bringas family, he despises them. He is corrupt, because he uses bribery and personal recommendations to thwart the legal system. He goes to Cándida's tea-parties and uses hypocrisy as skilfully as all the rest. He becomes curator of the Palace after the revolution, even though he is clearly as sceptical about democracy as he was about the Monarchy; the thank-you present he gives to the monarchist Bringas for favours received takes place on 4 October, *after* the revolution and the exile of the Queen. Clearly the narrator assiduously cultivates political allies on both sides of the fence at all times, so that he can get the best out of every situation.

The narrator's ironic exposé of Madrid life in the 1860s seems to establish a safe distance between himself and the complicit reader on the one hand, and the characters whose faults he details on the other. This arrangement is, however, shown to be a mere illusion, a trick of perception, at the end of the novel, when we realise that he has been concealing the fact that he has had an affair with Rosalía during the course of the novel and that he too was manoeuvring, just like Pez, for a position in the Revolutionary Junta. His mordant irony is thus ultimately self-inclusive. He who lampooned Pez's participation in the old-boy network has participated himself; he who feigned such moral concern about Rosalía's deceitfulness is himself duplicitous; he who mercilessly exposed Rosalía's selling of herself to Pez – and even laughed about it with him – as himself had an affair with her. The narrator finally lets us see him as a double of the cynical, unsinkable Pez. The novel thus serves as a warning against inveighing too complacently against the moral failings of others and the plight of Spain, and a *post-factum* analysis of why the revolution failed: because it was taken over from the start by amoral opportunists. Unlike Flaubert, Tolstoy and Alas, the other great novelists of adultery of his day, Galdós's view of the subject and its consequences for the body politic is both hard-headed and humorous rather than tragic. Sex, money and vanity, not souls, are at stake here. Rosalía emerges from her 'fall' triumphant: majestic and serene, although sadder and wiser, a veteran of the survival game like all the other inhabitants of her, and our, world.

References

1 Peter Bly, *Galdós's Novel of the Historical Imagination, A Study of the Contemporary Novels* (Liverpool: Francis Cairns, 1983), p. 63.

2 *Ibid.*, p. 65.

3 Philippe Ariès, *The Hour of Our Death*, trans. Helen Weaver (New York: Random House, 1981), p. 461.

4 Gerald Gillespie, 'Reality and Fiction in the Novels of Galdós', *Anales Galdosianos*, Vol. 1 (1966), p. 29.

5 Arthur Ramírez, 'The Heraldic Emblematic Image in Galdós' *La de Bringas*', *Revista de Estudios Hispánicos*, Vol. 14.1 (1980), pp. 67–8.

6 Michael Nimetz, *Humor in Galdós* (New Haven: Yale University Press, 1968), pp. 62–3.

7 Jo Labanyi, 'The Problem of Framing in *La de Bringas*', *Anales Galdósianos*, Vol. 25 (1990), pp. 26–7; see also Hazel Gold on the opening chapter and its significance for the novel in 'Narrative Beginnings in *La de Bringas*', *The Reframing of Realism: Galdós and the Discourses of the Nineteenth-Century Spanish Novel* (Durham and London: Duke University Press, 1993).

8 Ricardo Gullón, *Técnicas de Galdós* (Madrid: Taurus, 1970, repr. 1980), pp. 113–14.

9 Ramírez, p. 67.

10 See also Peter Bly, 'Lo acuático en *La de Bringas*', *Revista de Estudios Hispánicos*, Vol. 20.1 (1986), pp. 45–57.

11 See chapter 3 of Aldaraca's book, extracted later, and pp. 85–95 of Catherine Jagoe, *Ambiguous Angels: Gender in the Novels of Galdós* (Berkeley and London: University of California Press, 1994), for a discussion of luxury.

12 Peter Bly, 'The Use of Distance in Galdós's *La de Bringas*', *Modern Language Review*, Vol. 69 (1974), p. 96.

13 Linda Willem, 'The Narrative Voice Presentation of Rosalía Bringas in Two Galdosian Novels', *Crítica Hispánica*, Vol. 12.1–2 (1990), pp. 75–87.

14 Pedro Ortiz Armengol, 'Tres apuntes hacia temas de *Fortunata y Jacinta*', *Letras de Deusto*, Vol. 4.8 (1974), pp. 241–51, shows that Bringas was the name of a well-to do merchant family in early nineteenth-century Madrid.

15 Jon Juaristi, 'Ironía, picaresca y parodia en *La de Bringas*', *Nueva Revista de Filología Hispánica*, Vol. 38.1 (1990), p. 292.

16 J. E. Varey, 'Francisco Bringas: *Nuestro buen Thiers*', *Anales Galdosianos*, Vol. 1 (1966), p. 63–9.

17 *Juaristi*, pp. 288–9.

18 *Ibid.*, p. 287. 'Pez' also has sexual connotations.

19 Hazel Gold says the effect is literally to make us cross-eyed, as 'the narrator's lens zooms in for a strabismic close-up', *The Reframing of Realism*, p. 34.

20 Peter Bly, *Pérez Galdós: La de Bringas* (London: Grant and Cutler, 1981), p. 29.

21 It is worth noting that Galdós was so fascinated by voice that several of his novels, such as *The Unknown*, are written entirely in dialogue.

22 Paul Julian Smith, *The Body Hispanic: Gender and Sexuality in Spanish and Spanish American Literature* (Oxford: Clarendon Press, 1992), p. 82.

23 Robert H. Russell, 'La voz narrativa en *La de Bringas*', *Anales Galdosianos*, Vol. 21 (1986), p. 136.

NOTE ON THE TRANSLATION

My translation is based on the first Spanish edition of 1884, published in Madrid by *La Guirnalda*, one of the journals Galdós worked for. Subsequent editions of the novel have introduced only minor variants, mainly in spelling and punctuation.

One of the peculiarities of Galdós's style is his heavy use of ellipsis points, amongst other things as a signal that the narrative has slipped into free indirect style, that is, it has become the thoughts or words of a particular character. I have maintained the ellipsis points to signal these changes of voice. As a further indication to the reader of the switch to free indirect style, I have followed Jo Labanyi's practice in her English translation of *Nazarín* of using contracted forms of speech, normally reserved for dialogue, such as 'hadn't' or 'don't', on such occasions.

Galdós was also a great devotee of synonyms, particularly as regards the names of his female characters. He uses the feminine article 'la' followed by an adjective or one of the character's names, a practice which has great linguistic flexibility and expressiveness in Spanish, conveying sympathy, familiarity, irony and scorn by turns. This flexibility is encapsulated in the Spanish title of the novel, *La de Bringas*, the single most difficult phrase to translate in the book, which, if it had an English equivalent, would lie somewhere between 'Mrs Bringas' and 'Bringas's old lady'. I opted for *That Bringas Woman*, in order to convey the slightly familiar and even derogatory tinge of the Spanish expression. In the text, I have tended to use simply *Rosalía* where the heroine's names are used, though I follow the Spanish when it uses an adjective or noun, such as the poor woman, the lady. I have Anglicised Spanish forms of address such as 'don', because I believe the social connotations of respect and affection are largely lost on a non-Spanish speaker. I have used, for example, either Mr Bringas or Francisco, depending on who was addressing him. However, I have kept the Romance-language aristocratic titles such as Marquesa and Condesa in

Spanish, partly because they reflect ranks that were not native to the English aristocracy.

I have also standardised some of the numerous units of currency into reals (the form mainly used in the novel) to avoid excessive footnoting of the respective amounts involved, since there is a veritable labyrinth of different units of currency in the original novel.

The most elusive thing for a translator of Galdós to capture is the particular flavour of his writing: the extraordinary panache, lightness, versatility, and wry ironic humour lurking just below the surface, and in particular, the ease with which he slips in between highly colloquial forms and rhythms of speech, and elegant, formal prose, often in the space of a few words. Galdós himself was, we should remember, criticised for his use of non-literary language and subjects in his quest to create a Spanish Realist movement. If the text reads like an amalgam of the slangy and the erudite, it is in part because this is just what the original does.

A further challenge that confronts the translator of any non-contemporary text is that it is not only geographically and culturally different, but that it belongs to another time period. This presents an intriguing series of linguistic choices. For a nineteenth-century reader, Galdós's colloquiality and slang would have sounded highly contemporary, thus one would be quite justified in producing a modernising translation. However, for a twentieth-century Spanish reader of Galdós, the text is a mixture of the colloquial and the quaintly archaic, with the latter demanding a consciously archaising translation. I have opted for a compromise approach. While I favour the modernising translation strategy, on the grounds that this simulates the effects that Galdós's work had on the readers of his day, I realise that highly contemporary slang can have an alienating effect on readers, because it dislocates the text too brutally from its time frame. Therefore, I have tried to use terms that are neither completely dated nor exclusively modern, ones that, while still in general use today, would not have been unrecognisable in the late nineteenth century. I have made exceptions to this rule wherever the thing referred to is something that existed in the 1860s but no longer does so today; for example, I use nineteenth-century terms to refer to the garments discussed by Rosalía and her women friends.

My thanks go to Penelope Ruddock and Rhian Tritton of the

Museum of Costume and Fashion Research Centre in Bath, who so generously pointed me through the maze of terms for nineteenth-century fabrics and fashions in the novel; to Victoria Soto Cabas, Professor of Art History at the Universidad Nacional de Educación a Distancia for her help with the art and architecture terms; to Concha Herrera for taking me round the upper floors of the Royal Palace; to my colleagues in Spain and America, Paco Tablas, Tino Borondo, José Ignacio del Barrio Barrero, Paco Caudet, Rodolfo Cardona, Pablo Domínguez González, Carmen Rosa Díaz Mallado, Carmen Pereira Muro, Elisa Martí, Mario Santana and Rafael Reig, for their help with linguistic queries; and to Professor Peter Bly for his careful reading of the manuscript.

THAT BRINGAS WOMAN

CHAPTER I

It was . . . how shall I put it? . . . an elegant and highly ornate funereal artefact of great architectural daring and grandiose design. Some parts of it were done in the austere, straight lines of the Vignola school,* while others were soaring, undulating and ethereal in the Gothic mode, with lurking touches of the Plateresque,* topped off with intricate cresting reminiscent of the Tyrolean style so popular on those oriental pavilions you see in the parks these days. It boasted a pyramidal staircase, Greco-Roman plinths, buttresses, pointed arches, pinnacles, gargoyles and canopies. There was a profusion of torches, urns, bats, amphorae, owls, wreaths of everlastings, winged waterclocks, scythes, palm fronds, coiled serpents and other symbols of death and life eternal on all sides. These objects were clambering all over one another as if they were battling amongst themselves for every available inch of space. In the middle of the mausoleum, a large and slightly tubby angel was leaning over a tombstone in a doleful and afflicted pose, covering his eyes with his hand as if embarrassed by his tears; which fact would seem to indicate that he was of the masculine variety. This young gentleman had a wing and a half full of tiny, curly feathers, which swept over his behind with swooning nobility, and his ladylike feet were shod with boots, buskins* or espadrilles; for there was a little of everything in that supremely elegant rendition of angelic footwear. Tossed over his head was a kind of garland of ribbons, which ended up wound round his right arm. Although at first glance one might have assumed he was groaning at the discomfort of being laden with so many things – wings, flowers, knick-knacks and feathers, not to mention a small hourglass – it soon became clear that the reason for his dejection was the painful memory of the virginal creatures who lay entombed in the sarcophagus. Their names were disconsolately broadcast by various mournful letters, from whose nether regions dripped large tears which appeared to dribble down the marble like slavers of drool. This behaviour on the part of the letters was designed to add to the overall melancholy effect.

But the best thing of all was perhaps the weeping willow, that sentimental shrub which acquired its name in antiquity and which has played a more or less criminal role in every elegy that has been committed since Rhetoric came into the world. The willow's trunk curved over the cenotaph, while from its high sparse branches hung a shower of faint, drooping, moribund leaves. One felt inclined to give it a good dose of smelling salts to make it wake up and snap out of its poetic swoon. The weeping willow was inevitable at the time, since no one had yet seen fit to take an axe to the Romantics' favourite trees. The ground was scattered with attractive plants and flowers growing proudly on stalks of various lengths. There were daisies, pansies, passionflowers, sunflowers, lilies and huge tulips, all with their heads respectfully bowed in sign of mourning. The background or perspective was made up of a procession of other, smaller weeping willows, sobbing their way off into the distance. Further off were gentle curves of mountains, which dipped and fell as if drunk; then there was a bit of sea, another bit of river, the vague outline of a city with Gothic towers and battlements; and up in the space designated for the sky, a disc that was supposed to be the moon, judging from the silver rays that glinted on the water and the mountains.

The colour of this beautiful work of art was chestnut, black and blond. The shading from dark to light gave an illusion of aerial perspective. It was enclosed in an oval frame, about sixteen inches across, and it looked less like a charcoal sketch than a drawing in which everything was expressed by lines and dots. Was it an engraving on a steel plate, an etching, a woodcut, or a drawing painstakingly executed with the point of a hard pencil or in pen and Indian ink? . . . Look at how meticulously, conscientiously and decisively it has been done. You could count the weeping willow's leaves one by one. The artist sought to create the overall effect by means of an accumulation of details, an autodidact copying Nature; and in order to make the foliage, he had the blessed patience to fill in all the miniscule leaves one after another. Some of them were so minute, you needed a microscope to see them. The effects of light and shade on the tomb were achieved by small patches of finely drawn lines that formed combs and crosshatching which were darker or lighter according to the varying density used. In the figure of our friend the angel, there were shades so light they consisted of a mist of tiny dots. It looked as if a drizzle of sand had fallen on to a white surface. The dots imitated a mezzotint, getting closer together on the dark bits and further apart and disappearing on the light ones, giving the illusion of depth by their careful spacing and distribution ... Anyway, this cenotaph I have been describing was a hair picture or a picture made of hair, an art form that enjoyed somewhat of a vogue for a while, and its creator, Francisco Bringas, demonstrated in its execution a monkish precision, sure hands and an eye so sharp it was, to put it mildly, astonishing.

CHAPTER 2

Our dear Thiers* was planning to use this exquisite gift to pay off various debts of gratitude to his distinguished friend Manuel María José del Pez. In March of that year (1868), this thoughtful man, a bureaucrat, had provided the Bringas family with fresh evidence of his generosity. Rather than wait for Paquito* to get his degree in several branches of Law, he had come up with a nice little job for him in the Treasury at five thousand reals* a year, not a bad start in government work for someone who had barely turned sixteen. The best thing about his landing the job was that the boy, who was still wet round the ears, had so much to do what with going to lectures at the University and reading up furiously on the Philosophy of History and International Law, that he only showed up at the office once a month to collect the four hundred and sixteen or so reals which we were kind enough to present him for the pleasure of it.

Even though Rosalía Bringas had got it into her conceited head that the letter of appointment was not a favour but merely evidence that Spain was doing its duty by its talented young men, she was extremely grateful to Pez for having been so diligent in making the nation see and fulfil that duty. Francisco, who was much more fervently grateful, was at a loss to find a means of expression that measured up to the intensity of his emotion. A gift, if it were to reflect the size of the favour, was out of the question, given the state of the family finances. The poor man had to come up with something wonderful, original and valuable which would not cost him any money, something which would spring out of his fertile head and take on life and shape under his creative artist's hands. The good Lord in his providence arranged things according to my friend's noble wishes. The year before, He had taken the Pez's oldest daughter, a charming maiden of fifteen, to grace His Heaven. Her grieving mother had kept Juanita's beautiful hair, and was looking for someone with the skill to make one of those commemorative ornamental works that you only see nowadays fading dustily away in the windows of old-fashioned hairdressers or in the odd niche in a graveyard. What Mrs Pez wanted was ... like turning lyrical prose into poetry. No doubt she did not find those thick locks, which were still slightly fragrant as if part of the poor girl's soul lingered on in them, to be eloquent enough in themselves. She wanted them to be pretty and to speak the same language as hackneyed verses, stucco, artificial flowers, gilt paint and easy Nocturnes for the piano. When Bringas found out about this hankering of Carolina's, he cried eureka from the very depths of his soul. He would be the poet.

'Carolina, allow me, allow me ...' he stammered, struggling to control the artistic fever that was rising in his soul.

'You're right ... You could do it, you know how to do such a lot of things. You're so clever.'

'What colour is the hair?'

'I can show you right now,' announced the matron, in an emotional voice, as she opened a little tin once used to keep sweets in, which was now the repository of poignant memories wrapped in pink and blue. 'Look at this braid. It's such a beautiful shade of chestnut.'

'Oh, yes, it's magnificent!' sighed Bringas, trembling for joy. 'But we would need some blond.'

'Blond? ... I've got all sorts of colours. Look at these curls; they belonged to my poor little Arturo. He died when he was three.'

'What a marvellous shade. It's pure gold ... and what's that pale blond?'

'Oh, that's Joaquín's hair. We had to cut it all off when he was ten. Oh, that was such a shame! He used to be pretty as a picture. It was agony to have to take the scissors to that lovely head of his ... but the doctor wouldn't hear of not cutting it. Joaquín was getting over the typhoid fever and his face was so skinny you could hardly see it in among that dazzling hair.'

'All right, then; we've got chestnut and two shades of blond.
A bit of black would come in handy for contrast.'

'We can use Rosa's hair. Bring me one of your hairpieces, love.'

Francisco, who was by now ecstatic and not just enthusiastic,
took the switch of hair.

'Now then,' he said, rather breathlessly, 'listen, Carolina ...
I've got an idea ... I can just see it now. It's a funeral monument
in a cemetery, with weeping willows and lots of flowers ... It's
night time.'

'Night time?'

'I mean, if the scenery in the background is going to come
over as melancholic, it needs to be sort of darkish ... There'll
be water, way, way off in the distance, all peeaceful and caaalm
like the surface of a looking glass ... Know what I mean?'

'What was all that about water and glass?'

'A lake, Carolina, a sort of bay. Just think: the branches of
the weeping willows will be hanging out like this ... as if they
were dripping. In between the leaves you can see the face of the
moon casting its pale rays over the mountaintops, and there's
the faintest ripple ... get the picture? ... a ripple on the
surface ...'

'Oh yes ... on the water. I'm with you now. The things you
come up with!'

'All right; but to get that nice effect, I would need to get my
hands on some white hair somehow.'

'Lord! White hair! Forgive me for laughing, but that's easy
enough to come by in this house. Here you go, Francisco. I just
wish I didn't have so much of those moonbeams you need. If I
give you this hairpiece (*unpinning a long, thick one from her
own head*), you'll have more than you'll know what to do with.'

Bringas took the white tresses and pressed them to his heart
along with all the others, in a fit of artistic emotion. Bliss! He
had two shades of gold, some clean, shiny silver, some ebony
and that romantic sienna brown which was to be the dominant
shade.

'I will ask one thing of you,' said Carolina, courteously
disguising her mistrust. 'Never to use hair that doesn't belong to
us. The whole thing must be done in the family hair.'

'For Heaven's sake, Carolina! Whatever makes you think I'd
use adulterous material?'

'No ... no, I didn't mean ... It's just that artists tend to get
carried away by inspiration and (*laughing*) then they lose all

notion of morality, and maybe in order to get a particular effect . . .'

'Carolina!'

Our good friend left the house in a feverish, trembly state. He was in the epileptic throes of artistic gestation. The work which had formed so recently in his mind was announcing, by the stirrings deep down inside him, that it was a living thing, growing forcefully, pressing on the walls of his brain and stimulating his nerve endings, which sent unfathomable instructions that made his breathing catch, his skin itch, and his limbs twitch, filling him with impatience and anxiety and a whole host of other feelings I shall not go into. At the same time, he savoured the image of the work-to-be in his imagination, thinking of it delivered whole and quivering and complete, in the shape of the mould in which it was cast. And then again, he would see it being born bit by bit, first one part coming out, then another, until the whole thing emerged into the light. My morbid idealist would see the cenotaph with its jumble of architectural styles, the sniffly angel, the woebegone willow with its drooping branches, like slobber dribbling down from the sky, flowers adorning the ground everywhere, and the views into the distance all full of lakish and lunar lugubriousness . . . Certain notions about the budget of the work tended to come flickering into the artist's brain like will-o'-the-wisps (the natural accompaniment to such a funereal subject) and interrupt this lovely vision of the unborn work. Bringas turned them over in his mind, paying them the attention of a practical man who does not ignore the periodic itch of creative genius. He uttered the following words as he added things up in his head:

CHAPTER 3

'Shellac varnish: two and a half reals. At most I might spend five reals on it . . . A pair of florists' tweezers, the ones I've got are too big: three reals. A sheet of nice clean glass, one and a half reals. Four dozen pistils, although I might be able to make them with hair, I'll have a go: two and a half reals. Altogether that's fifteen reals. Then there's the most expensive part, the piece of convex glass and the frame; but I'll take the one off that tapestry dog my cousin Josefa gave me and touch it up with gilt paint. What with the paint, the convex glass, a hook and some left over for miscellaneous expenses ... it should come out to twenty-eight or thirty reals.'

The next day, which was a Sunday, he set to work. Since he did not care for any of the drawings he had of funeral monuments, he decided to do his own; but since he was not gifted with invention, he used bits of various different works in order to create the perfectly assembled product that I have already described to you. The willow came from Napoleon's *Tomb on Saint Helena*,* the angel with the quivering lip from the monument they built at El Escorial* for the funeral of one of Ferdinand VII's wives, and the background from a print in some revoltingly sickly book imitating Lamartine.* The flowers he culled from a garden in an illustrated tome called the *Language of Flowers*, which belonged to Cándida.

The artist spent about half a week on this initial phase, and when the drawing was ready he was so pleased with it that, behind a shield of false modesty, he privately gave himself a hearty pat on the back. 'It's come out just right,' said Rosalía Pipaón,* full of intelligent enthusiasm. 'You can just see the water, all smooth, and the moonbeams sort of playing on it.'

Bringas stuck his drawing to a board, and put the sheet of glass over it, adjusting it and fixing it so it would not move. Once that was done, the rest was just skill, patience and neatness. It consisted of sticking hairs on the glass above the lines of the drawing beneath, a really hairsplitting task, given how difficult it is to work with something as fine and slippery as human locks. Doing the main outline was not so bad; but when he had to represent shadows, using a series of finer strokes, the artist had to use sets of hairs trimmed to exactly the right size, which he would stick carefully on with heated varnish to get the effect of the marks of an engraver's burin on steel or boxwood. For the very delicate shades, Bringas had refined the technique to such an extremely subtle degree that he was working on a microscopic level. He was an innovator. No capillary artist* had ever worked out how to make dots with hair, chopping it very fine with scissors to get minuscule pieces the size of molecules, and then sticking these dots on one after another, each one in a slightly different place, so that they would look like an engraver's marks. For this, he used tiny paintbrushes, and even birds' feathers moistened to a point with saliva; and once he had cut up the hair into tiny pieces on a piece of glass, he would put each dot in its place, which he would have prepared beforehand with varnish. The mixture of shades heightened the complicated subtlety of the picture, for in order to achieve the desired effect, he needed to put some chestnut here, some black there, some blond over there, gold for the angel's hair, and silver for whatever was subject to the moon's rays. But the blessed man came out triumphant every time. His hands never seemed to touch the material he was working with; his eyes were as sharp as can be, and his fingertips must have been like the gentlest breeze that caresses the flowers without damaging them. What a man! He could have made a rosary from grains of sand, had he felt so inclined, or a model of Toledo cathedral in a hazelnut shell.

He spent the whole of March on the cenotaph and the willow, making its leaves come out one by one, and by mid April the angel had arms and a head. Everybody who saw this marvel was struck by its beauty and originality, and told Francisco what a superb artist he was. They all said that if one of those foreign types saw it, maybe one of those filthy rich Englishmen who come over to Spain to buy stuff, they would pay the earth for it and take it back to countries where they appreciate works of art. Bringas's studio had a huge bay window that looked out over the Campo del Moro . . .*

For the family lived in the Palace, in one of the apartments on the second floor that house the Royal Family's staff.

I was so taken up with the hair picture I forgot to mention that in February 1868 Francisco was made senior clerk in the Royal Heritage offices, which came with a salary of thirty thousand reals a year, as well as a number of other perks associated with living at court, such as free housing, a doctor, a pharmacy, water, firewood and so on. This sinecure represented the dream of a lifetime, and Thiers would not have swapped his lofty, safe and prestigious job for the throne of Primate of all Spain. The only thing spoiling his happiness was all the talk going on that dreadful year of '68 about whether there would or would not be tremendous upheavals, and the fear that what they were calling a revolution might finally break out. Even though the idea of doing away with the Monarchy always sounded absurd to him, as if they were talking about the planets getting out of phase, every time he found himself in a café or a discussion with friends where they predicted trouble ahead, announcing that *this was it* or commenting darkly on how bad things were looking for the government and the Queen, he would give a shiver and feel his heart shrink to the size of an acorn.

Francisco had to go up the one hundred and twenty-four steps of the Ladies' staircase to get to the second floor of the Palace from the central courtyard. The second and third floors make up a city in their own right, perched above the magnificent ceilings of the royal residence. This city, where the aristocracy, the middle and the working class intermingle peacefully, is a true republic which the monarchs wear as a crown. It boasts specimens of every class of person entangled in its vast domains. The first time that Manuel Pez and I went to visit Bringas in his new home, we got totally lost in that maze, neither of us having been there before in our lives. When we entered the outer circle, via the Ladies' stairway, a cerberus with a tricorned hat* checked our credentials and then gave us directions to our friend's house. 'Take the first on the left, then bear to the right ... Go up the stairs. Then you have to go down again ... It's number sixty-seven.'

CHAPTER 4

Famous last words! ... We set off down the red tiled corridor, which was so large it was more like a street or an alleyway, thanks to the gas lighting in places and all the turns and bends. From time to time we would come across open spaces that were just like small squares, full of sunlight, which came in through big openings on to the courtyard. The daylight reflected off the white walls and advanced into the passageways, alleyways, tunnels or whatever you want to call them, where it got lost and started to falter, until it died away completely at the sight of the reddish fans of gaslight flickering inside their sooty glass cylinders crowned by brass hoods.

All around us were panelled doors, some freshly painted, others discoloured and wormeaten, each of them numbered; but nowhere could we find the figure we were looking for. On one there was a luxurious piece of silken cord, taken from one of the Palace tapestries; on another a fraying rope end. Some of the homes signalled cleanliness and order, others disorder and hardship, and the bits of mat or carpeting that we glimpsed beneath the doors also told us something about the particular conditions of the lodgings within. We came across empty homes, with cobwebby doors, rusty bars, and the chill breath of abandoned rooms issuing forth through holes in the wall covered with fraying wire. Some of the parts we walked through seemed to be deserted, and the uneven roof arching over our heads sent back our footsteps with a melancholy echo. We climbed one staircase, went down another, and then, if my memory serves me right, went up another one, since we were determined to find the wretched number by ourselves; rather than ask a passer-by, we preferred the pleasurable task of exploring those mysterious places on our own. We were not too worried about getting lost, because we were already anticipating the satisfaction of finding our destination without anyone's help, by virtue of our own topographical instincts. The labyrinth appealed to us, drawing us on and on for ever; we kept going round more corners, which took us from sunlit parts to places where there was only gaslight. From time to time, a large window opening on to the terrace would provide help in our bafflement, since we could take our bearings from the chapel dome and work out where we really were.

'You can't come in here without a map and a compass,' said Pez impatiently. 'This must be the south wing. Look at the design of the roof over the Column Room and the staircase . . . What massive pieces!'

He was right: great big pyramidal blocks covered in lead sheeting marked the spot where Bayeu's angels* were performing their acrobatics across the ceilings below.

We kept on walking endlessly, but every now and then we would come to a dead end, illuminated by skylights in the roof, and we would have to retrace our steps, looking for a way out. The Royal Palace looks so perfectly sturdy and respectable from the outside that you would never suspect what a chaotic warren is built into its upper floors. For a whole century, people have been making endless haphazard alterations to the original building, putting up walls here, knocking them down there, blocking up stairs, expanding some rooms at the expense of others, extending some apartments into the passageway and putting thoroughfares through others, knocking holes in walls in some places and filling them up elsewhere. There are staircases that start and never finish; entryways and squares that bear traces of whitewashed ceilings which once belonged to the rooms of someone's house. There are dovecotes where there used to be drawing rooms, and rooms that once used to be elegant stairwells. Every so often, you come across spiral staircases that go nowhere, doors that have been bricked up, and gaps fenced across with wire, through which you can see nothing but emptiness, dust and gloom.

We came to one place where Pez said: 'This is a working-class neighbourhood.' We saw half a dozen little boys playing soldiers, wearing paper caps, swords and bamboo rifles. Further on, in an open space lit up by a huge barred window, we had to bend over to avoid the lines of clothing hanging out to dry. The walls were covered with caricatures and lewd scrawls. Many of the doors of the homes were open, and we could see pots and pans steaming on the hob and kitchen dressers decorated with paper borders. There were women washing clothes in kitchen sinks; others were doing their hair in the doorway, that is to say in the middle of the street.

'Are you lost?' asked a woman holding a chubby baby boy attired in yellow flannels.

'We're looking for Mr Francisco Bringas's house.'

'The Bringas's? . . . I know where that is,' said an old lady sitting next to an iron railing. 'It's quite close. You just have to go down the first spiral staircase and it's just off to the side . . . Bringas – he's the sacristan of the chapel, isn't he?'

'No, he certainly is not. We're looking for the senior clerk in the Royal Heritage offices.'

'Oh, that must be downstairs on the terrace. Do you know how to get to the pump?'

'No.'

'Do you know the Cáceres stairway?'

'No.'

'Do you know the chapel?'

'We don't know where anything is.'

'What about the chapel choir? And the dovecotes?'

All in all, we were completely clueless about the design of that labyrinthine city made up of cubbyholes, recesses and surprises, an architectural whim that thumbed its nose at symmetry. But, in our ignorance, we turned down the boy who offered to be our guide.

'We're in the Plaza de Oriente* wing, on the opposite side to where our friend lives,' said Pez, with the geographical airs of a Jules Verne character. 'We need to get over to the West wing; we can take our bearings from the chapel dome and the rooftops over the stairway. Once we've succeeded in taking the West, we'd have to be idiots if we couldn't find Bringas's house. And I'm not coming back here without a good map, a compass . . . and marching rations.'

Before setting out on the second stage of our journey, we took a look through the window at the lovely view of the Plaza de Oriente and the part of Madrid you can see around it, with over fifty domes, steeples and belfries. Philip IV's horse* looked like a toy, the Royal theatre a shack, and the topmost cornice of the Palace a wide bridge over a precipice, where someone not given to vertigo could run around quite happily. Below us, the pigeons were nesting; we could see them launching off into the great abyss of the plaza in pairs and in flocks and swooping swiftly back up again to perch on the ledges and mouldings of the pillars. Their cooing seemed as integral to the building as its very stones. The myriad hollows of that man-made mountain are inhabited by a republic of wild pigeons, who occupy the Palace with undisputed monarchic powers. They are the parasites that live in the folds of skin on the giant's body. It is well known that they could not care less about revolutions; there is nothing in that free air, on that age-old rock, to disturb the august reign of those unchallenged and unchallengeable queens.

We went on. Pez had picked up some notions of Geography from bits of things he had read in Verne; he rather fancied himself as a navigator and kept up an endless running commentary as we walked along. 'Now we're going through the South wing . . . The way through to the West wing has got to be on our right . . . We might as well take this spiral staircase down to the second floor . . . All right, now . . . Where are we? You can't see the dome, or even a damn lightning rod from here. We're down in the gaslit netherlands . . . Let's take this staircase right here and go back up . . . Now what did we do there? Are we back in the East wing again? Yes, we are, because if you look through this window on to the courtyard, the dome is over on our right . . . I'm beginning to get ill looking at that forest of chimney pots. I feel as if I'm out at sea and the whole mass is going up and down like a boat. It looks as if the pump is on this side, because there are women going to and fro with jugs. Right, that's it! I give up, bring me a navigator, I'm not going another

step ... We've walked at least a mile and a half and I'm
exhausted. Bring me a guide and get me out of here.'

Providence answered our prayers in the august personage of
García Grande's widow,* who suddenly emerged from one of
the ugliest and shabbiest doors around.

CHAPTER 5

Naturally, we were delighted to see her. She, on the other hand,
seemed unpleasantly surprised, as if she did not wish to be seen
in a place unbecoming to her rank. She stammered a muddled
greeting, and her first words confirmed my hunch.

'I won't ask you to come in, because this isn't my house ...
I'm just here temporarily, while they're doing up the rooms
down below, where the general's wife used to live. This place is
awful, dreadful ... Her Majesty wouldn't hear of me not living
in the Palace, and I just couldn't refuse ... "Cándida, my love,
I can't have you living so far away from me ... Cándida, my
love, come and live here ... Cándida, my love, you can have
any of the empty apartments upstairs." So there it is, I had to
move to the Palace. I got all my furniture into seven removal
vans, and I find the general's wife's place full of builders ... It's
a real mess! One of the partitions was falling down ... the
plaster was destroyed ... The floor-tiles jiggle when you walk
on them ... So I had to put all my precious belongings in this
place, it's quite big, but it won't do for me ... You should see
my two Raphael* paintings lying on the floor amongst all the
crockery; the big canvas by Tristán* leaning against the wall; all
my china in boxes of straw; the tables stacked upside down; the
lamps and the screens and everything else all topsy turvy,
waiting to be sorted out, all messy and horrible ... It's driving
me mad, as you can tell. I can't stand being so cramped, so short
of space, when I'm used to having everything all neat and tidy
... And you can't imagine how much I hate this neighbourhood,
all full of charwomen, concierges, kitchen boys and toilet-
cleaners. May Her Majesty forgive me; but I wish she'd left me
alone in my house on Cruzada Street; it was a bit on the big side
and rather chilly, it's true, but it was so comfortable ... I had
lots of room for everything and space to hang up all the

tapestries. Here I just don't know ... It looks as if I'm going to be really short of space in the rooms I've been given ... But, if that's the way the Queen wants it, what can you do? Her Majesty's a law unto herself.'

All this was uttered with cheerful resignation, like a person who is sacrificing her preferences and her comfort to the Queen's loving whim. She led us along the corridor, and when we came out on to the terrace to cut across, she pointed importantly to a line of doorways. 'That's where I'm going to be. Porta's wife has moved over to the other side to make room for me ... I'm going to knock down some walls to join up two of the rooms and give myself an entryway on the Cáceres stairway, and that way I can go straight down to the main hallway and get into the Royal chamber ... I'm going to have three more fireplaces put in and a set of screens ...'

Manuel, who was a consummate politician, agreed with everything she said; but he knew only too well who he was talking to and how seriously to take her airs of grandeur. I, on the other hand, barely knew the widow at that point, and I swallowed it all hook, line and sinker. My dealings with her only came later, when I became friends with Máximo Manso;* and I was convinced I was talking to one of Her Majesty's closest relatives. I was so naïve that all that about knocking down walls and having alterations done and bringing in the movers seemed like a Royal decree issued from the very threshold of the throne. I was struck dumb with awe.

In the end we arrived at Bringas's home. We realised that we had already been by it unwittingly, because you could not make out the number. It was a beautiful, spacious apartment with huge rooms, whose size made up for the fact that there were not very many of them. Our friend's furniture was somewhat lost in the vast drawing room with its high arched ceiling; but the knowing gaze of Juan Pipaón, whose portrait hung opposite the entryway, told every visitor, 'We're doing very well, thank you.' Light streamed cheerfully in through the windows that looked out over the Campo del Moro. The apartment lacked a study; but Bringas had improvised a really cosy one in the bay window of the main sitting room, by curtaining it off from the rest with felt. He had plenty of space in there for his work desk, two or three chairs, and his shelves of tools on the walls with all kinds of bits and pieces from his various hobbies. Paquito had set up his desk in the window of the sitting room on the left, which he had filled with a medley of books, papers and copious class notes, which were getting as voluminous as the Simancas archives.* These two rooms were spacious, with lofty ceilings, and on the far wall of both of them, as in the drawing room, were doors on to various cathedral-sized bedrooms, with bare, whitewashed walls and rope matting on the floors. The three bedrooms got their light from the doorway and from skylights with wire mesh screens which opened on to the main corridor-street of the Palace city. Even at midday you could see gas light through some of those skylights. They had set up the master bedroom off the right-hand sitting room; the bedroom off the drawing room, which was larger and had better lighting, had been converted into Rosalía's wardrobe and sewing room; and the bedroom off the left-hand sitting room had been turned into a dining room, because it was so close to the kitchen. The children slept in two rooms at the back.

I am not sure if the idea of naming the rooms of this humble abode after famous rooms in the main part of the Palace came from Bringas's fertile imagination or from Paquito's pompous comparison. A month after moving in, all the Bringases, great and small, were calling the drawing room the Ambassadors' Room, because it was used for formal visits and special occasions. The sitting room on the right which contained Thiers's study and the master bedroom was called *Gasparini*,* doubtless because it was the most attractive room in the house. The other sitting room was baptised the Little Room. The dining room was the Column Room; the wardrobe-cum-sewing room was nicknamed the *Camón* after a guardroom in the Palace, and the ironing room at the back of the house was called the *Furriela*.*

Francisco did not have to use the street to get to work. He would go down the Cáceres stairway and across the courtyard, or, if it was rainy, he would take the upper route through the city to the Ladies' stairway, and go along the galleries to the Royal Heritage offices. Since he hardly ever went out into the street, even his umbrella had become superfluous in that wonderfully convenient dwelling, which suited all his tastes and desires so well.

There were some families in their neighbourhood whom even Rosalía, for all her snobbishness, had to admit were of superior standing. There were others who were well below her Pipaonic rank; but she knew them all and paid them each a call in return for their ceremonious inaugural visits when the Bringas family moved into the town above the Palace. Cándida . . .

CHAPTER 6

But before I go on, I want to rid this narrative of my personality, which I shall do by briefly explaining the reason for my visit to Bringas. I had auctioned off a couple of plots of timber and hay in Riofrío;* and since there were certain serious breaches of procedure in the sale, I ran into trouble with a Royal auditor, which meant that I was in danger of being sued. When I began receiving the unpleasant attentions of a magistrate, I decided to solve the matter by going straight to the top. Manuel Pez, Mr Fix-it, the eternal issuer of recommendations, he of the little notes and memos, offered to help me out of my predicament. I owed him a few favours; but the ones he owed me were bigger and more important. He decided to put us on an equal footing by personally accompanying me on a visit to the senior clerk of the Royal Heritage offices, so as to make his recommendation more meaningful and effective. Everything turned out beautifully. Good old Bringas was so helpful and attentive that two days after our meeting with him I was out of trouble. On his saint's day, 4 October, I gave him two Bayonne capons and a dozen bottles of wine from my own estate, and even this thoughtful gesture seemed inadequate compared to the favour he had done me.

Now I shall return to Cándida. What a woman! What a way with words she had! She was very fond of the following line: 'I've got to go, the man who manages my estate is coming to see me and I don't want to keep him waiting. He's such a busy man.' And here is another one: 'My tenants are a bit late with the rent for my houses.' Once Máximo Manso gets going about her, there is no stopping him. In 1868, the lady was still almost as queenly as ever, leading the same high society life she had during the five years O'Donnell was in power.* But by this time, she was working her way rapidly through the remains of her husband's money, and every day a piece of jewellery or art or furniture would be dispatched from the house, charged with the mission of bringing back money to solve her domestic needs. I shall not go into the arguments she had with her landlord, whom she owed six months' rent. The Queen got her out of that one by coming up with the back payments and offering her rooms in the upper regions of the Palace, which the poor woman accepted on the spot. 'I'm stuck in this hovel just to keep Her Majesty happy and be near her, while they do up the rooms on the terrace ... What a hopeless man that architect is! ... Just wait till I see him ...' She was always going on in this vein, but months went by and the illustrious widow never left her makeshift accommodations. The time Pez and I met her, and she paid us the honour of showing us the way to Bringas's house, those famous Raphael paintings of hers, the Tristán canvas and the many other valuable things she had which were not, by some miracle, in museums, had been rotting away abandoned for over a year.

Cándida was one of the Bringas's most assiduous visitors. Rosalia treated her with respect and affection, and listened to her submissively, taking her for a great authority on social matters and on all that was elegant and refined. It seemed to Thiers's wife as if gleams of Cándida's brilliant past, though fading fast, still bathed the noble widow's Roman bust and haughty manner in a glow of prestige and nobility. This halo fascinated Rosalía, who took her respect for fallen majesty to extremes and appeared to take seriously Cándida's line about *the man who manages my estate, my houses* ... Cándida always spoke with an ease and an assurance and a superciliousness that brooked no contradiction. She lived in the East wing, the poorest area in what we have decided to call a city; but none of its other inhabitants paid more visits or spent as much time out of the house as she did. She spent the whole day long going from house to house, knocking on different doors, paying calls, chatting, going to every part of the Colossus, from the kitchens to the dovecotes; and she would get back to her makeshift accommodations at night as exhausted as if she had walked halfway across Madrid. Her only relative was a niece called Irene, of about nine or ten years old, the orphan of one of García Grande's brothers who had been the Queen's equerry. This little girl was a great friend of the Bringas's daughter, and you would see them in the evenings with their dolls in one hand, munching a snack and playing on the terrace or in the lightest parts of those long, covered streets.

The most prestigious person living there, a woman who in

Rosalía's eyes was only one step away from the Royal Family, was General Minio's widow, chief lady-in-waiting to Her Majesty, an extremely distinguished and virtuous lady in all respects. In town she was known by the friendly and familiar name of Tula; but Rosalía never used that form of address, opting instead for '*Condesa* this, *Condesa* that'. This generous and noble lady was the sister of the Marquesa de Tellería* and Alejandro Sánchez Botín,* that gentleman who has been elected to parliament so many times and has been a member of half a dozen political parties. The Sánchez Botíns are landed gentry from Bierzo, I believe, and distant relatives of the Aransis family. The two sisters got married the same day: Milagros to the Marqués de Tellería, and Gertrudis, the eldest, to Colonel Minio, who was soon promoted to general by dint of winning courtly battles in the Palace antechambers. Every time anyone in the Royal Family had a birthday, he would land a cross or a promotion. When they could not give him anything higher in the military than the two gold epaulettes, they came up with the title of Conde de Santa Bárbara (an estate of his in Navarra), a name that went well with his office since it carried a faint odour of gunpowder – although they used to say the only gunpowder he had ever smelt was from the official salutes.* His reputation for bravery must have been based on his extraordinary ignorance. Our values are so confused that people who can barely write their own names are continually becoming heroes. But clearly Pedro Minio, Conde de Santa Bárbara, cut an imposing figure on the parade ground, inspecting the troops in the barracks, or emitting military bellows in the various high offices he occupied. Apart from participating in a few minor skirmishes in the first civil war,* he remained entirely mute in the military annals of this country. But he will go down in history for uttering various famous phrases such as the *sword of Demosthenes*, *Pentecost's veil*, and *Garibaldi's soul*,* as well as having sailed for Havana via the Philippines, and a host of other delicious anecdotes much treasured by his subalterns. The Queen knew them all by heart and told them very wittily. But let us not stir the ashes of this nonentity, whom the countess in her heart of hearts thought of as a brute in uniform; we shall turn to his widow.

CHAPTER 7

She was so unlike the Marquesa de Tellería that it did not seem possible they shared the same mother. Nor was she at all like her famous brother Alejandro Sánchez Botín, that man of great means, either physically or in her temperament. The rare qualities with which she was endowed were complemented by that other form of human distinction, misfortune, which is the privilege of the almost perfect. She had two sons, real treasures the pair of them, who had inherited the general's name, vulgarity and solecisms. The things their poor mother went through to get them through their training in the Cavalry! She spent five or six years struggling bitterly against the boys' utter ignorance and laziness, and had exhausting battles with their teachers; but thanks to the family name and the little notes the Queen would write for them every year, they made it through. Both of them were safely commissioned at officer's rank when a fresh set of problems appeared to try Tula's patience. Not a month would go by without one of her beloved offspring doing something scandalous. Brawls, duels, drunkenness, military tribunals, gambling houses, and cheating at cards were everyday occurrences, and Mama had to fix everything by coming up with letters of recommendation and sums of money. She got to a point where she was so tired that when her eldest son, who was also called Pedro Minio, said he wanted to go to Cuba, she lacked the strength to contradict him. The other one wanted to marry a woman with a bad reputation. In order to prevent this, his mother had to go into battle once again, deploying all the resources her worldly knowledge and her contacts could muster. The lady came out with a remark that made a deep impression on all of us who heard it, the absurd cry of pained egotism against motherhood, which would have constituted a blasphemy against Nature and the human race were it not such a paradox. They were talking of children and mothers who wanted to have them, as well as mothers who had too many. 'Oh, children!' said Tula sadly. 'They're an illness that lasts nine months and a convalescence that lasts your whole lifetime.'

But while the lady's own children were stupid, squalid and

ugly as sin, her sister Milagros, on the other hand, had given birth to four angels, who were singled out from birth by their beauty, grace and manners. There was little Leopold, so sweet and mischievous; darling little Gustavo, who was so good and bright and precocious; mystical young Luis, who seemed to be turning into a budding saint, and most of all, María,* with her green eyes and classical profile, like Venus herself recovered from the ruins of ancient Greece, a perfect living statue. What mother would not be delighted with children like that? Tula adored her niece and nephews. For her, they were children who had caused her no pain. Someone else had to deal with their problems; she only saw their good side. She worshipped María, who had just turned fifteen, with the devotion of a grandmother – a mother twice over – and she had made her rather spoilt and coy. The lovely girl used to go and spend Sundays and Thursdays with Tula; she also used to go on Tuesdays and Fridays, and sometimes on Mondays and Saturdays too. On holidays, various young friends of the general's wife would come to visit, for example Buenaventura de Lantigua's girls and one of their cousins, whose name, I believe, was Gloria, daughter of the famous lawyer Juan de Lantigua.*

They made quite the gathering out there on the terrace. There were nymphettes in short dresses which would soon be full-length, and others in long skirts which had been short only a fortnight earlier. Those who had been officially ordained as women walked around arm-in-arm in groups, practising serious-ness and calm, measured conversation. The younger ones ran around with half their legs showing, and needless to say little Isabel Bringas and Cándida's niece were some of the noisiest. Whenever one of the girls' bittersweet beaux, some callow suitor with a walking cane, a loud tie, a light hat and maybe even a cigarette in an amber holder, managed to slip in through the galleries . . . Lord! You cannot imagine the giggles, the games of hide-and-seek, the awkwardness, the innocent banter, the delicious silliness of those fresh young souls who had just opened up their petals to the sun of life. The short phrases they exchanged so lightly were the most banal examples of stilted social intercourse, and at the same time the artless grunts of the primitive. The beginnings of the World, the dynamic of Cre-ation, the wish to be someone,* are replayed in every such encounter.

The playful band of young women-to-be would invade Bringas's home. Rosalía, who was always delighted to see Tula, the Tellerías and the Lantiguas, would welcome them with open arms and give them sweets, which she had ordered from the Palace confectioner's shop. 'Go ahead and play, be as naughty as you want. Shout and run around, I don't mind at all,' said Bringas cheerfully from the window, where he sat drowning in a sea of hair. They never needed telling twice; they would open the piano right away and one of them would start strumming out a polka or a waltz while the others, clasping their partners in their arms, would dance and skip around happily, laughing, squealing and kissing one another.

'Dance all you want, run around; make yourselves at home, my dears,' said Thiers, intent on the atoms he was sticking on to the glass. And they took him so much at his word that they would go skipping from *Gasparini* to the Little Room and bounce on into the *Camón* and the Column Room. And then ... when they got into Isabel's dolls, they would be there for ever. The biggest girls were precisely the ones who devoted the most enthusiasm to this wonderful simulacrum of domestic life, dressing and undressing those little women made of porcelain and tow, tucking in babies with glass eyes and fiddling with things on the tin stove or in a cardboard study. The thing that fascinated them most of all, and even caused some rivalry, was a huge doll that Agustín Caballero* had sent Isabel from Bordeaux, a marvellous creature; she could move her eyes, say Dada and Mama, and had joints you could bend into all sorts of positions. There was only one step left between her and a real child: suffering. That afternoon they dressed her in traditional Madrid costume.* When a certain petulant murmur indicated the proximity of the youths in the passageway, and they could hear them guffawing close by, trying to sound like men of the world, in voices that had only acquired their masculine gruffness a month before, the girls stuck the doll up through the high, barred window of the *Camón*, provoking all kinds of horseplay from the lads and much innocent amusement for themselves.

However much Francisco claimed to be pleased to have his house full of these angels, they were occasionally a nuisance. Whenever they happened to gather round his desk to admire the hairy work he was engaged on, the great artist, overwhelmed by the throng of beautiful heads crowding in on him, would say with a laugh: 'Girls, for Heaven's sake, move back a bit. You don't need to stifle me to see ... or to spill my varnish. Gloria, be careful please, you've got some hairs stuck to your sleeve. They're for the trunk of the weeping willow. Careful now, María, you're making those white hairs blow away ... Back you go, now, my dears, please ...'

CHAPTER 8

Meanwhile, they would be exclaiming: 'Oooooh, that's really pretty, that's really lovely ... Goodness meee ... your fingers must be as light as an angel's! Mr Bringas, sir, you'll go blind doing that ...'

All these things took place in the spring of 1868, and the Thursday before Easter that year was a particularly eventful day for the girls. Francisco came to the religious ceremony in the chapel in a full dress suit, cross and all. His presence made the holiday a truly sacred occasion. Rosalía also made an appearance in the Royal abode, in the belief that her presence was indispensable if the celebration was to have all the suitable pomp and circumstance. Cándida did not go, ostensibly because she was 'tired of ceremonies', but in fact because she did not have a dress to wear. The Lantigua girls and María Sudre* had invaded Tula's apartment at an early hour, and Tula herself came down dressed to the nines because of her Royal office, leaving the charming flock in the hands of her companion. They had a wonderful time that day, tormenting León, Federico Cimarra, the de Horro boy,* and a bunch of others just as good looking and daring! They invited the boys up into one of the high dovecotes, under the pretext that you could see into the chapel from there, and then kept them locked up there for half the afternoon.

Since the girls were friends of the sacristan, who was a neighbour of Cándida's, they could stand on the chapel staircase, which gave them a glimpse through the half-open doorway of the Bishop's mitre, two extinguished candles,* an altar covered in purple cloth, the bald heads of some of the chaplains and the chests of a number of aristocratic chests freighted with crosses and sashes; but that was it. A little later they managed to see a bit of the beautiful ceremony of the paupers' feast after the Washing of the Feet.* On the south wing of the terrace there are some big glass skylights, protected by wire netting, that look out over the main stairway, the Guard Room and the Column Room. When you look out through them, the domed roof is so close that the figures adorning it seem monstrous and crude. Huge angels and nymphs flex their vast limbs for the benefit of the masses, mounted on clouds that look like bundles of grey cotton wool. Some of the other figures look as if they are supporting the whole roof by virtue of their colossal muscular strength. On the other hand, the flowers on the carpet at the bottom look just like miniatures.

Crowds of citydwellers of all classes had been waiting since early that day to get a place at the skylights of the Column Room to watch the paupers' feast. The women clustered close to the big circles of glass, and since there were plenty of gaps, those who managed to make their way to the front by dint of judicious use of their elbows could enjoy that ceremonious ritual of Royal humiliation, which each person may interpret as they wish. Some of them even cut the glass with their diamond rings to make spyholes. What a disorderly hubbub all those impatient, noisy people made! Some of the outsiders, who had been invited to the city, were impertinent enough to want all the best vantage points for themselves. But Cándida, with the authority she could wield whenever the occasion required, ordered them to move away from one of the skylights so that the Tellería, Lantigua and Bringas girls could enjoy complete possession of it. What a lady! She threatened to have all the outsiders put out on the street if they did not do as she said.

Seen from the roof, the spectacle in the Column Room was a bizarre one. The table of the twelve beggar men was scarcely visible; but the one with the twelve old women was right opposite the skylight and you could see everything. The poor things were so awkward in their black wool dresses, new shawls and scarves! What a feeling, to be surrounded by such pomp, waited on by the Queen herself, when just the day before they had been begging for small change at the doors of some church! . . . They kept their eyes fixed on the table, except to dart glances of awe at the people serving them. Some of them were in tears, more out of nervousness than gratitude, because their treatment at the hands of the mighty of this world, clad in evening dress and dispensing charity, was more humiliating than flattering. If all the efforts of the imagination fail to allow us to imagine

Christ in a coat and tails, there can be nothing to convince us that this Palace comedy has anything to do with the Gospel.

The important personages who were to act as waiters during that pious event picked up the plates of food in the doorway, from the servants. Then the ladies and gentlemen passed them down the line till they reached the hands of the King and Queen, who presented them to the paupers with a certain kindly courtesy, the only bearable note in that whole farcical scene. But the paupers could not eat, they seemed incapable of managing it. Probably their clumsy hands could not remember how to put food in their mouths. Once the food was put on the table, a servant would take it and put it in the baskets behind each of the paupers' chairs. A little later, once the Royal Family and the nobility had left the room, the paupers would file out with their baskets to the Palace kitchens, where the innkeepers of Madrid and other unsavoury characters would be waiting to buy the whole lot for a few reals.

The pretty spectators kept up a ceaseless stream of chatter while the meal was going on. María Egipcíaca said she wanted to be down there, wearing a long dress with a train and passing trays. One of the Lantigua girls ventured the opinion that the whole thing was just like bad theatre, while the other was only interested in the fine dresses and uniforms.

'Look, there's Mother. Can you see her? She's wearing a peach dress. She's standing next to Mr Pez, talking to him.'

'Yes . . . now they're looking up at the ceiling . . . They know we're here. And there's Mr Bringas, over there . . . next to the steward. My mother's standing next to him.'

'The Marquesa looks so lovely in her purple dress and shawl! . . . Oh, Tula, Tula . . . If only she'd look up, she might see us . . . We're up here . . .'

'It's really hard on my aunt every time they have one of these things. She gets terrible headaches. You'll never guess how many recommendations she gets . . . For twenty-four poor people, there are about three hundred recommendations. Every day she gets letters and messages from the Marquesa and the Condesa. You'd think they were giving out jobs in the ministry!'

'Yes, tell me about it,' said Cándida in a bored voice. 'Yesterday and today have been awful. Tomasa, my neighbour, the Queen's chambermaid, had to clean up the twelve old women and change their raggedy old clothes for those beautiful clean dresses they're wearing today. Those poor women! It's only the second time they've had a bath in their lives and it would be the first if they hadn't been christened. Oh, my dears! ... You'll never imagine the fuss this morning! They must have used up an entire bathtub full of eau-de-Cologne ... I tried to help out a bit, to follow Our Lord's example. If I hadn't been there, they'd have been scrubbing away till lunch time ... To tell the truth, if I were poor and they brought me to this ceremony, I wouldn't like it a bit, because really, what they give them doesn't make up for the fright they go through and the discomfort of having to get so clean.'

Cándida's practical assessment, which was based on experience, meant nothing to the elegant lasses, who were at that tender age where the spiritual and the imaginary are all-important. To them, it all seemed fine and proper, a fitting symbol of the twin powers of Church and Crown.

Little Isabel Bringas was a puny, weak wraith of a thing, with a tendency to epilepsy. Her sleep was often disturbed by terrible nightmares, followed by vomiting and convulsions. Sometimes these symptoms did not appear, but then the incipient attack would take on a much more alarming form. She would go all stupid and slow, and lose all her childish vivacity. When this happened, it was no use scolding her, and her teacher had strict instructions not to punish her or insist that she pay attention and work harder. If she saw something during the day that overstimulated her sensitive mind, or she overheard a sad story, she would replay it all at night in her troubled sleep. This was aggravated if she ate too much or ate something that did not agree with her, for then the poor child's digestive system would be overwhelmed. That Thursday, Tula gave a superb lunch for her young friends. Bringas's little girl loved the milk pudding and ate far too much of it, something the poor child was to pay for later. Fifteen minutes after going to bed, she became feverish and delirious, and started seeing and hearing all the incidents, people and objects she had witnessed while she was on the go during the day, having so much fun; but this time they were all mixed up with the most crazy things. She replayed the games on the terrace; she saw all the girls, hugely disfigured, and Cándida like a great big black shepherdess guarding her flock; she went back to watching the paupers' feast through the skylight, and the painted figures on the ceiling came alive and started reaching out with their great hands to scare off the onlookers ... Then she heard the royal march being played. Was that Her Majesty coming up on to the terrace? No; there was her mother coming through the door on to the Ladies' stairway on Pez's arm, and her father arm-in-arm with the Marquesa de Tellería. How pretty the two women were with their huge long trains! . . . And how distinguished the men looked and how well they held themselves! . . . They were coming to have a rest and refreshments at Tula's house, before going off with *Madam* and the rest of the Court to say their prayers in various chapels. The upper floors of the Palace were overrun with men in livery, lots of blue and red cloth, lots of gold and silver stripes, endless tricorned hats* . . . In her delirium, she saw the city done up in bright, gleaming colours. It must be a doll city; but what dolls! . . . All around her were white wigs, and out of all the doors of the rooms on the second floor came pretty figures of wax, flax or porcelain; they were all running about in the passageways, shouting: 'It's time, it's time . . .' Military stripes going up the stairs ran past military stripes going down them . . . All the dolls were in a hurry. One of them had forgotten this or that, another would have lost a buckle or a feather or a piece of braid. Some of them called to their wives to bring something, and all of them kept saying, 'It's time!' . . . Then they milled about down below on the main staircase. Royal guardsmen crowded around in the main courtyard with the coachmen and footmen. It was like a great big saucepan in which human limbs of many colours were boiling away, writhing in the heat . . . There were her mother and father again . . . Oh, they were looking so smart today! But her father would look even better when they made him Knight of the Holy Sepulchre. The King was all for it, and had promised to give him the uniform and all the accessories – sword, spurs, the lot. How wonderful her father would look in that white coat and tails . . . all white! . . . At this point, the idea of whiteness completely swamped the poor child's senses. Just then she started to gag on a horrible obstruction, as if everything she was reliving in her head, all the dolls and the Palace, had got stuck inside her little stomach. She threw the whole lot up in racking spasms. Her delirium promptly receded and she started to feel a great deal better . . . Her mother had jumped out of bed to come and help her. Isabel, who was now wide awake, could hear her loving voice saying: 'There, there, love. It's all over now.'

CHAPTER 9

Milagros's looks had not yet gone into the decline in which we were to find them during the sad story of her son-in-law,* from '75 to '78, but she was getting further and further away from the heyday of her life. The restoration work she carried out with such consummate skill had not yet started to show, like white-wash that does not stick because of the poor state of the wall to which it is applied. Her ingenuity and elegance, her refined taste in sartorial art and her popularity among those who did not know her very well all combined to defend her from the ravages of time.

All these qualities held Rosalía Bringas in thrall; but the one that was clearly paramount was Milagros's exquisite taste in fabrics and fashions. This gift of her friend's was like a blazing sun to Rosalía, upon which she could not look without being dazzled. She revered the Marquesa's opinion on matters of this sort so much that she did not dare express any opinion that was not a reflection of the solemn truths proclaimed by Milagros. Any time there was the slightest doubt over the colour or cut of a dress, Milagros would solve it at a stroke. That lady's pronouncements became legal precedent for anything that might happen in the future, and since she not only passed the laws but backed up her doctrine by her own example, dressing impec-cably, Bringas's wife – who during the period this story takes place had developed a veritable passion for clothes – worshipped Milagros in the privacy of her own soul. García Grande's widow had seduced her friend with her prestige as a historical figure. Rosalía respected her as if she were one of the gods of an ancient religion; but she acted as if Milagros had all the authority of current dogma and contemporary gods. No one in the world, not even Bringas, had as much power over Rosalía Pipaón as Milagros. Although she was bossy and rather rude to her equals and inferiors, she would be overcome with shyness in the presence of her idol, who was also her teacher.

Agustín Caballero's little gifts, and the finery he had laid on for his wedding and subsequently donated to Rosalía, awoke in her a passion for clothing. Her former modesty, which stemmed more from necessity than from virtue, was put to a test which it did not pass. In the past, Thiers's caution had succeeded in restraining her appetite for luxury, leading us all to believe that it did not exist, when in fact it was simply that she was unable to satisfy it. We are back to the founding incident of human history, the perennial problem, *the* problem: human fallibility. As long as the fruit stayed untouched, forbidden by the domestic god, everything was fine. But the apple was bitten, without the devil taking the shape of a serpent or any other vile creature, and that was the end of her modesty. After trying on so many beautiful outfits, how could she ever get used to wearing her old stuff again, and never changing styles? It was simply not possible. Poor old Agustín, in all ignorance, had corrupted his cousin by his generosity; he had been the well-meaning serpent who had beguiled her mind by sowing in it some of the most dangerous vanity that can swell a woman's head. His little gifts were the fruit whose sweet taste destroyed her innocence, and thanks to them an angel with a satin sword threw her out of Paradise, where Bringas had kept her well and truly under control. Really and truly . . . it is hard to believe that the story of Eve happened so long ago. For all the evidence to the contrary, one would think it only happened yesterday, it is such a burning contemporary issue. It seems as if it just came out in yesterday evening's news.

Since Bringas disliked his wife making new dresses and spending money on finery and trimmings, she pretended to despise fashion; but she was forever making alterations to her dresses in secret, combining different fabrics and coming up with her own rather free interpretations of the latest fashion-plates. When Milagros came to see her, if Bringas was away at the office, they would talk for ever, each of them giving free rein to the passion that ruled them both.

CHAPTER 10

But if the saintly gentleman was in his niche by the window, engrossed in the microcosm of the hair work, the two ladies would shut themselves up in the *Camón*, where they could talk all they wanted without anyone interfering. Rosalía would open drawers very gently so as not to make any noise: and out would come skirts, bodices waiting to be altered, lengths of material and pieces that had already been cut out, and strips of velvet or silk. She would lay the whole lot out on the sofa or over the chairs and trunks, or on the floor if she had to, and they would begin a feverish consultation over what to do to get the best effect, one that was striking and distinguished at the same time. These consultations used to go on for ever, and had they been recorded they would have constituted an intriguing encyclopaedia of this female passion, which does more damage in the world than revolutions. They both talked quietly, so Bringas would not hear what they were saying, in rapid, stifled, vehement whispers that sometimes betrayed hesitation and nervousness, and other times the joy of having hit on a good idea. The French words that gave their conversation such a special flavour strained at the fabric of our language; but even if I have to stick them down with pins, I want to capture them so as not to lose the peculiar quality of that exotic language of materials.

ROSALÍA [*looking at a fashion-plate*]: I must say, I just don't understand this. I've no idea how you're supposed to join the skirt-tails at the back of the French military *casaque*.*

MILAGROS [*slightly at a loss, but relying on her infallible instinct*]: Forget the fashion-plate. If you follow them too closely you end up looking silly and overdone, anyway. Let's start by choosing the fabric. Do you want to use the white muslin faced with the silk foulard? Because if you do, you can't use the *casaque* pattern.

ROSALÍA [*decisively*]: No; I'm definitely going to go for the *gros glacé* silk, in a rose-grey shade. Sobrino said I could bring back what I didn't use. He's charging me twenty-four reals a yard for the *gros glacé*.

MILAGROS [*thinking it over*]: All right then: supposing we go for the *gros glacé*, then I think I'd put four tiers of four-inch flounces on the bottom of the skirt. What do you think? No; make that five- or six-inch flounces, with a band of spring green *glacé* silk cut on the bias at the bottom . . . How does that sound?

ROSALÍA [*rapt in contemplation of what is still all in the imagination*]: Lovely . . . And what about the bodice?

MILAGROS [*taking a half-sewn bodice and skilfully draping the fabric to make the lapels and the skirt-tails*]: The French *casaque* has a heart-shaped neckline with lapels, and it has three or four green buttons on the side of the waist . . . right here. The skirt-tails open out at the front . . . get the idea? . . . like this . . . so as to show the lining, which is green, like the lapels; and the flounces are all drawn together at the back over the bustle. [*The lady bunches up her own dress with her hands in that protruberant region where the skirt-tails of the casaque are gathered.*] See what I mean? . . . It'll look lovely. Now I told you that the jacket is lined in green *gros* silk and there's a band of ruched ribbon over the top of the gathers, just like on the flounces of the dress . . . Well? Oh yes, don't forget that you'll have to have a pleated batiste chemisette* with a ruff of *Valenciennes* lace at the neck . . . and loose cuffs; they should fall over your wrists.

ROSALÍA: Oh! I've got two or three different kinds of chemisettes.

MILAGROS: I've seen the one Pilar San Salomó ordered from Paris to go with the evening dress for going out to dinner and the theatre. [*She closes her eyes, overcome with aesthetic emotion.*] What a dress! It's so beautiful . . .

ROSALÍA [*eagerly*]: What does it look like?

MILAGROS: It's got a pink satin skirt, down to the ground, trimmed with a flounce covered in lace. It's so chic! The flounce has eight black velvet bows on it . . .

ROSALÍA: Does it have any puffing?

MILAGROS: Four sets. Then, on top of the skirt, fitted at the waist [*mimicking the action of the material with her hands round her own midriff*], like this, see? . . . There's one of those Court overskirts . . . It comes in here and falls like this, and then it's gathered at the back into a big *pouff*. [*Enthusiastically*]. It's so original! Under the *pouff* there's a long train of material with puffing in like the skirt. It's just brilliant! Utterly gorgeous! . . . Look . . . like this . . . and the same here . . . joining them up with a tuck . . . That is, the overskirt has a basquines and the points go just here . . . under the *pouff* . . . See what I mean, my dear?

ROSALÍA [*entranced*]: Yes . . . yes, I do . . . I see what you mean. It must look lovely . . .

MILAGROS [*with a grand gesture to demonstrate where the thing she is describing goes*]: There's a big satin bow on the puffing . . . The effect is fantastic.

ROSALÍA [*devouring all she hears*]: And what about the bodice?

MILAGROS: It's got a very low neck with straps on the shoulders that are joined by bows . . . But those bows never fall off the shoulder . . . The chemisette is the latest thing, puffed silk with little velvet ribbons threaded through it. It's got long sleeves . . .

ROSALÍA [*trying out different materials and pieces of fabric together to see the effect*]: I've just had an idea for a chemisette to wear with this dress. If I do get the rose-grey colour [*She pauses and thinks for a minute.*] I'm useless at these decisions! In the fashion plate ... [*Quickly grabbing everything together in a fright*]. 'I think I heard Bringas coming. I do so hate having to hide like this ...

MILAGROS [*helping her to stuff everything back into the drawers*]: Yes, I can hear that little cough of his. My dear, that husband of yours is worse than the Customs men, the way he goes after materials ... We'll have to hide the loot.

Some of Rosalía's happiest times were when she was talking to the Marquesa about ways to alter her dresses. But what she loved best of all was going shopping with her friend, even though she tended to get sad because she could not buy any of the lovely things she saw. Time would fly by without their realising it. Milagros would ask to see everything in the shop. She would dig around and compare, going from fits of sudden enthusiasm to cold disdain; she would bargain, and in the end she would take things and charge them to her account. If Rosalía ever bought anything, she would think it over for a long time first and agonise over the cost, and she always paid in cash. For the most part, her purchases consisted of bolt-ends, scraps or pieces of old fabric, which she would combine with the good pieces she had at home to make them seem new and distinguished.

But one day, in Sobrino Brothers,* she saw a shawl! ... It was a lovely thing, an apple fit for Eve! The passion of the collector when confronted with a rare item, the enthusiasm of the hunter who sees a fine, handsome beast, can give us no idea of the tremendous love of clothes in some women. Rosalía could not take her eyes off that magnificent garment; the assistant kindly showed her a whole selection, stacking them up on the counter as if they were empty sacks. Timidly, she asked how much it cost, but did not dare bargain for it. The enormity of the price terrified her almost as much as the beauty of the shawl seduced her, with its peculiar combination of velvet, cloth and gleaming braid. When she got home, she could not stop thinking about the wretched thing the whole day and night, and desire burned in her blood with such fury that she was afraid she would break out in a rash if she did not satisfy it. She went back to the shops with Milagros the next day, determined not to go

into Sobrino's, where the great temptation lay; but the devil saw
to it that they went in, and lo and behold, those white boxes
reappeared on the counter, those glossy cardboard coffers that
house ladies' dreams. The assistant took the shawls out one by
one, making a pile of black. Out came her favourite, with its
elegant shape and luxurious woven fringe, in which the black
beadwork glinting against the plush fabric confirmed everything
the poets have ever said about the mantle of night. Rosalía
started to feel a chill at her breast and a fever in her head, and
the nerves in her shoulders conjured up the feel and weight of
the shawl so vividly that she thought she was already wearing
it.

'For goodness' sake, go ahead and buy it!' said Milagros to
her friend, in such a convincing tone that the shop assistants
and Sobrino himself were obliged to lend their support to her
judicious declaration. 'Why should you do without something
that looks so good on you?'

When the shop assistants had moved off in the direction of
another group of lady clients, the Marquesa carried on lecturing
her friend in a whisper: 'Don't go without buying it if you like
it . . . really and truly, it's quite cheap . . . You won't even have
to pay for it now, because you're with me. I'm one of their best
customers. They won't send you the bill for a few months, till
the beginning of the summer, maybe even the end of the year.'

The idea of having that much time to pay off the sum made
Rosalía hesitate and inclined her all the more towards the
purchase . . . Really, one thousand seven hundred reals wasn't
such an exorbitant sum of money for her, it should be easy to
find, if she could get the pawnbroker to sell a few things she
didn't wear any more; she could save some money too, if she
was patient and determined about spending less on the housekeeping. The worst thing was that Bringas would never authorise such a huge expense for something that was not an absolute
necessity.

In the past, she had always made her own polkas* and shawls,
borrowing one to use as a model. She would buy the stuff
cheaply on Santa Cruz, stick various pieces together, cover up
the mends, and come out with something satisfactory for a lot
of work and very little money. But how could you compare her
pathetic efforts to that exquisite thing from Paris? . . . Bringas
would never authorise such a luxury, no doubt he'd think it
utterly exorbitant, and she would have to deceive him if she

were to get away with it . . . No, no; she couldn't buy it. It was
far too serious a step, and a waste of money that broke with all
the family traditions. But the shawl was so beautiful! . . . The
Parisians had made it just for her . . . Should she get it, or not?

CHAPTER 11

She did get it in the end, and in order to explain how she had
come by such a magnificent accessory she had to resort to the
by now rather well-worn excuse of Her Majesty's generosity.
Such a coincidence. Rosalía just happened to be in the Royal
Chamber when they were opening up some boxes that had just
come in from Paris. The Queen had just tried on a canezou*
that was too small for her and a bodice that was too big. The
Royal couturier was there, making observations about how to
coordinate the items. Then, out of a beautiful box lined with
cretonne inside and out, material that looked like satinette . . .
they took out three shawls. One of them looked marvellous on
Her Majesty; the other two did not suit her.
  'Try this one on, Rosa, my love . . . How does it look? Oh,
that's absolutely lovely on you.' And really, it might have been
made to measure. 'Let me see, turn round. You know, I don't
think I can take it away from you. No, really, keep it.'
  'But Your Majesty, really . . .'
  'No, leave it on. It's yours by right of conquest. You've got
such a perfect figure! Wear it in my name, and let's hear no
more about it.' The sovereign lady was always graciously
presenting her friends with magnificent gifts of this sort . . . Our
friend Thiers almost wept as he listened to her telling this
wonderful story.
  If I am not mistaken, the passing of this huge lie down
Francisco's receptive gullet took place in April. Rosalía had
relaxed, confident that she would not have to pay for a long
while, and convinced she could get the money together in a
couple of months, when, at the beginning of May . . . wham!
The bill arrived. Princess Isabel was about to get married, and
Rosalía was absorbed in following all the preparations, oblivi-
ous to her debt and the bill at Sobrino's. She was paralysed with
shock when she opened it, and gazed at the paper in stupefac-

tion, unable to think of an answer or even an observation, because she had no idea where she was going to find the money ... She had never been in such straits before, because Bringas's method was never to buy anything without paying the full amount in cash. Finally, stammering, she told the wretched man who had brought it that she would stop by the shop and pay it 'tomorrow ... no, the day after; anyway, some time soon.'

Luckily, Bringas was not at home. Rosalía spent two or three days in great trepidation. Every time the doorbell rang, she thought it was going to be that stupid man with his nasty receipt ... If Bringas ever found out! When she thought of this, her anxiety became real terror, and she began to think of ways to get out of her predicament. A few days earlier, she had had almost half the money; but she had spent it on bits and pieces for the children, confident she was not going to get the bill just yet. Not content with dressing elegantly herself, she liked the children to look smart too, so they did not let her down in front of the other families in town. The week before, she had spent over six hundred reals on nonsense like new collars, getting a hat mended, navy blue stockings, red gloves, a sailor's cap with *Numancia* on it in gold letters, and two leather belts; and the only way she had come by that sum was by a long spell of substituting brains or tuna omelette for the family's main dish of brisket of veal, on alternate days.

The investigation of her purse yielded only one hundred and twelve reals, and she had already gone into the red at the grocer's without Bringas knowing. Heavens, what was she going to do? She absolutely had to find that money somehow. She dropped some discreet hints to Milagros, but the Marquesa was suffering from an extraordinarily persistent intellectual deafness that day, and did not pick up on anything. Her oddly absent-minded behaviour translated as follows: 'My dear, try someone else.' But who? Cándida? Rosalía tried her, and found the noble widow would have loved to help her; but unfortunately, it just so happened that her administrator hadn't brought her the rent from her houses ... And she'd laid out a lot of money on some repairs ... Clearly, there was no hope of salvation from that quarter. In the end, Providence sent Rosalía the help she prayed for, in the form of Gonzalo Torres,* an old friend of the family, who often visited them at the Palace, as he had in the past at their old home on the Costanilla.

Torres was used to handling other people's money, and

sometimes he had rather large sums in his possession, which he would make the most of while he had the opportunity. Rosalía took advantage of her husband's absence to explain her dilemma to him with force and sincerity, and good old Gonzalo calmed her down instantly. To put it poetically, he soon put the roses back in the lady's pale cheeks. Fortunately, Torres had access to a sum of money that belonged to Mompous y Bruil: but he could easily delay paying it back for another month. If Mrs Bringas promised to return the one thousand seven hundred reals to him within the space of thirty days, he saw no reason why he shouldn't let her have the money. On the contrary, he would be delighted. A whole month! Thank heavens! She didn't even need that long, she could easily get the money by squeezing the family budget implacably, or by selling some of her stuff that had gone out of fashion. Oh, yes! Of course . . . Not a word of this to Bringas . . .

Now that she was sure she could pay Sobrino Brothers, a tremendous weight was lifted from her conscience. Now she need not catch her breath in fear, thinking that the man from the shop might turn up with the bill when Bringas was at home. She regained her lost appetite and her peace of mind. The truth was, she had started having dizzy spells that looked like a really serious illness, and she had a hard time convincing her husband not to call the 'family' doctor.

She was just putting on her cape to go out and pay the bill (since Torres had brought her the money that afternoon), when Milagros came over. She was looking so beautiful and elegant that day! 'Look . . . I've brought this blue ribbon for the canezou. It's a brand new shade shot with green that . . . see the way it changes? I'll just sit down for a minute and then we can go out together. I've got my carriage. Oh yes! You should see the lovely hats they've got in *Las Toscanas*!* There's one that a model could wear, gorgeous, really unique, out of this world. Imagine . . . it's a *Florian* in Italian straw, done up with wild flowers and black velvet. On one side, there's an aigrette* with black at the bottom, stuck in this way. At the back it has a black veil that falls over your shoulder. But they're asking an eye tooth for it.'

ROSALÍA [*feeling her head start to whirl, as she imagines, with admirable hallucinatory powers, the parts and the whole of the hat that Milagros has just described so well*]: Even though we're not going to buy it, we might as well just go and have a quick look.

They went out together and got into the carriage, which was waiting at the Prince's gateway. Milagros chattered on endlessly. She talked about the things she had seen, the summer fabrics which had come in at Sobrino Brothers and what she planned to do with her wardrobe that season, with the pittance she got from her husband. Suddenly, she remembered that she had to go and pick up a brooch from the jeweller's, which she was having mended and redone ... Oh, drat! She'd gone and forgotten her purse, and there was no way they'd give her credit at that place, because of an unpleasant little encounter she'd had a long time ago with the owner ... No need to worry about such a little thing. Rosalía had money on her. 'Oh! Well ... all right, then. I'll pay you back tomorrow, or the day after ... Anyway, the next time I see you.'

For a moment, the good lady was perplexed and disconcerted, unsure of whether to repent of her offer or to congratulate herself on the noble service she was doing her friend. But the human mind is an infinite source of remedies for its own sufferings, and Rosalía's confusion was cured by a line of reasoning which conveniently popped into her head, and which went something like this: 'I'll pay half the bill at Sobrino's and I'll promise him the other half next month, without fail. I'll give poor Milagros the six hundred reals she needs and then I'll still have some left over for the piece of foulard, a few feathers for Isabel's hat and the mother-of-pearl buttons. I really and truly can't do without them.' And that is exactly what she did, following a plan whose logic was born in the jolting of a carriage that took her from shop to shop under the intoxicating influence of an overdose of fripperies.

CHAPTER 12

Francisco was entirely absorbed in his hair work, and never left it for a moment, devoting all the time left over from his very undemanding job to it. He had reluctantly called off his customary evening strolls; and his friend Manuel María José Pez, on

finding himself deprived of his usual companion on their hour-
long constitutional, promptly switched locations to the Palace
so as not to miss out on Bringas's company.

The walk from the Ministry to the Palace, and up the Ladies'
stairway – no mean feat – provided sufficient exercise to do him
some good; and if, in addition, he went out with Francisco and
his wife to do a few turns round the magnificent terrace that
overlooks the main courtyard, he was guaranteed a decent
appetite at mealtimes. Not even the most affectionate of scold-
ings managed to drag Bringas away from his labours while there
was still daylight. Neither by begging, nor reprimanding, nor
telling him that he would get sick, develop migraines or go
blind, could they get him to stop his feverish though disciplined
pace of work. Pez would spend some time chatting to him about
politics; but, usually, he would go out for a stroll on the terrace
with Rosalía. It was a peaceful and enjoyable walk, because
although the sides of the building were high enough to protect
the terrace from gusts of wind, there was plenty of air. The
Palace and its built-in city get the purest, freshest air from the
mountains, being sufficiently removed from the thick fumes of
the metropolis, and high enough up that not even the pigeons
and the sparrows enjoy such a healthy and constantly recharged
atmosphere. The stroll along that monumental walkway stimu-
lated the lady's imagination, bringing to mind the architectural
backdrops used by Rubens, Veronese, Van Loo* and other
artists to make their figures seem larger and more aristocratic.
Pez and Rosalía imagined themselves to be beautifully set off by
the balustrades, mouldings, sculpted arches and amphorae, an
assumption that made them unconsciously stand up straighter
and move in a way more in keeping with their majestic
surroundings.

Pez was the most respectable-looking man you ever saw, a
perfect example of the type of official known as *high* because he
has one of the larger shares in the allocation of State handouts;
a man who, both in physique and manner, embodied government power and the time-honoured maxims of the Civil Service.
He was extremely pleasant and cultured, good at small talk, and
capable of making a witty comment about anything, no matter
how far removed from his field of bureaucratic expertise. He
had been a hanger-on of politicians all his life, and had
accumulated a vast knowledge of contemporary history, which
on his lips was composed of an endless stream of personal

anecdotes. He was a scholar of political jokes, and wielded the encyclopaedia of parliamentary phrases with astonishing ease. Underneath this wordy exterior lay a sterile cynic, a moral atheist and a believer in the *fait accompli*, a disease all too common in those raised on Spanish politics, which is ruled by opportunism. He was a man hardened within and without, incapable of real enthusiasm for anything; but his face, peculiar though this may seem, revealed a tranquillity reminiscent of the saints in heaven above. Indeed, Pez's face said: 'I'm at the most comfortable time of my life. I'm just where I belong.' It was the face of a man who was determined never to get upset about anything, nor to take things very seriously, which is one way of solving life's greatest problem. As far as he was concerned, the Civil Service was just a cover-up, a lot of empty formulas created to conceal the real system of personal favours, which worked by bribery and recommendations. No one helped his friends as effectively as Pez, which was how he got his reputation as such a nice man. He had a unique talent for pleasing everybody, and he had a lot of followers, even on the revolutionary side.

His character shone through on his friendly face, which was wrinkle-free and incredibly well preserved, like one of those English countenances that have been weathered by fresh air and exercise. He was fifty, but looked a lot closer to forty; half a century adorned by sidewhiskers and a moustache of dark gold with a light sprinkling of silver, which were clean and shiny and whose gleaming condition suggested that they received their fair share of attention in front of the mirror. His eyes were pure Spanish; they held such serenity and sweetness one could not help thinking of Murillo's interpretation of St Joseph.* If Pez had not been cleanshaven and had been dressed in a tunic and staff instead of a frock-coat, he would have been the spitting image of Our Lord's father, as represented by the painters. Those eyes said to all who looked into them: 'I am the voice of sleepy, saintly Spain, which prefers to be fortune's toy and never interferes in anyone's business as long as it's allowed to eat in peace; in which nothing works, which expects nothing and lives happily in the present, gazing heavenwards with a flowering staff* in its hand; which submits to any who wish to rule it, whoever they may be, and professes mild socialism; which knows nothing of ideas, or action, or anything except daydreaming and digesting.'

The gentleman in question dressed extremely fashionably. It

was a joy to see how immaculately he was turned out. His clothes had the knack of never getting rumpled or dirty, and they hung on him beautifully. Morning and night, Pez always dressed with the same care: a double-breasted wool frock-coat, a pair of trousers that looked brand new, and a gleaming top hat, without any of this ever seeming affected or revealing the slightest effort or discomfort on his part. Just as the extraordinary polish of great writers comes over as perfectly natural and easy, in him formality came over as studied casualness. Wherever he went, he looked as distinguished as if he were going to the office, and you would have thought that the frock-coat, the trousers and the top hat were an integral part of the office itself, of Management, or the Civil Service, just the same as the letterhead, the portrait of the Queen, the velvet armchairs and the files tied up in red tape.

When he talked, people listened with pleasure, and he too enjoyed listening to himself, because he could watch his interlocutors' faces to see the effect he was having on them. His language was a model of the political style created here by journalists and orators. Since his mind had been formed by the propagators of florid prose, he could never manage to say anything clearly and simply, but always had to give it in triplicate.

Here is an example:

THIERS [*not looking up from his work*]: What's going on with those generals who've been banished?*
PEZ: At this point, my dear Francisco, it's impossible, it's tricky, it's very risky to venture an opinion. The revolution we've all laughed at, we've scoffed at, we've made fun of, is progressing, is mining away, is forging ahead, and the only thing we can wish for, the only thing we can pray for, is that they don't declare utter incompatibility, open struggle, open war between this revolution and the state, between these new ideas and the Crown, between these vital reforms and the person of Her Majesty herself.

CHAPTER 13

Pez and Rosalía, as I said, often went out for a walk round the terrace. The Rubens nymph, all plump and rounded, and the spiritual St Joseph, in a frock-coat and minus his staff of lilies, looked sublime against that architectural backdrop of white stone that looked like uncut marble. The train of her elegant dress swept along the clean paving stones asphalted together, while he walked along with his left hand in his trouser pocket underneath his frock-coat, gesticulating with the right one, in which he was holding a walking cane. Sometimes their attention was distracted by noises in the courtyard, and they would look over the balustrade to see what was going on. It would be the Princess and her relations going out in their carriage, or the Minister of State coming in in his. At times they would stop in front of Tula's apartment, where friends of theirs would wave frantically to them through the windows. Or they would stop and talk to Antonia, the cloakroom attendant, as she drew her blinds and watered her flowers; or they would be joined by some distinguished personage from the neighbourhood, the wife of the King's amanuensis, the sister of the Assistant Chief of Administration, the Inspector General and his daughter, and they would walk along together, making smalltalk. When they were completely alone, the good bureaucrat would confide in Rosalía about his marital problems, which had reached the point recently where they were beginning to disturb his natural equanimity.

Oh! The great Pez was not happily married. Mrs Pez, whose name was Carolina, a cousin of the Lantiguas (although there was a mistaken reference to her in another story as a descendent of the mighty Pipaón tree), had become very religious. She used to be all sweetness and light, but these days she had become snappish and unbearable. She got irritated about everything and was forever nagging her husband. She made such a show of moral rectitude and was so obsessed with religious observances that she was driving him mad with her vile temper, her inquisitorial prying and her harsh criticism of other people's behaviour. Months would go by without the two of them exchanging a single word. Their home was like a club for perpetual bickering and arguments over the slightest little thing. 'If it were just between her and me,' said Pez, 'I could put up with it; but recently the children have got mixed up in this too.' The poor girls had no desire to follow their mother down the road to salvation ... Naturally, they were young and enjoyed going to the theatre and socialising. The conflict between these worldly pleasures and what the girls' mother saw as their religious obligation caused endless rows, rages and tears. There seemed to be a commotion every day, and one of them would throw a fit and they'd have to call the doctor and send out for some drug or other ... Pez tried to smooth things out and get them to make it up, but he never succeeded. When it came down to it, he tended to side with the girls, because he hated to see them praying all the time and doing stupid penances. They were Christian girls and good Catholics, why try and force them to be saints and martyrs? As far as he was concerned, religion was a form of control that was vital to the maintenance of society and law and order. He had always defended religion and had no problem with the government protecting it and persecuting its opponents. He even admitted that a certain sanctimoniousness on the State's part was vital to the political régime of the day, but he couldn't stand sanctimoniousness in the privacy of his own home.

The worst thing of all was Carolina's struggle with her sons. The little one was still tied to his mother's apron-strings, and spent the whole day in church with a prayer-book in his hand. But how could Joaquín, who was twenty-two years old, and a lawyer, philosopher, economist, author, columnist, historiographer, poet, theogonist, and member of the Atheneum,* be submitted to obligatory confessions and mass every Sunday? Federico was very precocious too, and was doing some little articles on the *Mahabharata*.* All hell would break loose every time one or other of them said something that sounded like blasphemy to their mother. Lord, the woman would go beserk! One day, at lunch, she snatched off the tablecloth, broke the plates, spilt everything that was on them as well as the salt and the wine, and shut herself up in her room to cry for three hours. She made poor little Rosa and Josefa, who were in short skirts until only last autumn, go to confession every single month! Poor girls! What sins could they possibly have to confess, when they didn't even have beaux yet?

The hardest thing was that the bad-tempered woman blamed Pez for his offspring's lack of religious sentiment. He was nothing but an atheist in disguise, a heretic, a rationalist, because he only went to Mass on Sundays and even then stood right in the doorway and talked politics with Francisco Cucúrbitas.* He thought if he bent his knee when they raised the host, knelt down at the altar and crossed himself from time to time, that that was all he needed to do. He'd be better off being a Protestant, in that case. The whole time they'd been married she'd never once seen him go up to the confessional. His faith was all for show, like carrying an axe in a procession or sitting in the front pew when a bishop was being ordained. Anyway, with all this nonsense from his wife, things weren't exactly going swimmingly for poor Pez;* in fact, he was at his wits' end and desperately tired. He knew perfectly well who had got Carolina started on this mysticism business; it was her cousin Serafina Lantigua, who had a reputation as a saint. To be frank, that cousin of hers was a disaster. Carolina and Serafina saw each other every day in church, at six in the morning, and they talked to their hearts' content there. At home, Mrs Pez, switching from the comminative to the comparative mode, told her children they should be imitating the virtues of little St Luis Tellería, who was a saint in swaddling bands and had already started flailing his own pink flesh. She told poor Pez he ought to try and copy Juan de Lantigua, a good Catholic and a good lawyer and writer, a pious man in practice and not just in theory, who never flouted the scriptures; his Christianity was not just a show, but true and sincere; he was a brave, upstanding man, who was not ashamed to follow his religion and spend three hours on his knees with a bunch of church-loving women. He wasn't like Pez, and all the rest of the Moderates,* who used their faith like a stepladder to get into high office; he wasn't like those men who use Church money to get rich themselves and then preach Catholicism, as if it weren't obvious to anybody but a fool what they were doing; like those men who have Jesus on their lips and the devil in their hearts, who think that if they give the odd donation to the Pope they've done their bit. What a joke, what a sham, what a disgusting scandal!

All in all, Manuel had come to hate his home and spent as much time out of it as possible. The only time he got any peace and quiet was in his office, where all he did was smoke and receive visits from friends; and in other people's houses, like the

Bringas's, for example. Oh, how he envied Francisco his peaceful home and the way he and his wife got on so beautifully together! He had been happy once too, but not any more. *Et in Arcadia ego.** He was an outcast, an exile, and he begged them to like him and look after him a bit, to make up for his stormy home life.

Pez told Rosalía all this in impassioned tones, and she listened to him with the greatest interest and sympathy. They would talk and talk, barely noticing the time go by, and when the shadows crept slowly up from the courtyard, mingled with a waft of cool, damp air; when the last rays of the sun lingered on the tops of the buildings and pale stars began to stud the sky, Francisco would abandon his labours with the hairs and appear, rubbing his eyes, to join in the conversation.

CHAPTER 14

Ever since cousin Agustín had emigrated to Bordeaux, Mr and Mrs Bringas went to the theatre very seldom, using tickets given to them by friends who were sick or who were bored of seeing the same play over and over again. Milagros was kind enough to host a series of little get-togethers at her home, on Mondays or Tuesdays, I forget which. Francisco used to take his wife to them; but he had been feeling so tired lately that Rosalía had started going on her own with Paquito. In May, that discerning young man could no longer neglect his studies because of the approaching exams, and he would accompany his Mama to the Tellerías' door and then return home to do his duty by his books. Pez was in charge of escorting Mrs Bringas back to the conjugal residence, at midnight or one in the morning, and in between the beginning of Atocha Street and the Palace, which is not a very long way, Manuel rarely missed the opportunity to intone a lamentation about his domestic difficulties. Every night he told a more pathetic story, and he called forth storms of compassion in Rosalía's heart.

When she got back to the house, Francisco would have worn out his eyes and his brain by having read two or three newspapers after working on the cenotaph, and he would be just drifting off to sleep in bed, coughing and snoring by turns. After checking the children's rooms to see that they were properly covered up and that Isabel was not having nightmares, Rosalía would chat with her husband for a while as she peeled off all her finery, her skirts and the machinery of her corset, after which her imprisoned flesh would visibly regain its freedom. Although she thoroughly enjoyed the gatherings at Milagros's house, the truth was that the routine of having to butter up her husband afterwards provoked rather the opposite sensation; but we can easily forgive her this, in view of the extraordinarily perceptive comments she made about the people and things she had seen in the Tellería household.

'If you don't come with me, my sweet, I'm not going back there. You can't imagine how much I hate those gatherings at Milagros's. They're not my scene at all. You should just see what goes on! By the way, something really funny happened today ... Poor Milagros, we're quite close and she tells me everything, I know as much about her money troubles as if I were going through them myself. It's so embarrassing. I don't know how she has the nerve to invite people over when she's so hard up. All she'd laid on tonight was a few sweet things and some snacks. It was dreadful! You can imagine what all the scroungers will be saying; you know, the ones who only go to these things to get a free dinner. I've never met a woman with more nerve. At seven o'clock, she still didn't know what she was going to serve for the buffet. She sent out to the baker's ... it's hilarious ... and they refused to charge twenty pounds of biscuits to her account. I don't know where she managed to get those leftover bits of cooked ham and that half-mouldy boar's head. It was disgusting. It's true she did have some good wines. Heaven only knows where she got them and who was fool enough to sell them to her. She's really at her wits' end, but you'd never know it! She was as cool as a cucumber; smiling at everyone; but when she went back into the kitchen she would metamorphose into a captain wielding the helm of a sinking ship. [*Indignantly.*] Oh! It's that pathetic, good-for-nothing Marqués's fault. He's up to his ears in debt, and when the collectors come after him, he's going to find himself without a shirt to his back. Poor Milagros is very sweet, she's as kind as can be; but the money that woman spends! If you put twenty thousand reals in her hand, she'll spend them in one day, just as if they were a hundred. I give her advice, I tell her off, I draw up budgets and plans for her to follow; but it doesn't do any good.

She's hopeless. Sometimes she seems to be doing better; but then she goes out, goes into a shop, sees some fancy thing she likes, and there goes her money! She loses her head, and goes on a buying spree. When I catch her doing it, I tell her: "You must be out of your mind." You can't imagine what she's like! It's the children I feel sorry for. This evening I went into Leopoldo's room; it looks like the doorway of a neighbourhood shoe-maker's. The wall is covered in silly pictures stuck on with tape: bull-fighting scenes and caricatures from the newspapers. It looks just awful, everything all over the place. It stinks of medicine, because the boy's a wreck; there are penny novelettes everywhere instead of textbooks; enough whips and sticks to start up a shop; and the bed was unmade because he didn't get up till six in the afternoon. He was limping around in shabby old boots, begging for something to eat and eyeing the sweets and the cold cuts, waiting to stuff his face at the first oppor-tunity, as if he were dying of hunger. Gustavo's a different kettle of fish altogether. He's so polite and well brought up! There he was talking to the men and using all sorts of impressive long words. He looks like a little doll from Scropp's* in his miniature frock-coat, and when he walks and talks he looks as if he'd been wound up with a key. María is beginning to look gorgeous. The Marquesa doesn't want her to celebrate her coming-out yet because it'll make her look old in comparison, which is a crying shame, because she's such a well-developed little woman already. She's got more bust than her mother, you know ... it's a real shame to see her in the back rooms, playing with her dolls, hanging around the servants and doing her French trans-lations. She had her hands full tonight, poor thing, trying to stop her little brother putting his filthy hands all over everything and touching the sweets and licking the ice cream. I ate a sweet that reeked of cod-liver oil, I bet that Leopoldo had been fingering it.'

[*Indignant again.*] And as for the Marqués ... what a creature! To listen to him, you'd think he was the wisest man in the world, if you didn't know him. All he ever talks about is the Senate and what they've said or are going to say there. What a talker! He would fix everything that's wrong with Spain given half the chance ... But since he doesn't get the chance, it's the nation's loss. According to him, he spends all his time on committees, doing reports on this and that. Milagros says he's been obsessed with maids for the last few months, and they can't have one in the house unless she's horrifically ugly. Underneath that gentlemanly appearance, he's nothing but a lecher. He can't stand me, because I'm always making little digs at him. Honestly, he makes me sick; I'm so sorry for poor Milagros. Poor woman, what she has to put up with! She's always broke because of that husband of hers, as she calls him, and she goes through hell to make ends meet. I wouldn't be surprised if she'd had a fling or two on the sly . . . I'm not saying she has, but other people do, and even though I'm repeating it in private that doesn't mean I believe it, because if . . .'

Francisco, who was fast asleep by this point, was as far away from these paltry incidents his wife was recounting as Heaven is from the Earth.

CHAPTER 15

The things she confided to him weren't always the same, for Rosalía's vivid imagination instinctively sought to vary those nightly doses of gossip with which she lulled her husband to sleep. Intent on playing the role she had assigned herself some time ago, and which had demanded a great deal of effort on her part since it drew further away from her real feelings each day, she pretended to be annoyed about things that, in fact, pleased her, *verbi gratia*: 'Oh, my dear! I thought our friend Pez was never going to stop telling me about the rows he's having with his wife! I do feel sorry for him. But the man drives me mad with his endless spiel of complaints! Carolina's acting dreadfully, it's true, and I wish to goodness she'd behave better, if only so that we wouldn't have to put up with all this from her husband.'

Francisco always fell asleep before her. Sometimes she would stay awake tossing and turning until very late, envying the good man sleeping peacefully, reclining on the soft pillow of his conscience like an angel on the clouds of Heaven. The ingenious lady found no such soft cushions in her own mind, but something hard and spiky that kept her awake all night instead. Her passion for luxury had unwittingly led her on to treacherous ground, and she had to hide the things she was continually acquiring by means utterly foreign to the Bringas family economy. The drawers of her bureau were stuffed with pieces of material, some already cut out and others waiting for the scissors. An enormous trunk of hers held all sorts of bits and pieces in suspicious secrecy, some of them old and reworked, and others new, all of them half finished, bearing signs that they had been hastily abandoned because of inconvenient interruptions. It was vital to conceal this from Francisco's financial vigilance; the man never missed a thing, and would question so much as a reel of thread that did not figure in his budget. Rosalía lay awake at nights trying to think up fibs to get her off the hook if she were ever caught. How on earth was she going to explain the huge rise in the quality and quantity of her wardrobe? The line about being a present from the Queen was wearing rather thin and she was in danger of running into trouble if she used it again.

One day, Francisco came home from the office earlier than usual and found Rosalía at her favourite occupation, working in the *Camón* as if it were a modiste's workshop, with the assistance of a dressmaker she had called in. The *Camón* looked less like a sewing room than a branch of Sobrino Brothers.

'Heavens above, woman, what's going on?' gasped Thiers, in a trance, like someone witnessing supernatural or magical events and unwilling to believe his own eyes.

There were about twenty-four yards of checked mozambique,* at eight reals a yard, a lovely gauzy fabric that our Rosalía dreamed of wearing night after night. The huge length of material ran the whole length of the room, clambered over the chairs, toppled over the arms of the sofa and sprawled out on the floor, where it was being cut into pieces by the dressmaker, who was down on her knees checking the pattern before cutting. There were strips and pieces of *glacé*, the strangest geometrical shapes cut on the bias, all over the trunk, waiting for a skilful hand to combine them with the mozambique. Gleaming bits of satin in bright colours for the warm tones, so far still in the artist's mind, confronted poor Bringas in disarray all over the room, in between half unrolled lengths of ribbon and scraps of lace. The two women could not walk around in there without their skirts getting caught up in the mozambique and in twenty yards of navy blue poplin which had fallen off a chair and got mixed up with strips of foulard. In all that artistic disorder you could smell that special clothes-shop smell, made up of leftover industrial dye mixed with paper and wood and packing material. On the sofa, half a dozen fashion-plates in improbable colours displayed those impossible, reed-thin, ramrod-straight women whose feet are the size of a finger; women with red smudges for mouths, dressed in paper and gazing at one another with imbecilic expressions.

Rosalía's first impulse on being caught *in fraganti* was to grab everything; but there was no time, and her terror caused her to come up with an excuse, a brilliant stroke of her talented imagination.

'Calm down, my dear, for goodness' sake,' she said, putting her arm round him and gently guiding him out of the *Camón* so that the dressmaker would not hear. 'I thought I told you about all this last night. These dresses belong to Milagros. The poor woman had a horrendous row with that oaf the Marqués yesterday, you've no idea. She told him he was the one that spent all the money, he said it was her, and they kept going on like that. They almost came to blows. I was there. I can tell you, I was seriously thinking of sending for first aid. Milagros can't order anything from Eponina's any more because her husband won't pay the bills, so she went ahead and bought some material and called in a dressmaker to help her make a couple of summer dresses ... A perfectly normal thing to do. The poor woman was making do with twenty-four yards of mozambique at eight reals a yard and twenty-two of poplin at fifty-six. She was being really economical. Well, anyway; in comes that good-for-nothing husband of hers, who'd probably just lost several thousand on cards, and the moment he sees the materials and the dressmaker, he starts swearing like a trooper. Dear Heaven! It was just awful ... There he was, stamping on the materials and kicking the fashion-plates, roaring away, I don't know, all about how poor Milagros had ruined him with her glad rags. Did you ever hear anything so ridiculous? Then he stopped talking and grabbed the dressmaker by the arm and put her out on the street without so much as the time to put her shawl on. See what a pig he is? Milagros fainted. We had to give her ether and all sorts of things to bring her round. Anyway, to get her out of the mess she was in, I said she could bring the materials and the dressmaker here and finish the work. Milagros will be over later to direct her, because really and truly I don't know much about those fancy, overblown dresses. That girl Emilia is excellent and not very expensive. She's a really down-to-earth little thing, but she beats Worth* hollow, for all he's so famous, you wouldn't believe it.'

Thanks to this ingenious display, the good man calmed down, and since the Marquesa showed up shortly afterwards and the three women shut themselves up in the *Camón* and spent the rest of the day chatting, cutting, measuring, trying out, unpicking and trying on again, Rosalía's story seemed perfectly acceptable. Nevertheless, the lady was worried about the insuperable difficulties that would arise when she first wore the new dresses, because then the stories she had concocted so carefully would be flying in the face of the evidence. She consoled herself by hoping for something that would be an easy and foolproof solution. González Bravo* had offered Francisco the governorship of a province. Pez was encouraging him to accept, saying he would do a great job and that any province that got such a well-liked and respected governor would be jumping for joy. But Francisco was put off by the difficulties of the post, and he had no desire to give up the quiet and peaceful life he enjoyed so much. If Bringas ever accepted the position, he could go off and live in his kingdom like Sancho Panza, and his disconsolate wife would stay in Madrid, where she would be free to wear as many new dresses as she liked. But since it was much more likely that the great economist would not accept, Rosalía racked her brains trying to come up with a way out of her dilemma, and eventually hit on a formula which she went over and over in her mind, rehearsing it long before the occasion came to try it out.

CHAPTER 16

'You see, my love,' she would say to herself a month ahead of time, 'something dreadful happened. I didn't want to tell you because I knew you'd get upset, after all, she is our friend and the work was done in our house. Emilia insisted on being paid in advance ... wouldn't budge an inch. And then all of a sudden, boom! The bill from Sobrino's came. Poor Milagros couldn't manage to pay either of them. You'll never imagine the scrapes she's gone and got herself into. I'll tell you one day. Anyway, to make a long story short, I took the dresses for less than a third of their value and did the alterations myself so as to save money. They were a gift, a real bargain. Emilia insisted I take them, she says I can pay her whenever I want. So you see . . .'

She rehearsed the script a million times so she would be ready when the opportunity came to perform it. Meanwhile, she worked non-stop in the *Camón*, assisted by Milagros, who would always show up with some new thing or clever idea, the latest product of her teeming imagination, *verbi gratia*: 'I can't afford to spend a lot on my summer wardrobe this year. So here's what I'm going to do. Rotondo and Sons* have given me twenty-four yards of really fancy barege*. The Marquesa de San Salomó says barege is in this summer. To tell you the truth, I was getting sick and tired of mozambique anyway. Yes, really . . . I'll have this dress made up in a very simple style, the shepherdess look. It's going to have three flounces, and trimmings in very fine silk. It'll have a little tiny frill covered in lace, and an embroidered panel for those jockey-style epaulettes . . . There's a lilac waistband with a little rosette at the front. You know, I think that hat is overdoing it a bit . . . I've got an idea for another one. Listen to this. I've got a toque left over from last year, and those velvet ribbons. All I need now is a plume and one of those new Marabou feathers* to go on the right-hand side, like this . . .'

At the beginning of May, Rosalía had to give up this delightful work, much against her will. The doctor had ordered that Isabel be taken for a walk every morning. The weather was absolutely beautiful and cried out for pleasant trips to the peace of the Retiro Park. The lady began taking Isabel and her little boy for morning walks, and from the second day they were joined by Pez, who was suffering from a chronic lack of appetite. Moreno Rubio* had prescribed getting up early, downing a big glass of water from the Egyptian Well or the Fountain of Health, and going for a two-hour walk before lunch.

The four of them would all trip happily off to the Royal gardens in the Retiro, which they were allowed into because Rosalía was from the Palace. The children had a wonderful time looking at the Poor Man's Cottage, the Smuggler's Den and the Persian Villa, throwing bread to the ducks at the Fisherman's House, running up the spiral staircase on the aptly named Artificial Mountain,* which is, indeed, about as artificial as you can get. All those Royal whimsies, like the Menagerie, were clearly built during the reign of Ferdinand VII,* a brutal time in politics and an utterly ridiculous one in the arts.

Rosalía and Manuel perked up considerably under the favourable influence of the garlands of vegetation, the fresh air and the warmth of the spring sunshine, and sometimes they became almost as childish as the children, chattering incessantly and walking with somewhat less than grown-up gravity, rushing about wildly and then suddenly checking themselves, while the children played hide-and-seek in the thick undergrowth. The glass of water worked miracles on the bureaucrat's mucous membranes and digestive system, achieving marvellous results. Once his vital functions were back in working order, he regained his good spirits and his extreme verbosity, to say nothing of his chivalrous instincts, which were not neglected in this matinal resurrection. It seems incredible that a glass of water could produce such amazing results. So many times the remedy for the most chronic ailments is right there in our hands, unbeknownst to us! ... Pez's fluent tongue skipped from one topic to another, and soon arrived at the chapter on compliments, which in this case were perfectly genuine. He promptly set about pondering the lady's youthfulness and charm. Everything she wore looked so fetching on her, and she carried herself like a queen! Not many people had her gift for dressing well, nor her knack of making anything she wore look elegant ... Rosalía almost choked on these wafts of incense; or rather, I should say that her store of vanity (a kind of bladder located in the chests of the vain) became so extraordinarily inflated that she could scarcely breathe. She too was secretly experiencing an itch to confide in him; but respect for her husband held her back. In the end, though, Pez's eulogies of her became so exaggerated, that indiscretion won out over prudence. I saw them several times on their way home. She was carrying a bunch of lilac, with her veil tossed back as if sacrificing formality to the freedom of country life; her cheeks were rosy from exercise and animated discussion. He was bearing an auxiliary bunch of lilac, looking like a boy, magically ten years younger; the children would be running all over the place, getting their clothes all muddy, whipping each other with wands they had cut from saplings, and jumping over puddles. Rosalía was always talking, disconsolately and with a certain gentle melancholy; but who but Pez could catch what she was saying?

The poor dear could never wear anything pretty, because her

husband ... First of all, she had to say that he was an angel, a marvellous person ... But that didn't stop him from being very tight with money and abusing her by keeping her so badly dressed that no one ever took any notice of her. And it certainly was not because they were short of money, because Bringas had plenty of savings that he'd built up bit by bit. And all for what? For nothing at all, just for the pleasure of hoarding coins in a box and getting them out to count and gloat over every so often. There was no doubt that the man ... he was a very good person, of course, a wonderful husband and an excellent father ... but he hadn't a clue how to keep his wife in the social position they now occupied because of his job. She had to deal with people at the highest levels, people with titles, even with the Queen; but Bringas, who saw everything through the eyes of a miser, insisted she stick to that horrible black dress and half a dozen dreadful old things she'd had for ever. Oh! It was unbelievable the things she had to go through, the things she had to stoop to to look halfway decent. The Lord only knew how much she'd suffered! Her husband kept track of everything, even the parsley they used in the kitchen got written down in his account book ... His poor wife, concerned for their social standing, was turning into a second Newton* thanks to the endless sums she had to do in her noddle to come up with something left over from the household expenses to help her eke out the meagre amounts that Bringas gave her to buy clothes. The distressed damsel worked her fingers to the bone sewing and fixing up her clothes; but he went through the accounts with such a fine toothcomb that she was at her wits' end to try and squeeze out three reals one day and two and a half the next; and sometimes she couldn't get anything at all. This sort of constant struggle made for a life of torment, and it wasn't that she wanted to live in the lap of luxury, no, that wasn't it; but she felt that her position and the contact she had to have with all sorts of important people created some inevitable obligations; she didn't think she and the children should have to be shown up in the houses they visited, and she didn't like the way her friends looked her up and down and whispered among themselves, when she turned up in a mended skirt, looking dowdy and old-fashioned. All the same, she loved her husband dearly, because aside from the fact that he was so mean, he was a perfect gentleman, as sweet as could be, good and kind, as honest as they come, a man who never did anything remotely underhand and who never ran after loose women or bet on cards, a man who was so easy-going that he'd do anything you said unless it happened to affect his budget in some way . . . In view of this, the poor woman put up with all the rest, the little problems with clothes, and did her best not to look as if she didn't belong in her high station. From all of which, it transpired that both Mr Pez and Mrs Bringas had their own respective motives for marital disagreement, he because of his wife's insane saintliness, and she because of her husband's petty pennypinching; which just goes to show that no one is entirely happy in this world, and that it is rare to find two people completely at ease and in tune with one another within the cage of matrimony, since the devil or society or God himself confounds and mismatches couples to frustrate them all, so that each caged pair can work on deserving its place in Heaven.

CHAPTER 17

By the time the conversation came round to philosophical matters of this sort, they would be leaving by the Glorieta gate. By then, the famous avenues of horse chestnuts had been cut down, the iron railings removed and the land put up for sale, an operation which had been dubbed a 'gallant gesture'.* This expression was an ill-fated one for the monarchy; being of greater antiquity than the horse chestnuts did it no good, for in the end it found itself hacked down and sold for firewood just the same.

When they left the Retiro for the city streets, the group recovered its composure. The children walked in front holding hands. The adults, now that they were in view of the city dwellers, halted the confidential discussions which had been the delightful product of the pleasures of the countryside. It was as if they were passing from a free country to another full of rules and regulations. At home, while she was working in the *Camón* alone or with Emilia, Bringas's wife would muse over the outpourings of that morning, adding some ideas of her own that never dared cross the frontier of the land of thought. As she worked away on her outfits, the lady would go off into another world in her dreams, exercising the right conceded to all those who think that they are not in the position they deserve or that they married the wrong people, to revise and rectify the social order in their own minds.

'Now, that Pez is a real man. Any woman with some intelligence and presence, with an air of nobility, could look good next to him. But since the world's all topsy turvy, he's ended up with that praying mule Carolina. Everything's back to front! What woman worth her salt wouldn't end up looking small and worthless next to my boring little Bringas, who can only see petty things and is incapable of carving out a brilliant career and a respectable position for himself? What can you expect from a man who, when he's offered a governorship, instead of jumping for joy, starts sighing and saying, "I prefer my tools to a staff of office." Oh, but Pez! There's a real man for you. And I know who he should have married, if things were working right in this world and everyone was in their proper place. A man like that needs a woman with principles and a way with words, a lady with exquisite manners, who would know how to make her husband look good by looking good herself; a lady who would do herself credit by making him great; because the key to a lot of men's brilliant careers lies in the talent of their wives. Paquito was only saying yesterday that Napoleon would never have been anybody if it hadn't been for Josephine. If Pez had married a lady who knew how to entertain all the top politicians in her house, instead of that religious fool, he'd be a minister by now . . . Really . . . If only I were married to a man like that! But just try making a minister out of Bringas; the man gets in a bad mood if he has to give sugar water to a visitor; he wants me to wear a nun's habit and have the children go round in espadrilles. Oh! You stingy skinflint, you'll never be anybody. Oh, Pez! If you were married to the right woman, there's no way you'd let her go out on the street looking a fright and letting you down. Bringas, you could learn a thing or two from a man with a salary of fifty thousand reals who pays twenty-four thousand reals' rent but lives as if he made two hundred and forty thousand a year. It's not that he gets into debt, he just knows how to sell himself and make the most of his position. A boring little man like you would never be able to do that in a million years, always nitpicking about this or that, and going on at me for three hours over whether I did or did not put seven extra chickpeas in the stew; a man like you would never understand that, because all he can see is his stupid little salary;

who's terrified they'll give him a medal because then he'll have
to buy the insignia; who doesn't want to be governor of a
province; who refuses to let the water carrier bring me up two
extra barrels of water because he thinks there's no need to do
anything more than give your face a quick splash; who's
convinced I shouldn't need more than eighteen yards of material
to make a dress, and suggests I trim the children's hats with the
damask ribbon that demobbed soldiers use to tie up their official
discharge papers; who maintains that cashmere is prettier than
silk, and says that carriage hoods are useless just because they're
not cheap; who won't let me fix up my robe with ottoman
ribbon and went so far as to suggest I use the yellow ribbons
from cousin Agustín's bundles of cigars . . .'

Some afternoons, when Pez and Rosalía could not go out on
the gallery because of bad weather, the three of them would stay
in and chat in *Gasparini*. They would be submitted to Manuel's
lavish praises of his friend's marvellous hair work. He would
stand next to Bringas, with his left hand in his trouser pocket,
chewing his moustache and gazing judiciously at the wondrous
sheet of glass, as packed with tresses as a human head, all hairs
and clean spaces, the whole lot looking freshly shaved, gummy,
sticky, and gleaming as if from the perfumed lotions of a
hairdresser.

'It's superb . . . You're so skilled with your hands, and so
patient! It ought to go in a museum.'

And to himself he would add, chewing harder on his moustache and digging his hand deeper in his pocket: 'What a
damnfool waste of time. Trust that thick head of yours to come
up with something like this. You're the only person idiotic
enough to dream up something this ridiculous, and my wife's
the only person who could like it. You're made for each other.'

When Francisco stopped work that day, he was more
exhausted than he had ever been before. He was seeing double
and his head was whirling as if he were on board ship. But he
told himself it would pass, and congratulated himself on how
fast he was working and how nicely it was turning out. The
angel was completely done already, with those incredibly tiny
dots of hair. The willow draped its weeping branches protec-
tively over the tomb, and it was too bad there was no such thing
as green hair, because it would have put the finishing touches to
the illusion. The background was completely ready; it was a
model perspective of melancholia, to such an extent that only

someone with a heart of flint could have contemplated it without
getting misty-eyed. All that was left now was the flowers and
the whole foreground area. Bringas had decided at the last
minute to put in some broken, tumbledown columns like those
of a ruined temple, so as to give an even stronger impression of
desolation.

By the beginning of June, the best part of the work was done,
but he still had to add a few odds and ends, such as minute
sunflowers and giant pansies, as well as a few sentimental
butterflies with black wings dotted about, sipping sweet nectar
from the flowers of the piliform flora. At about the same time,
certain things happened of which the worthy artist was completely unaware; but for this very reason they should be
explained here. As the appointed day drew nearer for Rosalía to
pay back Torres's money, she became so dejected that, to look
at her, you would have thought that she had been robbed or
suffered some terrible outrage. She racked her brains trying to
come up with a solution to the fearful problem, but the numbers
refused to add up to the sum she needed ... She had an idea.
Should she try Mr Pez? Oh! If she knocked at that door she was
sure of a hearing, but she dared not do it. Anyway, Manuel was
just about to leave for Archena* where he was going to take the
waters (since if he didn't get a complete overhaul twice a year
he was a wreck), and wouldn't be back until the twentieth. On
the twelfth, Torres showed up, with his eyes like hardboiled
eggs that radiated mild astonishment. He looked like the pleas-
antest man in the world caught in the act of being garrotted. His
sickly sweet smile affected Rosalía like a noxious vapour,
permeating her whole being and making her ill. He was so
impertinent with his little nose and that irritating habit of
stroking his beard, as if he were going to produce something
from it! That rather good-looking man, who had always left
Rosalía cold, seemed to her just then like a handsome hangman
who had materialised before her with his rope and sack.

CHAPTER 18

And talk about being persistent! ... The man would not budge
an inch. He had to have it by the fourteenth without fail. He

could not postpone it by a day or even an hour, because his reputation with Mompous was at stake, and if Rosalía could not come up with the money, he would have to ask Francisco for it.

'Merciful Heavens ... don't even think of such a thing, Lord! You must be out of your mind,' stammered Bringas's wife, tense and trembling.

She went over her accounts for the hundredth time. Even if she sold things she didn't want to sell, she couldn't come up with the money. The pawnshop had yielded a little; but the good lady had already spent some of it on bits and bobs to make the children look nice. If only Milagros would pay her back the six hundred reals she had borrowed to pay the jewellers ... Well, now she would just have to. She would demand the money back. If only, by some devilish ruse, or rather by a miracle of Her Divine Majesty, Cándida turned out to have some money ... ! Cándida owed her one hundred reals which Rosalía had lent her when she needed change for a thousand. Those waylaid reals would have to be brought back to the fold too. Vowing to be firm, she went to pay a visit to the Marquesa. But unfortunately, her timing was out. The Marquesa was at a church service which she and some other ladies were paying for. It was a novena* dedicated to some saint or other, with an adoration of the eucharist, stations of the cross, rosary, sermon, novena, verses in honour of the saint, communion prayers and ritual replacement of the blessed sacrament. Rosalía went straight there, anxious to see her friend that very afternoon. The street was packed with elegant carriages. The church, which was resplendent with gold, had been decorated with cheap velvet curtains, gold paper trim, endless oil-lamps, huge bouquets of artificial flowers, and draperies that looked like props from a third-rate theatre. It was so full that it was hard to get inside the door. Rosalía managed to squeeze her way through the elegant congregation, but she could not get as far as the Marquesa, who was perched up near the altar, next to the priests. A long, long time went by, during which Rosalía listened to half a sermon, delivered in a whining, high-pitched voice, a mishmash of clichés seasoned with theatrical gestures, followed by some droning chants. Finally, it got so late that she despaired of these tedious proceedings ever coming to an end, and had to leave without seeing Milagros. The poor lady was a martyr to her husband's insufferable ways, and could not risk getting home late, for if lunch was not on the table at exactly the appointed hour, Francisco would start huffing and puffing and saying rather nasty things, like, 'Well, dear, I must say I'm quite faint with hunger. Next time you might let us know, so we can have lunch without you.'

She spent a very restless night, and at twelve o'clock the next day, 13 June, she was just getting ready to go and see her friend when Milagros herself showed up, in a great commotion. It was clear from her face, as well as from her lack of make-up, the tremor in her voice and other signs of turmoil, that something untoward was up. Rosalía became as anxious as her friend when she heard the following words: 'Oh, Rosalía! My dear, I'm in a terrible mess! You've got to help me or . . .'

'Me?' said Bringas's wife, recoiling, as she realised that her friend had money problems just like herself. 'You haven't exactly chosen a good time . . . If only you knew . . . I was just coming to see you.'

'At home? . . . I'll tell you what's the matter and I hope you feel really, really sorry for me. Tomorrow I'm giving a ball and a dinner, a big family occasion, absolutely vital. I've already sent out the invitations . . . What a mess! Oh Lord, would you mind pouring me a glass of water, my dear, I can't speak. I've got a sort of lump in my throat . . . [*Swallows a few sips of water.*] I was going to have Bonelli cater the dinner, to save myself trouble. I sent for him yesterday. I thought it would all be perfectly straightforward to arrange; but he had the unbelievable impudence to demand I pay him for the other three dinners I owe him. I wish I could; it's not as if I like being in debt . . . Believe you me, it's that wretched husband of mine who's to blame for us living like this . . . But anyway. Where was I? You can't imagine the state I'm in. Oh yes! Well, given the way Bonelli was behaving, I sent for Trouchín* this morning, you know, the one on Arenal Street, he's never catered for me before; I asked if he could do tomorrow's dinner for me, I suggested a price, we came to an agreement; but then, would you believe it? The dreadful man said very politely and in a roundabout way that if I didn't pay him first, he wouldn't do it . . . I was mortified. It's the first time such a thing has ever happened to me . . . Let me tell you, those caterers are a right bunch. No doubt Bonelli went and warned Trouchín and told him I owed him three dinners. It's a conspiracy against me, a plot . . . To tell the truth, my dear, they're right, you know; but it's not my fault. It's that useless little man I'm married to! ... You just can't say enough bad things about him. He's impossible to slander ... Yesterday I had to pay a bill from his tailor, who wouldn't stop ringing the front door bell. So you see what a pickle I'm in: what do you think I should do, can you see any way out?'

Rosalía said timidly that she had no idea how to guide her friend through the maze, especially since she was in a jam herself and had been relying on Milagros to pay back the ... that sum of six hundred reals that very day.

'Oh! Yes, I remember perfectly ... I put the money in my purse just the day before yesterday to bring you ... I'm sorry ... but before I even left the house, the church accountant showed up with the bill for my share of yesterday's service, and ... My dear, I had to cough up ... And by the way, I did see you in church yesterday, I'm sorry we weren't sitting together, I kept wanting to say things to you. The service itself was lovely, but have you ever seen such a bunch of idiots in the congregation? Cucúrbitas's wife came in that overpowering brown dress that makes her look like a member of the Tobacconist Order.* The uniform of the place. San Salomó overdid it too, I've never seen such a huge bustle, and even if it is fashionable to wear them bigger every day, I do think she might have toned it down for church. And what about those amazing puffs on her dress ... And that train? As for me ... did you see what I was wearing? The simplest outfit I could find ... But to get back to the point, my love. Can't you give me some advice? Tell me what to do, because I've come over all stupid. If I don't find a solution by tomorrow, I'm done for ... This is the sort of thing people commit suicide over.'

Out of curiosity, Rosalía asked her friend how much she needed, and when she learned it was about nine or rather ten thousand reals, she looked so annoyed that Milagros's distress doubled.

'Oh! You're not being very encouraging ... And to top it all, yesterday afternoon Eponina gave me a horrible shock. I tell you, I have the worst luck ... She sent me some bills that were absolutely exorbitant ... Two thousand reals for making up a dress! And one thousand five hundred for some alterations to a day dress. Just for alterations! ... I could have killed her ...'

'Ten thousand reals!' muttered Rosalía, staring at the ground and counting the syllables like coins. 'Just a fifth of that would be enough for me.'

'How about asking Francisco?' began Milagros, determinedly, giving to understand that dear Bringas must have some savings.

'No, don't even mention it, for Heaven's sake! If my husband ever finds out ...' the other woman replied, in a panic. 'This sort of thing drives him mad.'

'What about Cándida?'

'Lord help us!'

'You never know, she might turn out to ... I forgot to say that if I pawn a few things, I could come up with four thousand reals. All I need is six thousand.'

'Absolutely no way.'

'And Torres ...' mumbled Milagros, whose throat was so dry that her tongue was sticking to the roof of her mouth.

'Heavens! Torres! ... Don't be ridiculous!' exclaimed Rosalía, who suddenly saw the image of her creditor before her in her mind's eye, like an apparition from the other world. 'I don't think I told you that tomorrow by twelve ... Oh! I was crazy to buy that shawl. You tell me ... what did I go and get myself in this mess for?'

'You hardly owe anything, my love,' said the Marquesa with that tone and air of indulgent superiority she could put on so well when she needed to. 'If I get out of this fix, I'll take care of that little trifle you're so worried about. [*Leaning over and squeezing her friend's arm.*] Francisco must have quite a bit stashed away, money that's not earning any interest, sitting around, hoarding it up like a peasant. He's so incredibly backward! That's why the country's in the state it's in, because capital isn't circulating, because all the hard cash is locked up, doing nobody any good, not even the people it belongs to. Francisco's the type who thinks money is for growing cobwebs on. He's just like a wealthy farmer. Why don't you make a suggestion? That he lend me what I need ... at a fixed rate, of course, with an agreement in writing. I've no wish to ... !'

'I don't think Bringas ...'

[*Fervently.*] 'But you must have some say over him, my love ... you must have. You'd be a fool otherwise. All you have to say is: "My dear, for Heaven's sake, you're not doing anything with that money." You have to be forceful, so he'll get the message. Or don't you have the nerve? I thought he asked your opinion about everything, and let you make the decisions, you're brighter and more decisive than he is ... well then, just go ahead and ask him. And don't forget, a deal's a deal: if he gives me the money, I'll take care of that little problem of yours. [*With a laugh.*] We can think of it as commission.'

'I really don't think my husband ... no, there's no way, it's out of the question!'

But even though she declared her ingenious friend's idea was out of the question, Rosalía thought about it. The very insuperability of the obstacles appealed to her, for weighty problems attract and fascinate great minds. For a while, the only thing to be heard in the *Camón* were Pipaón's sighs, and a few little coughs from the Marquesa, whose bronchial tubes were not in the best condition. Since the two friends had the house to themselves, Bringas being at work still and the children at school, they could talk freely about their problems without having to disguise them at all. Tellería's wife went over her proposition again, supporting it with some shrewd reasoning (Oh! Money that's left idle is the cause of all this country's problems!)* and with all kinds of sweet-talking and flattery; but Bringas's wife still saw the proposal as one of the most difficult and thorny enterprises the will of man could have dreamed up. Even to attempt it was to scale the very summits of heroism.

They were still in this frame of mind when Cándida appeared, smiling and looking very pleased with herself. She had just come from talking to the Queen and Tula, and then she went to the kitchens, where the head chef had insisted on giving her three *entrecôtes* and a couple of partridges. 'That Galland is such a nice man.' He was always giving her things, and she had had them sent up to the house so as not to offend him.

'I'll send you over a partridge and two steaks later on,' she said to Rosalía, giving her a friendly tap with her fan. 'No, don't thank me ... I don't know what to do with it all. I've got plenty of meat in the house ... Yesterday I gave the neighbours a superb sirloin that I'd ordered from the Plaza del Carmen, thinking I was going to have guests ... You should have seen how grateful they were, poor things! My house is like a soup kitchen. The day I move out, they'll be heartbroken.'

CHAPTER 19

And then, changing the subject to something completely unrelated to charity, although just as interesting, she let slip the following faithfully recorded enquiry: 'Would either of you happen to know where and how I might go about placing some money I've got on my hands? It would have to be very reliable and yield a moderate interest.'

These phrases did not have quite the galvanising effect on the two friends that one might have expected. Rosalía's face registered indifference and incredulity, rapidly followed by alarm, as she remembered that Cándida's request for a loan of one hundred reals the previous month had been preceded by exactly the same opening preamble. Milagros did not put much faith in García Grande's statement, but suspected that there might possibly be a grain of truth in it, and she clung to that absurd hope the way a desperate man will grasp a red-hot nail.

'Now be honest, Cándida . . . do you really have that kind of money?'

'Don't be such a materialist, my love. I don't have it right here in my pocket, but it's just as if I did. Muñoz y Nones is bringing it to me some time soon.'

[*Disheartened.*] 'Oh . . . some time soon . . .'

'And I always like to plan ahead. Because, to be honest, I don't feel comfortable having large sums of money in the house, there are all sorts of shady characters around, even in the Palace.'

Unimpressed by Cándida's investment schemes, Milagros scrutinised her attire that day. At that point in time, the noble widow began to carry herself with less assurance and her clothes were becoming somewhat shabby and disreputable, although she was still a long way from the dreadful state of abandon in which we were to see her later.

The children came back from school and Rosalía went to get them a snack.

'Isabel is such an adorable little thing!' said Cándida to Milagros, and then disappeared into the Column Room, abandoning madam the Marquesa to her agonised reflections. Milagros could hear the little ones chattering away, their mother scolding them for being impatient, and Cándida giving them big, smacking kisses. Shortly afterwards, Rosalía reappeared in *Gasparini*, half frowning and half smiling, as if she could not help laughing at one of those amusing incidents that often happen in the midst of the most painful circumstances.

'This is hilarious,' whispered Rosalía in her friend's ear. 'She asked me very discreetly in the dining room if I would be so kind as to lend her another hundred reals.'

Milagros smiled, like an invalid trying to take her mind off her sufferings. Then she fell back into that deep depression that was eating away at her like consumptive fever. She was imagining the terrible ordeal of tomorrow night, the guests arriving, the rooms filling up, herself in her long, pink satin skirt with its huge bustle and gigantic train, and the problem of dinner still unresolved. Because this time she couldn't get away with serving a few snacks . . . What an excruciating thought! Rosalía saw her friend's eyes fill with tears, and tried to console her.

'That despicable, amoral, useless man . . .' was all she could think of to say.

Francisco came in shortly afterwards, rather less lively and affable than usual. Milagros greeted him very affectionately, and proceeded to complain of her dreadful bad luck and how hard God was on her, causing her nothing but problems and more problems. Bringas tried to comfort her with Christian precepts, although he held a now long-standing grudge against her for not having given him the Christmas present he thought he deserved for having made her a little marble box. But my friend had almost got to the point of forgiving her, although he had not forgotten the offence; and if the truth be known, he was none too happy that his wife was so close to that particular lady, even if all they talked about was dresses.

'Shall I have the pleasure of seeing you at my house tomorrow?' asked the Marquesa.

Francisco gallantly excused himself, and began to get ready to start work again on his magnum opus. He had started noticing that going out at night did not seem to suit him . . . His head was not too good these days. He put it down to tension, and perhaps the weather too, since it always seemed as if the heavens were about to open, although they never actually did. He had felt quite ill in the office that morning . . . The chief said it was all in his stomach, and recommended taking a dose of aloe with every meal. But he did not go in for medicines, and had decided not to do it. Since he was indisposed and wasn't going to be able to go to Milagros's soirée, he'd just have to make do with reading all about it in the newspapers.

'We'll see, we'll see,' said the distressed damsel, in a tone of deep sadness. 'I don't know, I really don't. There may not be anything at all. I'm going through the most terrible time right now. Don't ask . . . It's my problem, I'll just have to deal with it. You'll forgive me if I don't breathe another word. That husband of mine is a real treasure . . . But it's not my job to sing his praises. Unfortunately it's public knowledge how he behaves. Don't laugh if you see me crying. There are some things that . . .'

Bringas was dumbfounded. He beat a hasty retreat, having given her hand a good squeeze and bidden her an affectionate farewell.

The two friends spent a while whispering in the drawing room and the passageway.

'I've laid the groundwork,' said the agonised Milagros. 'Now you try . . . Be brave. I'm sure . . .'

'Oh! My dear, you're delirious, you're dreaming. I know him . . .'

'Then you mean there's no hope for me?' said the distressed lady, throwing herself into her friend's arms and clinging to her.

Rosalía was too moved to speak.

'At least,' the Marquesa stammered, 'you could just tell him what's happened to me . . . Maybe God will soften his heart.'

'I'll speak to him as soon as Cándida leaves. But I really and truly don't have much hope! In fact, I don't have any. And what about me? I'm in just as dire straits as you are. What I am going to come up with between now and tomorrow? Now that I think of it, why don't you try your sister?'

'Lord, woman, how can you say that. My sister! She's already bailed me out so many times! I've really abused her! I just can't. We aren't on speaking terms any more. We had a falling out a little while ago. In any case, before I ask my sister, I'll ask Her Majesty, I'll throw myself on her mercy.'

'Yes, yes, you're quite right. That's the best thing to do.'

'No, no, no. I hope I die of agony overnight. Is the chapel open? I'm going to go and pray for a while and see if the good Lord can help me. Goodbye, now. I'll be back tomorrow, to see if there's any hope at all.'

Rosalía's dejected face clearly showed that any such hope was just a dream in that crackpot brain. It should be said that madam's pain was caused by her own difficulties and not by her good friend's. She had such faith in Milagros's bizarre talents, that she said to herself: 'I've no idea how, but she'll come up with some way out.'

As the Marquesa was squeezing her hand for the last time, Rosalía said: 'Tomorrow you'll be telling me all about how you solved it.'

But when she went to Bringas's cubbyhole to tell him what had happened, he forestalled her with the following acerbic comment: 'What's that Tellería woman up to now? The same as ever: she's got money problems. There's no one left gullible enough to lend them so much as two reals. The morons of this world are becoming extinct because of all the nasty lessons they've been getting.'

Rosalía's lips were sealed. She did not dare say a word. Fixed in her mind like an *Inri* was the image of Torres and the deadly figures of the sum she had to pay him. Confessing to her husband the trouble she was in would be tantamount to declaring a series of clandestine attacks on the household economy, which was Bringas's second religion. But if God did not send her a solution, she would have to face up to that painful remedy of confession and all its consequences, which would be awful. Heavens, no; it was better to invent something, keep looking, rummage through half the world, delve deep into the dark heart of the problem to find a solution. Rather than sell the secret of her purchases – perhaps the most glamorous thing in her dull and humdrum existence – to the economist, she preferred to sacrifice her finery, to rip out those morsels of her heart in the shape of fabrics, lace and ribbons, and toss them to the voracious maw of the pawnshop woman, who would sell them for next to nothing. She needed to be heroic, not tearful.

When this course of action occurred to her, she went into the *Camón* to think it over, because she always found she had more clarity of mind there. Cándida, after playing with the children for a while, went in to chat to Bringas. Rosalía could hear her from her workshop, but all she could make out were odd words like *administrator* and *government bonds . . . Consolidated . . . Revolution . . . Generals in the Canaries . . . Montpensier** . . . *God help us*. They were talking of high finance and petty politics. Suddenly the lady heard a violent crash, as if a piece of furniture had fallen over and broken some china. The thud was followed by a cry from Bringas that was so loud and agonised that it took Rosalía's breath away. She went cold all over, unable to move. What could it be? Had the roof caved in and crushed the best of husbands?

CHAPTER 20

Once she recovered from her momentary astonishment at hearing such unusual noises, Rosalía ran to *Gasparini*, only to be faced, Lord help us, with an incomprehensible spectacle. Bringas was in the middle of the room, his face distorted and deathly pale, his hands clenched, and his eyes almost starting from his head. A little bench next to the table, which had been holding the pot of shellac varnish and the spirit lamp he used to heat it up, had been knocked over by the artist when he leaped up out of his chair. Flames flickered on the carpet where the spilt alcohol had caught fire. Cándida had promptly set about putting them out, and had lifted her skirts almost up to her knees in order to do so. She was hopping about trying to smother the most intense flames; but since the hot varnish, a very sticky substance, had also run on to the carpet, the soles of that respectable lady's shoes were sticking so fast to the floor that she had to exercise considerable effort to raise them.

Rosalía went straight to her husband, who, sensing her near by, clutched at her in convulsive anxiety, his eyes darting from side to side as if searching for something he could not see. His face registered a naked terror his wife had never seen in him before. Aghast, the only word she could formulate was: 'What . . . ?'

Bringas rubbed his eyes, opened them again, and blinking repeatedly, like poets when they read their own work, exclaimed in a heart-rending voice: 'I can't see! I can't see!'

Rosalía could not think what to say, she was so horrified. García Grande, who had managed to put out the fire, although she could not stop her boots from sticking to the carpet, came up to the pathetic pair.

'It'll turn out to be something minor,' she said, contemplating Francisco's bizarre eye movements.

'Where's the window, the window?' groaned the unhappy man, in terrible desperation.

'Here, here, can't you see it?' cried Rosalía, turning him towards the light.

'No, I can't see it, I can't see you, I can't see anything at all. It's completely and utterly dark. Nothing but black . . .'

'Oh! It's that wretched picture of yours. I told you so, we all told you so. But you'll get better.'

Rosalía was half dead with fear, unable to think, stifled by emotion. Cándida, who was calmer, started giving orders.

'Let's sit him down on the sofa. We should call the doctor.'

They led him over to the sofa and the invalid collapsed on to it in despair, as if he were tumbling into his coffin. He kept feeling the things around him, as well as his wife, who was at his side the whole time.

'We did warn you,' she repeated, choking on her tears and trying to hide the tremor in her voice. 'That wretched hair picture . . . Working away on it all day long . . . If you could tell your eyes were tired, why didn't you stop?'

'My children, where are they?' murmured Bringas.

Little Isabel and Alfonso were standing in the doorway, terrified, wordless, not daring to move; the little boy was chewing slowly, clutching his sandwich; the girl, with her hands clasped behind her back, was staring in consternation at the sad spectacle of her dismayed parents. Rosalía told them to come over. Bringas felt them, covered them with kisses, lamented he could not see them and prophesied he would never be able to see them again. The poor man shed more tears in that fifteen minutes than in the whole of the rest of his previous life, and Rosalía, as she considered the sudden misfortune that God had sent her, took it as a punishment for the sins she had committed. In the end, she had to send the children out of the room. Prudencia was put in charge of keeping them in the *Furriela* and not letting them out. They were afraid that Isabel would have a worse fit than usual, because of the shock. Meanwhile, García Grande's wife, who was more obsequious and helpful with her friends in times of great need, did all she could to be useful.

'I'll go and fetch the doctor myself. He'll say it's nothing, just you wait and see. I had a similar thing myself when I was learning to do needlepoint. All of a sudden, I got the strangest disturbed vision; then I started seeing things cut in half. It ended in a horrible headache. Ophthalmic migraine they call it. I remember the doctor saying you can sometimes lose your eyesight completely for a few hours, or for a day. Calm down, Francisco, my dear, and have a glass of water with a dash of wine in it. I won't be long.'

She went diligently on her way, with a sincere desire to help, and since the resident physician was not there, she went to fetch the one who was on duty. While they were alone, Bringas and his wife barely said a word to each other. She gazed at him continually, hoping that just when they were least expecting it, those staring eyes of his would regain that precious gift they were designed for; he was beginning to use that sense peculiar to the blind, touch, and he used his hands to see her with, either squeezing hers, or touching her slowly and lovingly. The odd word, sighs and laments from the poor invalid were the only verbal expressions in that sad tableau, all the more eloquent for its silence.

Finally, the doctor arrived. Cándida had refused to let him out of her sight until she got him into the house. He was an affable, elderly gentleman, one of the old school, an excellent diagnostician, conservative as regards prescriptions, and, according to rumour, rather unlucky. Once he had taken down the particulars of the case, he described it as *retinal congestion*.

'If it's in the retina,' said Cándida, 'it'll pass. You'll get your eyesight back; but you can forget about that hair picture, my friend.'

'I told him so, I warned him,' said Bringas's wife forcefully, somewhat relieved by the hope the doctor had given them. 'And now what should we do?'

The doctor prescribed complete rest, a special diet, and something to draw the humours the following day. He also ordered a black eye-bandage, a mild sedative in case he could not sleep, and offered to come round first thing in the morning to give the patient's eyes a thorough examination. It was getting late by this point, and the last rays of the sun were fading mournfully from the room. When the kindly old man left, Bringas and his wife were more cheerful.

'It'll be all right, there's no need to worry, my dears,' said Cándida, whose useful officiousness was a great comfort to them both. 'Now off you go to bed, and see if you can get some sleep. You're not to be frightened, nor to think about things that aren't going to happen. You've got to be calm and have some patience. It's a matter of hours or a couple of days at most. I'll take care of bringing you the medicines and anything else you need. I'll stay here all night and keep you company, if you like.'

When the helpful lady got back from the pharmacist's, Rosalía had already put her husband to bed, and bandaged his eyes with a long strip of black taffeta. Like all those suffering from incipient blindness, Bringas pretended not to need any help getting undressed, but realising how anguished his wife was, he was heroic enough to try and cheer her up with affectionate remarks, as if he were quite healthy and she were the one who was sick.

'This will probably blow over. But it's a real nuisance. It's no joke, this not being able to see. Just you calm down, now. I intend to be patient, and I'm almost beginning to get used to it already. But I'd much prefer not to have to see one of those ophthalmologists, because even though they cure you, they cost an eye tooth.'

The night passed without incident; Bringas was extremely restless, with an excruciating headache and eye pain; Rosalía lay awake, dividing her care and attention between her blind husband and her epileptic daughter, who had even worse nightmares than usual, because the scenes of the evening before had overstimulated her. Fortunately, Cándida stayed with her afflicted friend all night, comforting her just by her presence, and being tremendously helpful. She was very good in this sort of situation, and knew a thousand little tips on home medicine. She always came up with a solution for every challenge, no matter how great; nothing intimidated her, and her bones were thoroughly inured to fatigue.

Around daybreak, Rosalía was overcome with sleep and dozed off in an armchair next to the double bed where our dear Thiers was lying, drowsy at last; and no sooner did the lady drop off than she started seeing Torres and his famous beard and nose. She also dreamed that the money she owed was rolling by in front of her, coin after coin, stretching lazily off into infinity, and she saw the dreaded appointment on that day which was dawning so fatefully. All of a sudden she came to and opened her eyes. She thought she had heard a groan from Bringas, but it must have been in her imagination, because the saintly gentleman seemed quite calm, and his measured breathing indicated that he was sleeping deeply at last.

'Torres . . . the money!' thought Rosalía, shaking her head to ward off the idea, as if it were a large fly that had landed on her forehead. 'And today of all days, my God!'

CHAPTER 21

But almost simultaneously, an idea of how to save herself shot into her mind, like one of those mystical bolts from the blue, a wonderfully easy and efficient solution, which sprang – oh, how peculiar life can be at times – from the very same affliction that the family was suffering from just then. Ah, the ways of the Almighty! Only He can fathom them.

She got up out of the armchair very quietly and slowly, so as not to wake the patient. She knew now what to do. It was obvious and easy. What she could not have done the day before, she would do on this fateful day. She had often thought of the silver candlesticks, but how could she pawn them without Francisco noticing, when his eyes were so sharp? . . . Well, now she could, now she could! . . . She would be very careful to put them back in their place, and to get hold of the money to redeem them as soon as possible; that way her husband wouldn't notice a thing when he got his eyesight back. Pray God and St Lucy* that would be soon! The price of the candlesticks might not be enough to cover her needs, since beside the money for Torres she had to come up with the second payment for Sobrino Brothers, so she decided to add to the aforementioned silver items the diamond earrings from Agustín Caballero that she was wearing in her ears. Bringas wouldn't notice the difference, and if by chance he did, while touching her face, she would invent some story, she would say that . . . That she had taken them off as a sign of mourning.

Cándida was the perfect choice for the financial operation she had in mind. She found her in the dining room, as lively and fresh as a daisy; one would never have guessed she had just passed a sleepless night. Rosalía took out the chocolate right away, so her friend could make her own, the way she liked it. While the respectable lady was going about this operation in her usual fastidious way, Rosalía expounded her scheme. There was a series of private whisperings and Cándida's head was seen nodding so affirmatively that it would have convinced doubt in person.

'It'll all be done by twelve o'clock. Don't you worry. I've got a friend who's really sharp who I always go to for things like this. He's discreet, efficient, intelligent, you name it; and he can get a thing like this done in no time.'

There is reason to believe that around that time, the second phase of her decline, Cándida was beginning to frequent pawn-brokers and moneylenders, either on her own initiative or to do some discreet favour for a really close friend. Máximo Manso used to call this *Cándida's middle period*, and I have to point out that there was a *mature period* yet to come that was even more pitiful.

The whole thing was resolved that morning as quickly and easily as García Grande had said it would be, because she was back with the money before eleven thirty. Rosalía seized it anxiously and was delighted to find she had enough to pay off Torres and Sobrino, and some left over for a few other little matters.

'I don't know how to thank you,' she said feelingly to her distinguished friend, taking her hands in her own. 'It'll all be back in the house soon enough, I don't like my valuables going off on these little excursions. I only did it because of the most pressing need . . .'

It is hard to tell how, but the conversation wound its way around to a certain little difficulty that had arisen because of the excessive sang-froid of a devious administrator . . . It was a matter of two or three days. How could she refuse this favour to someone who had been so kind to her? Rosalía felt as if she were ripping out a piece of her own flesh when those two hundred reals left her hands to calm her friend's monetary thirst. But it could not be helped. Cándida went jubilantly off to look in on Bringas, who said he felt better, although his head wasn't too good. The doctor had examined him that morning and the prognosis was reasonably favourable. He would get his eyesight back quite soon, and . . . He thought he could see a little already if he moved the bandage . . . What he needed was to rest up, be patient and take his medicines methodically at the proper times.

'Who was that who just came in?' asked Bringas, sharply.

'I think it was Mr Torres,' Cándida replied, 'he just stopped by to ask after you.'

'My mind is so weak and confused that I could have sworn I

heard money being counted out. Even though I try not to worry, and the doctor's ordered me not to, I can't avoid being aware of everything that happens in the house, I can't help it. I've got very sharp ears, and I don't believe I miss a thing, even when I'm asleep.'

She remarked sagely that a diseased brain needs rest; that he needed to train himself to lie still and pay no attention; that while he was still in bed nobody was to come and talk to him, and that not even his children were to be allowed into the bedroom. He agreed to it all, heaving a great sigh, and claiming that what was going to take the most patience and willpower of all was squashing his urge to keep tabs on everything and always be telling people what to do.

While all this was being said in the dark bedroom, Rosalía was carrying on a whispered conversation with Torres in the Little Room. However much care she took not to make a sound as she counted out four hundred reals in silver coins, the odd chink sounded in the room and reverberated faintly through the house until it reached Bringas's highly trained ear. Torres, who was deeply concerned about his friend's illness, expressed his hope that it would turn out not to be too serious . . . Mompous's accountant had had a similar problem with his eyes once. 'There he was writing one day, when all of a sudden he went blind. At first they thought he had a damaged retina; but after ten days of wearing an eye patch and taking various medicines, he got better, although his eyes were still rather on the weak side. He wasn't completely cured until he went to the baths in Quinto . . .' The gentleman went on his way as happy to have recovered his money as he was distressed to hear of Francisco's plight.

They sent Isabel off to Cándida's house for the day to play with Irene and the other girls from the neighbourhood, since the child was depressed and off her food because of what had happened. Alfonso went to school, but Paquito, who was quite miserable because of his father's illness, stayed home and refused to eat a thing at lunch. Cándida was the only person present who demonstrated a decent appetite.

'You should eat, even if you have to force yourself,' she said to Bringas's wife. 'Don't let yourself go like this. You need to build up your strength so you can stay awake at night and nurse him and deal with whatever comes up . . . I don't feel like eating either, but I make myself, my dear, I force myself to eat, because I have to.'

Shortly afterwards, our friend got a note from Milagros saying that everything had turned out all right in the end, and that she was looking forward to seeing her that night. The letter exuded relief and satisfaction.

'Poor Milagros has no idea what's been happening,' said Rosalía, tearing up the letter. 'The poor woman's begging me to go there tonight. Would you mind going over there and telling her what's happened, son? ... And on the way back you could stop by the Pez's house and tell Carolina, too. It's all her fault, with her hair pictures. What a dreadful woman!'

The dressmaker came that day; but the lady of the house sent her away with the message that she was in no mood for dresses just then, and to come back next week. In the afternoon, Milagros showed up, very contrite for not having found out earlier, so she could rush over and comfort her friend. Her remorse was genuine, but not strong enough to mask her overwhelming satisfaction at having successfully resolved the financial crisis of that crucial day. How and why she'd solved it, she would reveal later on, there was no need to bother Rosalía's poor head right now with that sort of thing. 'And what does the doctor say?' The good lady hoped that his blindness would just be a trifling ailment. She begged God would cure him, for Bringas was so kind and such a model family man ... 'I'm so sorry you won't be able to come to my house this evening! All the best people are sure to be there, and the buffet supper is going to be superb ... One of these days I'll tell you how ... It's a long story.'

As she said goodbye in the doorway, she could not resist a few spontaneous outbursts of her reigning passion. She told her friend, as if she were letting on a terribly important secret, that that night she was going to wear the white muslin dress with the lilac foulard lining, and that she had added a band of embroidery and a little Watteau* casaque ... At the last minute she had managed to make up a chemisette like the one they sent San Salomó from Paris ... She had decided to wear her hair waved and swept up, with a big braid wound round her head and long ringlets at the back. 'But anyway, you can't be in the mood to listen to all this ... Goodbye, goodbye ... I'll come over tomorrow to see how Francisco's doing and to tell you all about it.'

Bringas, who always knew what was going on, said to his wife: 'I heard you whispering with that Tellería woman in the hallway. How is she? Did she manage to convince some naïve fool? Poor woman! I tell you, we're better off eating bread and onions in peace and quiet than living the way those people do, in dying grandeur . . . So there's a big do on tonight! I swear, I feel sorry for them.'

CHAPTER 22

He was much more cheerful these days, because when he lifted the bandage a little, ignoring the doctor's instructions, he could see the light, even though it was rather blurry and painful. At any rate, he was convinced that his sight was not lost and that, sooner or later, he would get back the use of that most precious of faculties. His eyes were very itchy and bothered him a great deal, as did the feverish perception of thousands of little shiny dots and faint, flickering, fleeting metallic lines, images of those unspeakably abominable hairs, which were being reproduced by his diseased retina. Nevertheless, our man bore his discomfort staunchly; but he did keep begging them to let him get out of bed, it being torture for him to have to lie flat on his back, sweltering under the sheets. The doctor let him get up after three days, but under strict orders not to move from his armchair and to keep quite quiet and still, to keep his mind quite blank, and not to have visitors, or any kind of activity whatsoever, and to wear a heavy bandage at all times. He got up and they put him in *Gasparini* in a comfortable armchair propped up with pillows. No one was allowed in to talk to him, and his pleas for Paquito to come and read him the newspaper at night fell on deaf ears. As for keeping him out of the household affairs, Rosalía was not so successful, because although he prided himself on leaving everything to her, he could not contain his domineering streak, which had been so heavily indulged over so many years, and every couple of minutes he would remember what good use he had made of his powers.

'Rosalía . . .'

'What's the matter, my love?'

'What's the main dish for lunch today?'

'Why do you want to know?'

'I thought I could smell beef stew. Don't deny it. This is when we most need to be economising by having potato omelette, stuffed artichokes, pork sausages, and, if we have to, sheep's liver, to say nothing of pig's jaw. If you rely on Cándida to do the shopping, she'll spend us out of house and home before we know where we are. That woman went through two people's fortunes on exorbitant meals, you know. Tell me something: you gave us fried hake for lunch yesterday, right?'

'I thought the doctor told us you had to have it. That's why I ordered it. Then I found out I was wrong.'

'And what about Cándida . . . Where is she now?'

'She's in the *Furriela*. You don't have to worry about her overhearing.'

'Can't you politely tell her to go and eat in her own home? I don't like these guests who stay for ever. A day or two's all right, but . . .'

'But, Francisco . . . She's been ever so helpful, poor thing! Tomorrow, maybe. I can't tell her to go, just like that.'

'What did Prudencia get at the Cebada market?'

'Three big sacks of potatoes.'

'How much per sack?'

'Six reals.'

'Listen, love, don't forget to write it all down, will you, so that when I'm better I can balance the accounts for this month. Did you remember to get olive oil? Don't buy any more wine, you know I'm not drinking it at the moment. The doctor told me to have a small glass of sherry every day, but don't bother buying any. If Tula sends you the two bottles she promised, I'll drink it, if she doesn't, I won't. If Cándida keeps on coming in the mornings and you have to give her a cup of hot chocolate . . . She can't hear me, can she?'

'No, there's no one around.'

'Well, I think you should start giving her the four reals brand, no doubt she'll think it's perfectly delicious; I doubt she ever has anything more than the three reals sort at home. I've been thinking about the present we'll have to buy the doctor, we're going to lose all our savings. And thank goodness he hasn't called in an ophthalmologist, because if he does, we may as well pack our bags and leave. I hope to God it won't be necessary. Yesterday, he was talking about sending me to take the waters at some spa. It make me shudder to think of it. All this nonsense about taking the waters is just something the doctors have dreamed up to squeeze a bit more out of their poor patients.

Spas didn't exist in my day, and there weren't any more diseases
around as a result. On the contrary, I think less people used to
die. If he says anything about spas to you, my love, don't give
him any encouragement, I don't.'

The most striking thing was that even in his miserable state,
the good Thiers still kept a vigilant eye over the housekeeping
money. While he was in bed, he gave the keys of the drawer
where he kept the money to his wife; but once he got up, he
insisted on taking back the reins of power and exercising that
royal prerogative which is the clearest sign of domestic authority. Undeterred by his blindness, his busy mind would overcome
his bodily weakness and he would get up from his seat, go to
the desk, groping for the furniture so as not to fall over on the
way, and open the drawer that held the little box with the
money in. His sense of touch, even after such a short period,
had already acquired the heightened sensitivity of the blind, and
he knew which coins were which by weighing them in his hands
and feeling them a little. He would sit with the box on his knees
and take out a niggardly amount, which he would count into
his wife's hands. She would venture a timid observation: 'We've
had to spend a bit more than usual these last few days, love.'

'Well, you shouldn't have to. Just make do . . . Oh yes! Today
is Saturday: you'll need to give the coalman twenty-four reals.
As for the water carrier, if he insists on bringing up more barrels,
tell him I'm only paying for the usual amount; the rest will have
to come out of his own pocket. Don't bring me any more
chicken broth, unless the head chef sends you some. Cut out the
quarter of a hen or half a chicken. Thank goodness I'm not a
finicky man. A bit of broth from the stew, with some nice tasty
bones and marrow, will do me just as well.'

Rosalía submissively agreed to all these instructions, so as not
to upset him. After giving her the housekeeping money, Bringas
would sit there for a while with the box on his knees, and lifting
up its false bottom, he would get out a well-worn old wallet,
whose folds revealed a number of banknotes. He would extract
them delicately one by one, unfold them and then carefully fold
them back up again, saying: 'This is the five hundred note; these
two are both four thousand . . .'

He knew what they were by the order they were in. Then,
after a respectful pause, he would put the whole lot back in its
place, put the box away and lock the drawer, stowing the key in
the left pocket of his waistcoat. His wife would help him back

to his armchair. All this was always done behind closed doors; for before scrutinising his treasure, he would order Rosalía to bar the door, so no one could come in.

After St Anthony's day,* that sad day for the household, a week went by without the patient showing much improvement. He was not getting better, although it was true that he was not getting any worse either, which was at least some consolation. There was no doubt that his optical faculties remained intact; that is to say, Francisco could still see; but he found light hurt his eyes so much that if he took off the bandage even for a second, he would feel an excruciating, burning pain that forced him to put it right back on again. His wife nursed him with a love and attention that cannot be praised highly enough. When he was in a lot of pain, she would put belladonna compresses on his eyelids and rub his temples with belladonna and laudanum.* Every night she would give him calomel powder, with a mild dose of opium in it if he could not sleep; but his solicitous spouse devoted her greatest energies to warning him never to lift his bandage. The poor man was so energetic that the moment he felt a little better, he could not wait to *take a peek at the world*, as he put it.

'For goodness' sake, Francisco, behave yourself. You're not doing yourself any good, you know. You're just like a little boy. Use your brain and act your age. The doctor tells you under no circumstances to take off the bandage, and what do you do . . . You're not going to get better if you go on like this. You've got to be patient, and soon you'll be able to take off that black rag and then you can look straight at the sun, if you want. But right now you're blind and you've got to stay that way for a while. Now be good, because if you go on *opening the window*, as you call it, I'm going to tie your hands up.'

'This wretched bandage is driving me mad,' said Bringas, with a sigh. 'I feel as if I'm buried under a castle rampart. You're right that the light hurts my eyes a lot; but I can't stand doing nothing, especially in the dark. It's a relief just to see something from time to time, even if it's just the shape of the room, with everything all confused and blurry. It's a relief to see you, and by the way, if this old retina of mine isn't playing tricks on me, you're wearing a silk robe, aren't you? Didn't you use the one Agustín gave you to make a dress for Isabel? *Ainda mais*,* the one you're wearing now is a sort of claret colour.'

Rosalía was just leaving the room when she heard this. At first, she was disconcerted, but she rapidly recovered her poise, and said with a laugh: 'Thinks I'm wearing a silk robe, does he? As if I were in the mood for silk robes. That's what you get for taking one of your little peeks out of the window. You see everything all mixed up and confused; you've got it into your head that wool is silk, and that this dark, dirty colour looks like red wine.'

'I tell you, I'd swear . . .'

'Don't swear, love, it's wrong. Silk robes! If only I had one!'

And she beat a hasty retreat. She changed the robe she had on in the *Camón*, and put on a very old one, the one she usually wore.

'Are you there?' asked Bringas after a while, beginning to wonder whether his wife was in the room or not.

'Yes, here I am,' said Rosalía, hurriedly. 'The baker just came. I only bought three pounds of bread today.'

'You know, I could swear that . . . I wonder if I'm seeing everything all wrong?'

'Are you still going on about my robe?' said Rosalía, going up and giving him a hug.

The blind man grabbed a handful of the fabric of her dress and fingered it.

'To the touch it's wool, there's no doubt about that.'

And after another pause, during which she said nothing, Bringas, spurred on by his congenitally suspicious nature, added, 'Unless you got changed while you were out of the room a moment ago. I thought I heard a noise and the rustle of material.'

'Lord! You heard a rustle. Well, you very well may have done. The dressmaker's next door, altering Milagros's dresses.'

Paquito, who had just got home, sat down next to his father to recount some gossip that was going round and to read him bits from the newspaper. That afternoon, Milagros stopped by; she had visited the previous few days too, demonstrating a truly sisterly concern for Mr Bringas's health. She spent a little while with him, but soon she and her colleague repaired to the furthest room, the *Furriela*.

The Marquesa never explained verv clearly to her friend how she had managed to get out of her famous tight spot on the fourteenth; but, as we shall see later, it must have been thanks to a very short-term loan. The dinner was truly sumptuous, and a well-known society columnist extolled it lavishly, in that effeminate style they cultivate, in a mixture of French and Spanish that I won't imitate for fear it would have the same effect on the good reader's stomach as an emetic. When the account of this glittering function was read aloud to Francisco, the worthy gentleman could only repeat: 'I'd just love to know who was fool enough to . . . !'

The first few days after her soirée, Milagros seemed very satisfied. Gradually, though, her happiness declined, and round the twentieth, you might have noted in her sudden fits of sadness. By the twenty-second, the deep sighs she kept heaving revealed she was under great stress. By the Feast of St John,* her tranquil periods had become rare, and the Marquesa announced to her friend that she had certain very disagreeable things to confide. Rosalía grew alarmed at these hints, and envisaged a cloud on the horizon even blacker and more threatening than the last one. In the meantime, Milagros had grown so extremely affectionate, that Rosalía did not know how to thank her. They often talked about fabrics and fashions, although Bringas's wife did not have much heart for it, while her husband was still sick. Fortunately, the doctor was forecasting a rapid recovery, and the lady was so relieved by this favourable prognosis, that in her mind she began to devote a largish space to matters of sartorial elegance. She was deeply touched by the little presents that Milagros kept giving her during that melancholy period. And they were not exactly mere nothings, those gifts. One day, as she was leaving, she said: 'Do you know, that Florián hat doesn't suit me very well? It would look just right on you. I'm going to have it sent over.'

And so she did. Another day, they were talking rather more animatedly about dresses. 'I don't like the cashmere one that's still half-finished. I'll send it to you tomorrow. Since you're bound to be going to a spa with your husband, you can wear it there. No, don't thank me. It's no use to me. I'll bring you the fichu with the green velvet ribbon and the felt toque, you should be able to fix it up quite easily. It would be really sweet for a spa. And I'll send you some flowers and feathers and *aigrettes*. I've got six drawers full of the things. The dressmaker brought the claret-coloured dress over today. Do you know, it doesn't look very good on me? That colour only suits full-figured women with young skin. Would you like it? You could alter it, have it let out a bit, and it would look fine. The material is gorgeous.'

And that is how all those beautiful things found their way into the house. Rosalía, as we have said, was too upset to wear them, and stowed them away in the *Camón*. Sometimes, when she was feeling calmer, because the doctor had said something encouraging, she would shut herself up in the room to try on the dresses and the hat. Unable to resist the temptation, she had Emilia make some alterations, lengthening some things and completely redoing others. Occasionally, she would get carried away in her excitement and would leave the *Camón* and take a few turns round the house wearing all her new trappings. She would always wait until the maid and the children were out of the house and Francisco was shut up in *Gasparini* with Paquito. Several times, she would parade in her finery before Cándida's admiring gaze, soliciting her informed approval and criticism. The widow was rather prone to fits of furious applause, and in order to prevent her from some noisy outburst, Rosalía would come up with one finger on her lips, urging her to repress any manifestation of amazement or surprise, so that no sharp ear would overhear what was going on in the Little Room. Then she would wend her way sadly back to the privacy of the *Camón*, and take off her fine clothes, saying regretfully: 'I'm so out of sorts these days. I'm just not in the mood for such foolishness.'

By the twenty-sixth, Tellería's wife was unable to contain the tidal wave of sadness that was inundating her afflicted heart, and she poured everything out to her good friend, after the following pathetic introduction, which history has preserved for us: 'I'll also send you the muslin dress with the mauve lining ... and all my Valenciennes, Alençon and guipure lace. What good is all that to me now? What little jewellery I have left will probably be yours one day. I'm ruined; all I can do is go into hiding, or go into a convent, or flee the country, I don't know ... It would be best if I could go into a convent. If only God would see fit to let me die, he'd be doing me a great favour! I don't know what I'm saying. You must be astonished to see me this dazed and hysterical and beside myself. You'll understand some day! It's raining disasters on me, the good Lord must be trying to test me. They say that way you get to Heaven faster, and they must be right, because otherwise, my dear, what could be worse than having to suffer in this life and the next as well? I was born unlucky. Up till now, if I was careful, I could just about make ends meet, despite all the problems that husband of mine has caused me. God knows how long-suffering I've been these last years, a real heroine. The things I've been through to save the family name, so that the children wouldn't have to do without! The effort I've gone to some days just so the servants could say: "The soup is served." I've had so many humiliations, so much suffering, so much struggle, my dear, so much struggle with lenders, with vulgar little people and no end of spongers asking for money! But when you go on accumulating difficulties, when you get too used to opening a hole here to fill up one somewhere else, and delaying and postponing, a day comes when the bottom falls out; it's like a very old boat that's been patched up too many times, that suddenly splits a seam and whoosh! . . . down it goes.'

When she got to the bit about the sinking ship, the poor lady's words became a protracted sob. Rosalía, who was almost as moved as her friend, encouraged her to explain why she was so unhappy, to see if a clear explanation of the facts would lead to an easy solution. But the Marquesa could not or would not explain in plain terms what was wrong. It was something to do with getting together a substantial sum of money by the end of the month. If she could not get it, she was going to find herself in the worst and the direst situation she had ever experienced in her whole life, and maybe, or forget the maybe, she would have to face the humiliation of being taken to court. But, what on earth had happened . . . ! Had some friend of hers offered to help and she'd gone and signed some wretched document . . . ? The silly woman! Why hadn't she cut her hand off before signing it? The fact is that if she had cut off that pretty little hand of hers, there would have been no dinner on the ill-fated night of the fourteenth.

Rosalía, who was more logical than the Marquesa, asked why she did not write to the manager of her estate in Almendralejo and ask him to send her an advance on this quarter's rent, even if it meant giving a discount. Milagros answered, sighing, that she had already put out some feelers in that direction and that there was no way she could have the rent before 15 July . . . But she would definitely have it by then, and she would pay whoever might lend her the money punctually on the fifteenth.

'But can't you postpone it?'

'It's utterly impossible, my dear. As impossible as pigs flying or my husband seeing sense.'

'And what about your sister, Tula?'

'That's even more absurd.'

Rosalía shrugged. She could see no salvation. But Milagros, who was trying to perform the delicate operation of persuading her friend to get her out of the morass she was engulfed in, threw her arms round Rosalía's neck, and choked out the following words, more tear-stained that the cenotaph that Francisco had worked on with such unfortunate results.

'You . . . My darling, you could save me.'

At which point, she was overcome by anguish and began twitching in what women term an attack of nerves, a name that will do as well as any other; and this was followed by one of those convulsions fondly known as a fainting fit.

CHAPTER 24

She had to bring her a glass of water and undo her corset and all sorts of things I shall not go into here.

'What do you mean, me . . . How?' exclaimed Rosalía in horror, much later. 'How can I . . . ?'

'Ask Francisco. I'll pay him interest, at whatever rate he likes, and we'll write up a formal agreement, signed and sealed. I'll bring the letter from my estate manager for him to see. It says I'll have the rent by the fifteenth. And my manager isn't makebelieve, like Cándida's, he's flesh and blood all right. I know, because I have to pay him twenty per cent interest on the advances he gives me.'

Rosalía shook her head energetically and tried to sound discouraging.

'Don't get your hopes up, my dear. My husband hasn't got a thing. And even if he had, he wouldn't give it to you. You don't know what he's like . . .'

The anguished lady countered this cogent argument with

others which bore witness to her shrewd and infinitely resource-
ful mind. It was a well-known fact that Francisco had money,
that was obvious. That being the case, the question was how to
get the elusive treasure into Milagros's needy hands. If a certain
faithful wife undertook the task, which shouldn't be that
difficult after all, the funds could be transferred without having
to go through Bringas at all. The faithful wife shouldn't suffer
any scruples of conscience at the thought of these rather
questionable and reckless proceedings, because the sum would
be back in place before the good gentleman had recovered
enough to notice it was gone.

'You don't think Francisco will be able to see again by 15
July, do you?'

Rosalía was quite hurt by this question, which had escaped
Milagros in the heat of the moment.

'I hope so, and even if he can't, I so much want him to be able
to see again that I'd really rather assume it won't take long.'

'I'm sorry, love, I didn't mean to be tactless. I say the most
stupid things sometimes. You can't imagine what it's like to be
in this position. You're living up there in heaven, and you have
no idea how we poor wretches writhe and burn and curse down
here in hell in Madrid. You'd never believe the things that pop
into my head! In a situation like this, and don't be too shocked
... believe me ... in a situation like this, I sometimes think I'd
be capable of taking things that belonged to other people. I'd
mean to give them back, of course. Dear me! Every time I come
home and see the concierge in his little room eating garlic soup
with his wife, I get so envious! I wish I could send him up to my
apartment and I could stay at his desk, even though I'd have to
sweep the hallway, polish the doorknobs and mop the entire
staircase every morning. All I say is, I'd be better off going into
a convent and leaving this world behind. But then what would
happen to my children, my poor children ... what would
become of them? Once I get María married off, you never know!
I might opt for the peace of the religious life, I just might ... At
least, I'll give up socialising and live a reclusive life in my own
house; I'll wear a nun's habit and nothing else, and that'll be the
end of it. I'll go to Mass every morning and visit a friend in the
afternoons, stay home in the evenings and go to bed early, that's
the best thing for you anyway. Oh, wouldn't that be
marvellous!'

After discreetly pressing her request a second time and getting nothing but frosty refusals from Rosalía, she suddenly said: 'I wonder if we could manage to go to one of the spas together. I hate to have to put it off, but I don't think I can get away before the beginning of August. Has the doctor said yet which of the waters would be best for Bringas? I'll go wherever you do, because no waters are going to cure what I've got. I just need to get out and about and away from this oven.'

Rosalía was more talkative about their little trip to a spa than she had been on the previous topic. She would love to go somewhere that summer, but the doctor hadn't said anything categorical yet. Bringas didn't want to go away to save money; but if the doctor ordered him to, he couldn't very well say no, could he . . .? A bit of relaxation and travel would do his wife good too. She was feeling rather fragile and under the weather . . . The topic of discussion moved from spas to dresses, and their remarks were pursued by endless tryings-on. Rosalía changed into the mozambique, which was almost finished by this stage, and her friend congratulated her so warmly on how wonderful she looked in it, that the noble scion of the Pipaón clan almost burst with vanity.

'Oh, you look so elegant! Whatever you wear looks marvellous on you. It's true, I'm not just saying it because you're my friend. I say the same thing to everybody: if you put your mind to it, no one could hold a candle to you. What a figure! What lovely sloping shoulders! Really and truly, every time you get dressed up, you put everyone around you to shame.'

Needless to say, Rosalía was delighted at this praise. It was ridiculous that someone of her calibre should have to hide her nice clothes, put them on in secret and dream up endless fibs to justify wearing garments which hung on her handsome body as if they had been fitted by the angels of fashion themselves. As she took off her fine clothes in front of her friend, she was thinking about the thorny problem of how to explain to her husband where she had got them, for eventually she was either going to have to wear them in front of him or not wear them at all.

Before Milagros said goodbye, she treated Rosalía to another affected rendition of her problems and the remedy she sought for them. In the end, Rosalía consoled her with a *we'll see*, and the Marquesa's face lit up with a gleam of happiness.

'Tomorrow,' she remarked in the doorway, 'I'll send you that écru lace you liked so much. No, don't thank me . . . It's I who should thank you, if you get me out of this morass . . . [*Giving her two loud and heartfelt kisses.*] If you do, I'll never forget it. Goodbye.'

Round about then, Manuel Pez came back from Archena, saying that the waters had done wonders for him. He had a good colour and an even better appetite, and was in great spirits. The first visit he paid was to Bringas, whose illness he had heard of at the spa. He tried to cheer him up, offering to come and sit with him morning, noon and night, and to spend all his spare time at his friend's side. He was as good as his word, and his presence in the household became so routine that when he was not there, it seemed as if something was missing. From time to time, he kept the invalid amused by describing what was going on in politics, telling him all sorts of funny stories; but he was careful not to discuss the dangers to the Monarchy nor the ominous course things were taking, because dear Francisco would get terribly upset every time anyone said anything about the *so-called* revolution, and he would heave heart-rending sighs. When there were other people around to keep him company in *Gasparini*, or when he thought they had been talking for too long for Francisco's health, Pez would go off to the Little Room or the Ambassadors' Room, where he would come across Rosalía and they would exchange a few words. The lady noticed that her friend seemed to regard her with mute reverence and the compliments he paid her were always very gallant and rather elaborate. Her feelings for him consisted of admiration of the purest kind; Pez grew larger and larger every day in her eyes. He was the epitome of an official personage, a senior civil servant, with lavish, cosmopolitan ways. In Mrs Bringas's mind, no ideal man was complete unless he basked in the golden rays of the government payroll. If Pez had not been a bureaucrat, he would have lost a great deal in her eyes, accustomed as she was to seeing the whole world as an office and to thinking of the national budget as the only source of income. And he was so elegant, with that immaculate, freshly ironed, wrinkle-free, buttoned-up frock-coat, which looked as if he had been born with it on; those high, stiff, snowy white collars; those trousers that one would have sworn were brand new on that day; and those carefully manicured, womanish hands . . . !

CHAPTER 25

And that way he had of doing his hair, that was so simple and yet at the same time so distinguished-looking; the way he wore just a trace of expensive aftershave; that Russian leather brief-case of his that always smelt so good, those perfect manners and that oratorical way of speaking, saying things two or three different ways so you could understand them better ... ! Whenever he spoke to her, he never failed to use some ingenious phrase with a double meaning. Rosalía might not have been so receptive to these remarks had she not been moved to indulgence by the thought that she deserved them, and that society owed her some sort of homage, which it had never paid her until then. Pez was simply acting as society's envoy and making amends by paying her that long-overdue tribute.

It was extremely hot, especially in the afternoons, since the appartment faced west, and the family sought refuge on the terrace. One afternoon, Francisco came out, with the doctor's permission, on Pez's arm, and took a few turns; but it made him worse, and they decided not to try it again until the invalid was stronger. But even though he himself was deprived of that form of recreation, he did not want the others to have to go without, and he often told his wife to go out and get some fresh air. 'My love, I can't bear to see you shut up in this oven. I don't feel the heat; but you must be sweltering, you do so much running around. Do go out on to the terrace.' Rosalía usually refused. 'I don't feel like going out. Leave me alone.' But sometimes she would go, accompanied by Mr Pez. One day, when he had stepped out first because he was stifling in the hot sitting room, he saw her appear in her claret-coloured robe, covered with lace, fanning herself. She was looking extremely elegant, a bit over the top, as Milagros would say; but very, very pretty. Listing Pez's compliments would turn this book into one long madrigal. Without knowing how, the lady gave way to a violent, spontaneous urge that had hatched in her heart, and told her friend the story of the robe which her husband had caught her wearing when he lifted his bandage a moment. 'Poor lamb! He doesn't like to see me wearing things that he thinks are exorbitant ... Maybe he's right.' The Pipaón woman moved on from this to general observations. According to Bringas, she should wear the same old things all the time, just keep doing them up, and make one dress last for ever by endless metamorphoses ... She had no idea what to wear. On the one hand, she was duty bound to obey her husband; on the other, she wanted to look decent and respectable ... for his own sake! 'If it was just for me, I wouldn't mind so much. But it's for him, for his sake ... so people don't say I dress like a fishwife.'

Pez was decidedly and even vehemently in agreement with all this, and he became quite indignant, holding forth against his friend for his miserly behaviour, which violated social expectations. 'The man doesn't recognise that for the sake of his own dignity, of his own reputation, of his own interests ... What kind of a career is a man like that going to have, a man who talks like that, a man who behaves in that way?'

Rosalía continued imparting confidences, telling him about the agonies she went through to prevent Bringas from finding out about the little purchases she was obliged to make. 'You have no idea what I suffer sometimes; I have to lie, I have to make things up.'

Pez was so noble and gentlemanly that after expressing his heartfelt sympathy for her, he offered his completely disinterested assistance, should his friend ever find herself in difficulties due to Bringas's incredible meanness ... 'We're friends, aren't we? We should be frank with each other. No one but the two of us would have to know about it. How can he not let you ... you who are so noble and so good, and with a figure most women would kill for, how can he not let you dress like a lady ... ?'

This was followed by such a flood of praise that Rosalía had to fan herself harder to counteract the bright colour that had risen to her cheeks. Her pretty chiselled nostrils flared almost to breaking point. 'I'm going to fetch him a cold drink ... it's seven o'clock,' she announced all of a sudden. She would have one too, she could do with cooling down.

The following day they were all very happy because of the doctor's assurances. Laughter was heard in the household again, and even the patient perked up and started brimming with impatience and energy. 'Next week,' the doctor had said, 'we'll take off your bandage. Things are looking good. The week after, you should just have some slight blurriness of vision and you'll be able to go out with dark glasses on. As long as you stay away from anything that might cause eye strain all summer, you should be able to go back to the office and lead a normal life again by the autumn, as long as you promise never to play around with hairs ever again. Mechanical tasks that make you use your muscles would be a good idea, like carpentry, for example, or lathe-work, or something physical in the open air. But nothing small-scale.' Bringas looked very put out when the doctor added that he recommended taking the waters at Cestona.* He came out with his usual line of it all being 'a load of nonsense; in the olden days no one went to spas and less people died,' and 'spas are just an excuse for people to spend money and for the ladies to get dolled up . . .' To which the good doctor replied with a vigorous defence of hydropathy as a treatment.

'There's nothing for it, my love,' said Rosalía, whose nostrils were more eloquent than her lips. 'It's doctor's orders, and that's that . . . What do you mean, it's all a load of nonsense? That's not for you to say. In this sort of situation we have to do everything he says so we won't feel bad if you get worse. The climate in the provinces in summer will do you the world of good. Oh! If it were up to me, I'd really much rather stay here, because travelling is such a bother, but the children . . . [*underlining her statement with emphatic gestures*] they can't go another year without going to the seaside.'

Although the prospect of this trip depressed him, with all the upheaval, the expense, the bother of having to ask for free tickets and all sorts of other irksome things, Francisco was overflowing with happiness, which spilled out on to his lips; he could not keep quiet for a second. 'As soon as I get better I'm going to do a spot of carpentry. I'm going to make you a wardrobe for your clothes that will be so huge and so famous that people will need a ticket to see it, like in the Natural History Museum and the Royal Stables. The man who's got logging rights at Balsaín* will give me all the pine I need. There is some mahogany stored down in the cellars of this building that is going rotten, and Her Majesty won't mind if I use a bit of it. The contractor who did the Royal Family's mausoleum at El Escorial has offered me all the marble I want. I'll make you a marble wardrobe . . . a pantheon for your clothes . . . no; I'll make you a superb washbasin and stand. And I'll make something for Cándida too . . . I haven't got all that many tools . . .

But I'll get hold of some more . . . or I'll borrow them from the contractor who's doing the work at La Granja.'* While they were discussing this, the widow chipped in, informing the artist that she could lend him the most magnificent, elegant models for his work. She had an inlaid sideboard that belonged to Grimaldi himself, and a wardrobe that the Princess of the Ursins* had brought from Paris. As for the workshop Francisco would need, they could easily persuade Her Majesty to give him one of the places that were sitting empty and unused on the third floor. In fact, next to the oratory there was a great big room with plenty of light, where there once used to be a dovecote, which would do him perfectly. Bringas rubbed his hands so gleefully that no doubt he could almost have set off sparks. 'Good, good. Once I get going, you'll see what I can do . . .' he said, over and over again.

I presume it is unnecessary to say that Rosalía was overjoyed too. Her beloved husband was going to be well again, and recover his eyesight, that essential feature of health and well-being, and would once again be able to fulfil his role as paternal sovereign of the household. But since no joy is complete in this miserable world, where happy events always bring sad forebodings with them, and every object casts a shadow, Mrs Bringas's pleasure was obscured by the presence of something disagreeable off to one side. Over that part of her mind loomed the recollection of the pawned candlesticks and the need to retrieve them before Bringas got his sight back, for with it would come the vigilant watch he kept, his interfering habit of checking up on her, and that implacable, inquisitorial, rodentlike curiosity of his. If the great day dawned and the candlesticks were not on the sideboard and the earrings in the lady's pretty ears, the first thing he would be sure to see with those eagle eyes of his would be the lack of those very objects. It was too dreadful to think of . . . ! Note how happiness itself engendered in her such an acute distress, that the poor lady found herself painfully perplexed. She described it to herself by saying that maybe she would be happy not to be quite so happy.

Bringas's impatience and energy manifested themselves in a fever of domestic interventions, in a sort of administrative delirium, overseeing things without being able to see and giving directions just as if he had his eyesight back. He kept on endlessly issuing decrees and answering his own questions.

Needless to say, this spate of words was driving his wife out of her mind.

CHAPTER 26

'Now you listen to me, love ... If we do have to go to that wretched spa, you've got to make do with the dresses you have. You can change them, alter them, take things off one and put them on to another ... and your dresses will look as good as new. Everyone will say you got them from Worth. Even duchesses do that, you know ... I'm counting on Her Majesty to write a note to the head of the railway company to tell him to give us all free tickets ... Oh, and another thing: if you put your mind to it, you could get the Queen to tell the people in Administration to give me double pay in July ... And why not August as well? You just have to go about it the right way, look upset when you mention our trip and say we can't go for financial reasons ... You have to catch her in a generous mood, which shouldn't be too difficult, because she's almost always that way. I'll leave it in your skilful hands. The children don't need new outfits. A little hat each, at most. Don't get anything without my seeing it first. You're capable of spending a fortune and dressing them up to the nines, with huge contraptions on their heads that will make them sweat buckets. I'll wear the panama hat that Agustín left behind, and that light serge jacket I had made six years ago, and my cotton suit, which always looks brand new ... they'll do me just fine. I'll tell them to give us a private compartment, so we can take our meals, a little stove to make hot chocolate with, a mattress, pillows, a carafe of water and a few other useful things. That way the trip will be bearable.'

He rattled on: 'What's that noise I heard? Who's gone and broken more of my things? Ever since I went blind, I've been keeping count of the plates and glasses that have been dropped, and it's at least a dozen and a half. When I get my sight back, I'm going to find the house in an almighty mess. Don't try and pretend otherwise. I can just imagine how chaotic it must be, and all the money you must be squandering. I have no idea why you're using so much oil, when I don't need any light. And are you keeping track of what Prudencia is spending? I bet you aren't. Since the master can't see, everything's topsy turvy. You say you spent twenty-four reals on lemons. What did you do, order the whole crop from Valencia? If we had to pay for prescriptions as well, we'd be out begging on the streets by now. Oh well, when I get better I can sort you all out. I get the feeling that ever since I've been ill, a lot of my orders are being ignored . . . I know, the master can't see, so . . . You haven't ordered the cheap stewing beef, and the soused fish, which is a good nourishing dish, has completely disappeared; and nobody's informed me whether we're still having those almond fingers that cost a quarter of a real a kilo for dessert. What you're all doing with your time, I don't know. You say you can't be everywhere at once, but what I'd like to know is, why can't Paquito clean the silverware when he gets back from lectures? Don't tell me it's beneath his dignity as a University student to do that sort of thing. His father's done it before and he'll do it again, as soon as he gets his eyesight back . . . And another thing, I'm convinced you don't make the children change into their old shoes as soon as they get back from school. I can tell from the sound of their footsteps that they're running around in their street shoes. You might have thought to buy them some espadrilles, which would be ideal for this weather. But I'll be able to see again soon, I warn you, and then we'll get things under control so we can keep our heads above water . . . And I get the impression that Prudencia isn't doing as much washing as she should be. It can't be for lack of soap, because we've used far too much of it these days, despite the fact that I haven't needed so many clean clothes and I haven't used any collars or cuffs at all . . . I'd swear that when you gave Cándida her coffee you didn't re-use yesterday's grounds, you made a fresh batch. I could tell by the smell. You're encouraging bad habits, you know, and that's the last thing we need around here.'

This sermonising did not go down too well with Rosalía, especially just then. She tried to get things running again the way they had before, and to abide by the numerous rules that flowed endlessly from that infinite source of domestic legislation. She bought espadrilles for the children, and Bringas decided they should stop going to school, because the excessive heat was bad for them, and a little break, besides being cheaper, would be better for their health. They were delighted, and spent the whole day in loose outfits of cotton twill, running around and playing in the corridors, or going up to the third floor to play with Irene and the other children. They were the happiest people in the place, almost as much as the pigeons nesting in the niches of the building and lulling the whole grandiose structure with their cooing.

Round about then, they had a visit which took them both by surprise and aroused in them a sentiment that was rather far from satisfaction. A person whose name they would have preferred to forget, Refugio Sánchez Emperador,* showed up at the house just when they were least expecting her. She seemed very intimidated, which made Rosalía think she was masking her usual impudence so as to be able to carry on a brief conversation with respectable people. She soon told them the reason for her visit. Her sister Amparo had written to her from Bordeaux ... Oh! She was so very sorry about Francisco's illness ... 'She says she's been worried to death ever since she heard.' She had asked Refugio to go and see the Bringas family right away, find out how the invalid was doing, and send her the news by return of post. She wanted to hear how he was two or three times a week, at least. Agustín was very worried too, and asked to be kept up to date ...

Bringas thanked her kindly and exaggerated his recovery to such an extent that Refugio must have thought he was wearing that huge bandage for the fun of it. 'Tell them I'm fine and that I'm very grateful for their concern ...' Rosalía was tempted to tell the woman exactly what she thought of someone like her having the effrontery to profane a decent house by coming to visit; but Francisco's composure and the girl's good manners restrained her. However, she could not bring herself to be polite to her; she greeted her curtly and did not shake hands. While the young woman talked to Bringas, the lady of the house came and went, ignoring the visitor. She scrutinised Refugio during the process, and noticed something that mitigated her hostility. It was not her courteous, grave manner; it was not the reasonable, judicious things she said; it was her dress, which was extremely elegant, the latest thing, beautifully cut, sewn, and trimmed. Rosalía looked at her out of the corner of her eye and could not help being astonished at the original, attractive shade of cashmere she was wearing, and the young woman's highly respectable appearance, her expensive gloves and even more expensive boots. 'She's rather charming,' she thought to herself; and kept wanting to ask where she had bought the fabric ...

Maybe Amparo had sent it to her from Bordeaux. And what a
chic little brooch she was wearing on her breast . . . ! How it
mesmerised Rosalía!

'And what are you doing with yourself these days?' asked
Francisco, turning his face towards Refugio as if he could see
her through the black bandage.

'Me?' the Sánchez girl replied, slightly disconcerted all of a
sudden, but overcoming it rapidly. 'Oh, nothing much: I'm not
working any more. I'm not all that well, you know; I keep
getting pains in my chest; sometimes I can't breathe properly
and it stops me sleeping at night. As soon as I lie down it's as if
I had a big stone right here, know what I mean? My sister sends
me what I need to live comfortably, without any problems. I live
with some very respectable ladies who are very kind to me. I
lead a quiet life . . . But anyway, as I was saying, my sister wants
me to have something to occupy my time. Since I can't do
needlework or use a sewing-machine, Amparo insisted I start a
little fashion business. She's sent me a crateful of bonnets, fichus,
straw hats, bows, cravats and chemisettes to start off with . . .
they're gorgeous. You've never seen such classy new styles in
Madrid before. I've also got a shipment of little straw and fabric
bonnets, and hundreds of different kinds of ribbons and plumes:
Marabou stork, egret, parrot, humming-bird, and toques and
little wing decorations, and all sorts of other chic things, you
name it, I've got it. I'm just trying my hand at it to see how I do
. . . I've advertised amongst the best families, and all sorts of
rich women have been to my house . . . They love my stuff. I've
had some business cards made up . . .'

And so saying, she took one out of her pocket to give to
Rosalía, who managed to stop glowering and take it, deigning
to bestow a gracious smile on the young woman, the first
Refugio had ever seen on those haughty lips. And while the
callipygian creature went on singing the praises of her new line
of work, Mrs Bringas listened to her with interest, possibly
moved to suspend her low opinion of the person in question
because of the lofty nature of the topic she was discussing. Just
as the Holy Spirit can come down and sanctify the lips of the
repentant sinner, so Refugio, in the eyes of her illustrious
relative, was redeemed by her divine discourse.

'So you've gone into the fashion trade, have you?' said
Francisco, waggishly. 'Good luck to you! You'll have to put up
with a lot of frustrations from your clients! People here indulge

in luxury in inverse proportion to the amount of money they have to pay for it. You be careful, my girl . . . If your dear sister doesn't send you an allowance, you'll starve on what you can make with the latest fripperies . . . And you're trying to sweet-talk us into becoming your customers? Try someone else, my dear, for Heaven's sake . . . Your line of business is ruining families and putting people in the workhouse. But I wish you all the best, and I recommend you be as hard-hearted as you can, unless you want to end up a pauper. You be tough on those women! Charge them forty for something that's worth twelve, and that way you can cover your expenses for the ones who never pay you at all . . . Lord, what a joke!'

The two of them laughed for a long while, and everyone joined in, even madam herself, who was kind enough to condescend to accompany Refugio to the doorway and exchange a few friendly words with her.

CHAPTER 27

'Did you ask her whether they're married yet?' Rosalía asked her husband, having rushed back to his side.

'It was on the tip of my tongue several times, but I didn't dare, in case she said no, because I would have thrown a fit.'

'I had to stop myself from having her thrown out of the house,' declared the lady, doing everything she could to seem possessed with holy fury, the legitimate product of her sense of dignity. 'She's got a real nerve coming into our house with stupid messages from that sister of hers, who's no better than she should be . . . The one's as bad as the other. What do we care whether Amparo's thinking of us or not! . . . And Agustín's reaction is pretty funny, too . . . That lot treat the Catechism as if it were a cartoon strip . . . I was furious listening to her. I don't know how you had the patience to sit through that load of lies and nonsense . . . And now she's going to start a fashion business . . . I'd like to know what kind of rubbish she sells! She really made me sick, I can tell you . . .'

The appearance of Mr Pez cut short the series of observations which were no doubt going to illustrate her point. A little later, Bringas, who never tired of issuing orders, decreed that from

then on, they would have luncheon at one thirty, like proper
Spaniards, and dinner at nine at night. This was not only more
appropriate in the heat, it would save money, because they
would use less coal. Dinner should be light. Our man recommended dishes such as lentils, chard and peas stewed in black
broth if necessary, and garlic soup, and forbade meat at night-
time. The only disadvantage of this plan was that their stomachs
required fortifying with a cup of hot chocolate in the afternoons
to fill them up, which was becoming an almost intolerable
burden because Cándida had taken to sticking to the family like
a limpit. But as it turned out, God came to Thiers's aid as
always, because Tula, who adopted the same culinary system in
summers, made the most wonderful hot chocolate every afternoon and always sent over a cup of it, generously furnished with
cup-cakes and slices of sponge, to her sick friend.

'I must say,' Bringas would remark when he heard their
neighbour's maid coming in, 'Tula's such a kind person . . .'

Rosalía would go over to Tula's house, and Pez rarely failed
to join them for chocolate at six-thirty . . . Various other
important people from the Palace city would show up, such as
the Head of Administration's sister, one of the chaplains from
time to time, the Second Steward, the Chief Inspector of Police,
the doctor, and so on. Milagros never went to her sister's,
because they had not been on speaking terms for some time.
Tula seemed rather reluctant to mention the Marquesa; but that
was all. María was almost always there, and everyone adored
her and fussed over her. Bringas's wife proudly displayed her
mozambique dress in public at these gatherings, and Cándida
wore her black grosgrain one, the only decent dress she had left.
Needless to say, since Mr Pez was present, no other mere mortal
dared try and show off his knowledge of politics or any other
weighty matter. As for me, I must confess that winsome and
well-spoken gentleman's conversation had a kind of soporific
effect on me. No sooner would he start explaining why he was
so important to the Moderate Party, then a sweet narcotic fluid
would begin to flow in my brain, and Tula's armchair would
caress me in its warm arms and urge me to take a snooze. For
politeness' sake, however, I was obliged to struggle against that
unfortunate urge to doze off, and I would end up in a state
similar to what the doctors call *waking coma*, seeing and not
seeing, going from real images to imaginary ones, hearing and
not hearing, aware of a general hum mixed in with particular

sounds. The attractive room, which was kept dark and half-shuttered because of the heat; the light filtering in through the gauzy curtains, creating a tropical effect thanks to the huge flowers printed on the fabric; the muted shades, like a faded tapestry, in that somnolent cavern; Cándida clearing her throat and discreetly stifling her yawns behind her hand; María Sudre's other-worldly beauty; the design of Rosalía's mozambique starting to swim before me; and finally the lulling creak of the rocking-chairs and the swishing of five or six ladies' fans, all acted as sedatives on my brain. The ideas sparkled like the spangles on some of the fans ... Summer had come early that year, it was going to be a long, hard one ... The generals had arrived in the Canary Islands ... Prim was in Vichy ... the Queen was moving to La Granja and then to Lequeitio* ... Women's trains were getting shorter, and you couldn't be seen in one in a spa nowadays ... González Bravo was having stomach problems ... Cabrera had been to visit Don Carlos* ...

Towards the end, Pez's voice would begin to dominate, sounding just like his golden moustache, whose whiskers were so perfectly trimmed that they looked artificial, and the soporific effect would intensify ... He couldn't help feeling rather bitter and sad about the way things were going, through the fault of both sides ... Between the revolutionaries with their *all or nothing*, and the Moderates with their *non possumus*,* they'd put the country on the edge of a chasm, the edge of an abyss, the edge of a precipice. The good gentleman was very disappointed, and couldn't see any way to salvage the situation at this point. The country was going to perdition, the country was in love with adventure, the country was torn between conspiracy and resistance. There was no chance of progress or improvement or reform or even of proper administration. He was always saying, 'We need more administrators, more administrators.' But he was a voice in the wilderness. All the public services were woefully inadequate. Pez's organising mind had come up with a wonderful idea; but how was he going to make it happen? His ideal was to set up the perfect civil service, with eighty or ninety main offices. According to him, not one single aspect of the nation's life should escape the wise tutelage of the State. That way, everything would work properly. The country didn't think, the country didn't act, the country was stupid. Therefore, the State needed to think and act for it, because only the State was intelligent. Since this was not possible, Pez had retreated into his shell, permanently saddened, and was trying to affect a lordly indifference to it all. He considered himself better than his superiors; at least he had more vision, he could sense there was a better way of doing things, but since he couldn't do anything about it, he was trying to be calm and resigned. He consoled himself by caressing his own ideas in his mind, amidst the general confusion. In order to contemplate his fantasy of a revitalised Spain, he had to turn his back on all the corruption and the contempt for the law which was becoming so rampant ... Oh! Pez was happy he had such a good store of moral principles himself. He loved pure morals and strict virtue, and his conscience protected him against the crimes he saw being committed all around him ... He hoped to God his idealism would never desert him ... that it wouldn't fade away in contact with so much petty crime; he hoped to God ...

I do not know how much time passed between that second hope of his and Cándida's discreet little tap on my knee ... 'You seem a little absent-minded,' she said.

'No, no, not at all, ma'am ... I was just listening to Manuel, he's ...'

'Manuel has just stepped out on the terrace for some air. It's poor Serafina Lantigua, who's talking about the death of her husband. I'm horrified.'

'Oh! Me too ... absolutely horrified.'

CHAPTER 28

Pez, Rosalía and the Chief Administrator's sister strolled lazily along the terrace, whiling away the time. The sister went off to the Lord Chamberlain's house, and the elegant couple remained alone ... Poor Manuel was really in a sorry state. His wife's religious monomania had reached such exasperating extremes that she had become unbearable. 'What can I say? Listening to Serafina's tired old line about her sufferings was driving me so mad I couldn't wait to get out of there ... That pious droning voice and those funereal sighs of hers set my teeth on edge ... I'm a god-fearing man and I believe everything the Church tells us to believe; but people like her who eat, sleep and breathe

religion make me really sick. It's that Serafina who turned my
poor Carolina's brain, she's the cause of my unhappiness and
the reason I hate my own household . . . Oh, my dear, you've
no idea how miserable and ill one feels when one hates one's
own home! . . . Fortunately, you've never felt that . . . I'd rather
be out the whole day and never have to go there . . . Without
realising it, I've got used to thinking of dear Bringas's house as
if it were my own, and I'm forever comparing the friendly
warmth I get here and the chilly reception I get there . . . I'm a
man who can't survive without affection. I need it just as much
as air, without it I'd choke and die. Whenever I find it, I set up
camp and there I stay . . .'

Isabel and Alfonso went running by. They were hot and
sweaty from having played too hard in the corridors on the third
floor with Irene and the head chef's little girls. 'My goodness,
look at you!' said Rosalía, stopping her daughter. 'You're as red
as a lobster . . . And there's a draught at this point . . . Go on in,
I don't want you catching a cold . . . And what about this little
rascal? Just look at him, will you? He's got so many tatters he's
as naked as Adam. Look at those knees . . . Even if I put him in
a suit of armour, he'd wear holes in it . . .'

'What a funny little scamp! He's quite the little devil . . . Now
there's a man for you,' said Pez, kissing him and the little girl
too.

'Got any spare change?' said the little boy, brazenly.

'See what a naughty little thing he is? . . . Now look here, my
boy! . . . What did you just say? . . . Don't take any notice of
him. He's got into the bad habit of asking for money from
everyone. I don't know where he learned that trick from. What
a joke . . . One day I took them along for Her Majesty to see
. . . I've never been so embarrassed in my life! I couldn't get
them to say a word, and then all of a sudden, this little rascal
stands up, stares at the Queen as cool as a cucumber, stretches
out his hand and says, "Got any spare change?" Her Majesty
burst out laughing.'

'All right, little Mr Precocious, here's something for you.'

'Oh, you shouldn't. He only wants it to buy trifles with . . .
And this silly goose never asks for anything; but if you give her
money, she's happy to take it. And she's no spender. Not her!
She saves it all up in her piggy bank and she's already got her
very own capital. She's just like . . .'

'Just like her father . . .'

'Go on off home now, both of you, before you get cold out here ... You're sweating so much, sweetheart! ... I'll be there in a little bit.'

In no time at all they found themselves at the top of the Cáceres stairway, which took them back to the house. Pez gave a sigh. Rosalía carried in her hand a half-wilted but still very fragrant rose, and she buried her nose in its petals from time to time, as if she wanted to inhale every bit of its scent. The flower set off her pretty nose beautifully.

'Because in the end,' said Pez, returning to his doleful theme, 'you'll have to ask me to leave ... It's rude for me to spend so much time here.'

She must have replied that she saw no reason for anybody to be ejected, and he cheered up and begged her pardon for his attachment to the Bringas family ... It would have been cruel to deprive him of the consolation of their friendship; although, to tell the truth, the focus of attraction ... Yes, that was the word, the focus of attraction ... 'lay not so much in my dear friend Bringas as in his incomparable wife. You understand me better than he or anyone else does. It's a curious thing; the day I don't exchange a few words with you I feel as if I'm missing something, as if the roots of life are thirsting for water, as if the sap of my being has run dry ...' Pez went on in this poetic and philosophical vein, and as Rosalía listened, her vanity and her nostrils swelled, and she crushed her nose deep into the flower whose fragrance enveloped them both.

'I am irresistibly drawn to you. If you forbid me to come, you'll blight a life that used to be devoted to the family and the service of our country ... you will do the worst possible thing to a man ... and all for nothing ...'

She cannot have replied in a very haughty tone, because he then went on to express his wish that they see each other more often ... When poor Bringas got better, why shouldn't they see each other more often and in a place where they could speak somewhat more freely to each other ... ?

There was still a lot to say; but their little stroll could not be prolonged any more. When they reached the door of the house, Isabel came out to meet her mother, shouting in innocent jubilation: 'Papa can see, Papa can see!' Rosalía and Pez rushed in, beside themselves with joy at this good news, and found Francisco walking up and down *Gasparini* with his bandage up, gesticulating, so tense and excited that he seemed almost insane.

'It just stings a bit, a tiny bit of pain ... But I can see everything ... My dear Pez, you look so much younger ... And my wife's lost fifteen years ... By all the saints! I'm mad for joy ... There's just a red rim around things, that's all ... The light bothers me a bit ... I'll be better in a few days ... Give me a hug, love, hug me, all of you ...'

'Don't count your chickens before they're hatched,' said Rosalía, suddenly transfixed by a sad thought in the midst of her happiness. 'You have to be careful of a relapse ... I wouldn't take off that bandage, if I were you.'

'What's all this?' said the doctor, who had come in unannounced. 'Having a party, are we? Why are you running around like this, my friend? Put that bandage back on this minute ... You've got to play safe for a while.'

'Of course, it's not a good idea to take it off ... But just be patient a little while longer, my dear. Then we'll go and take the waters.'

'What waters? ... I'm not taking any waters,' asserted Bringas, allowing the doctor to replace the bandage. 'I don't need them. I don't want to hear any more of that nonsense.'

'We'll see about that,' said the doctor, good-naturedly. 'Now back to prison with you. And don't go escaping again, or you might find your sentence extended. We're doing very well so far, and we'll make it just fine as long as we take things slowly.'

The late evening light, in which our dear Thiers had tested the return of his optical functions with such immense pleasure, was slowly fading. At last, the room was lit up only by the glow left in the sky by the sun as it went down behind the Casa de Campo, a glow so strong it was like the flickering of firelight. Rosalía went to light the lamps; but Bringas quickly forestalled her with the observation that there was no need to bring in a light ... 'A lamp's just what we need in here, so we can all bake to death ... Forgive me, Manuel; but I think we're better off in the dark ... Paquito, open the window wide. Let's have some air in here, air, air ...'

A little later, Bringas, tired of listening to his son's student tales, said loudly, 'Mr Pez ... Is he there?'

'No, he's not,' replied Paquito.

'Rosalía!'

'Mama!' called the young man.

A little later Rosalía appeared. Her majestic figure, a ghostly white in the shadows, brought a touch of theatrical mystery to the solitude of the room where father and son sat, invisible in the gloom.

'Has Manuel left?'

'No, he's on the balcony of the Little Room, watching the . . . I'm sorry you can't see it . . . Watching the glow in the sky to the West . . . It's as if half the world were on fire.'

'Off you go then, don't leave him alone . . . Today I had a little word with him about the boy's promotion, and I think he took it all right. He said *we'll see* in a way that sounded to me like *yes* . . . Oh! And don't forget we're to have dinner at a quarter to nine.'

At which time Pez departed and Rosalía changed her glamorous robe for an old one and her low-heeled shoes for some cloth-soled slippers, and set about organising dinner. She complained of a bad headache and would only have a plate of mixed vegetables herself. Her husband told her she ought to go to bed; but she had too much to do to go to bed so early . . . Oh! The tea-party at Tula's house, with Pez and Serafina both going on endlessly, had left her with a splitting head . . . And Manuel was capable of giving the Holy Spirit itself a migraine with his spiel of lamentations. Job was nothing next to all the calamities that had befallen that man.

'Well, dear, why don't you go to bed and have a rest after all that nonsense . . . You have to be patient and listen to whatever Pez feels like telling us, because you know what he says. We're his shoulder to cry on, this is where the poor man comes to get his problems off his chest.'

In the end, Rosalía did as her husband told her. Once the tables were cleared and the lights out, and Paquito had been instructed to give his father his medicine later on, the noble lady's head sought rest among the pillows. However, sleep only came after a long period of concentrated brooding.

CHAPTER 29

The silver candlesticks . . . the danger of her husband finding out they had made a trip to Pawnsville* . . . how to avoid this . . . Mr Pez, her ideal . . . What an extraordinary, fascinating man! What vision, what a superior being! . . . To think he was capable, if given the chance, of organising a civil service with eighty-four main offices, it just went to show what that superb brain of his could do ... And what cultivated, distinguished manners and gentlemanly generosity! ... She was quite sure if she were ever in a pinch that Pez would help her out with that tactful gallantry that was so alien to Bringas; he had never once shown it, not even when they were engaged, nor on their honeymoon in Navalcarnero* ... How vulgar her whole life seemed to her now! Even the village chosen for the initiation of their married life was horribly uncultured, unattractive and contrary to all notions of good taste ... The lady remembered the awful place well enough; they had stayed at an inn without one single comfortable chair to sit in, that reeked of cows and hay, and been served wine that tasted of tar and chops that tasted like leather ... And Bringas was so dull he could only talk of the most prosaic things. In Madrid, the day before the wedding, he wasn't man enough to spend one and a half reals on a bunch of sweet roses ... In Navalcarnero he'd given her a little ceramic wine jug and taken her out for walks in the fields, going so far as to pick bunches of poppies, which dropped their petals right away. She did not care for the country very much and the only thing which might have made it tolerable was hunting; but shooting frightened Bringas, and once, when the mayor had taken him on a hunting expedition, he'd ended up almost killing the mayor. His aim was so bad he couldn't even hit the wind ... When they got back to Madrid, they'd begun that regimented, oppressed matrimonial life, composed of hardships and pretences, a domestic comedy by day and by night, caught in the methodical, routine flow of time and small change. Subject to such a crushingly ordinary man, she had come to learn her uninspiring role by heart and played it automatically, unaware of what she was doing. That dummy had made her the mother of four children, one of whom had died in infancy. She loved them dearly, and thanks to that, she began to feel a real and growing genuine appreciation for the dummy ... She hoped he would live and be healthy; his faithful wife would stay by his side, playing her role with the skill she had acquired over so many years of hypocrisy. But for herself, she desperately wanted something more than just life and health; she wanted a little bit, just a tiny little bit of what she had never had: freedom, and an escape, even if only a figurative one, from those irksome constraints. Because, to be quite honest, she was jealous of the beggars; they at least were free to do what they liked with the spare change they were given, whereas she . . .

Sleep overcame her. She did not even feel the mattress dip as Bringas got into bed. When she awoke, the noble lady's first thought was for the captive candlesticks.

'How do you feel?'

'I think,' said her husband with a great sigh, 'that I'm not as well as I'd hoped I would be. I've been awake since four. I've heard the clock strike every single hour, half hour and quarter hour. My eyes sting and ache, and I can't bear the thought of light on them.'

They spent the morning in great uncertainty until the doctor came. He seemed discouraged and somewhat perplexed, hesitant about the medical reasons for this relapse in poor Thiers's condition. Was it the result of having eaten a bit too much . . . ? Was it a side effect of the belladonna that would disappear if they reduced the dosage? Was it . . . ? In a word, he should keep on resting, try not to get agitated, protect his eyes completely from the light, and since he could not bear to stay in bed, he was not to move from his chair or do anything or have anyone talking to him in the room . . . My good friend received these instructions with indescribable dejection. 'You see?' said his wife, flaring her nostrils enormously. 'That's what you get for fooling around, for wanting to get better in two days. I told you so, but you . . . You're just like a child . . .'

The unhappy man was too downcast to say a word. He spent the whole day in his armchair, with his hands clasped, twiddling his thumbs. His wife and son tried to comfort him with affectionate words, but he would not be comforted; it was as if their verbal palliatives exacerbated his pain. That afternoon, the intelligent Pez discussed the matter with Rosalía, and came up with this eminently sensible observation: 'I don't know why you didn't call in an ophthalmologist right from the beginning . . . I get the impression the poor doctor here knows as much about eyes as a mole.'

'That's just what I said,' replied the lady, attempting to express with an elegant grimace and a shrug of her shoulders just how mean her husband was. 'But just try going to Bringas with that idea. He refuses, and says that ophthalmologists are only after your money . . . It isn't as if he were hard up. He's got his savings . . . but he won't agree to use them on his own health unless he's at death's door, when the disease tells him: "Your money or your sight."'

Manuel was most amused by this colourful interpretation of his friend's avarice, and later, while he was talking to him, he brought up the idea of consulting an eye specialist. This time the patient seemed to accept the suggestion. Disheartened and impatient, he decided that his savings were well worth a ray of light, and all he said was: 'Do as you wish.'

That night, Milagros came over to keep her co-religionist in clothes company. Since they had not seen each other since the week before, Rosalía thought the financial problem which had so afflicted the Marquesa at the end of June must be solved. Frankly, I thought so too. But both Rosalía and he who has the honour of writing these lines noted with surprise that her aristocratic face was not glowing with that light of contentment which is the sure sign of a recent victory. Indeed, Tellería's wife soon declared that her little problem was not solved, just postponed. She had begged so hard, she had been awarded an extension until the tenth. It was already 7 July and there were only three days left. She begged her friend, by all the saints, by everything she held dear, to . . . !

Rosalía put her finger on her lips, recommending discretion. Isabel was somewhere in the vicinity, and the child had the irritating habit of recounting everything she heard. She was like a repeating watch, and you had to be extremely cautious when she was around, because she always went straight to her father with the story. A few days earlier, she had made the good gentleman laugh with this innocent revelation: 'Papa, Mr Pez says I'm just like you . . . because I hoard all the money people give me.'

CHAPTER 30

This earned her a loving squeeze and a kiss from her dear father.

And that night, hearing her come into his room, he called to her and sat her on his knees. 'Where's Mama?'

'She's in the Little Room with the Marquesa,' replied the child, who spoke clearly and rapidly. 'She told me to come over here. The Marquesa was crying because it's the seventh.'

'It's the seventh,' Milagros had said to Rosalía, clasping her hands in despair, 'and if by the tenth I haven't come up with it ... I'm going to have a heart attack! ... You've no idea what a state I'm in.'

They had shut themselves up, and, alone in the room, with no light, because the master of the house was a frenetic devotee of obscurantism in all its manifestations, the afflicted lady freely unburdened herself of all her wealth of grief, displaying it a thousand different ways, with flowery and elegiac inspiration ... She found daytime hard, and preferred the night for abandoning herself to the contemplation of her sorrows. When she looked at the stars, she thought she could feel an inexplicable sense of consolation ... It was as if the stars were promising something hopeful, or casting a certain metallic gleam into her mind ... It is very peculiar, that relationship between the stars and freshly minted gold ... The poor woman had no hope from anything or anyone except from her dear friend ... She'd been counting on her to save her ... How? That she didn't know. But she'd appeared to her in dreams with that angelic smile of hers and that distinguished air ...

'For Heaven's sake, my dear,' said Rosalía, 'don't get your hopes up; I can't, I can't, I can't ...'

'Yes, you can, yes, you can,' replied Milagros, whose insistence held a certain fascination for the other woman. 'You just have to want to ... It's not so very much money. I've managed to come up with five thousand reals; I just need another five thousand. Bringas ...'

'I don't know how to make you understand that it would be easier for us to drink the ocean dry.'

'I forgot to tell you that I brought the letter from my estate manager, promising that between the fifteenth and the twentieth ... You can't have a better guarantee than that. Besides, you'll get a formal agreement ... If I don't solve this, I shan't be able to bear the shame ... They'll find me dead for sure when they come looking for me. Sometimes I think, "Why can't there be a cataclysm or an earthquake or something before the tenth!" I think about the revolution, and believe me ... I wish it would happen ... All I need is a week of uproar and shootings when people can't go out into the street ... But even that's not going to happen, my dear. Did you know that General Serrano, Dulce and Caballero de Rodas have been arrested, and they say they're to be sent to the Canary Islands, and that the Duke of Montpensier is being exiled too? With all those precautions, nobody's going to lift a finger, unfortunately.'

'To the Canary Islands? I wish they could send them to hell!' exclaimed Rosalía jubilantly. 'That's wonderful; send them a long way away and then we can all stop worrying. Let's see them plot away now. And so the Duke is being sent away too . . . ? I'm going to tell Bringas, he'll be as pleased as punch.' The lady ran off to bear him the good news, and he was as overjoyed as if he had won the lottery (well, not quite, but almost), welcoming the event with the warmest words.

'Good, good, good. That's proper government for you. And to think they say that Ibrahim Clarete* is gaga; what he is is sharper than ever, you rogues. All right, now just try plotting against our wonderful Queen . . . So they're off to jail, eh? What a tough man that prime minister of ours is . . . ! I'd like to give him two big hugs . . . ! Off to the Canaries with them, it's as good as being shipped to another country! And if the ship with them in it goes down, so much the better . . . I can't help it, I feel like going out on to the terrace and shouting *Long live the Queen!* at the top of my lungs.'

And he almost did. A while later, Milagros played up to Bringas's dynastic passion with a colourful line demanding not just one death for the generals, but a hundred, and the gallows for all the conspirators. The invalid became very animated discussing all this; but, alas! the following day was one of the blackest in his whole life. Poor man! After spending a restless night, he found in the morning that he had almost entirely lost his eyesight. The doctor was so stunned that he could not even come up with those evasive formulae physicians use when they do not want to admit defeat. But he was a conscientious man and opted to abdicate his authority before he made things worse, saying, 'You must see an ophthalmologist. Ask Golfín to see you.'

Francisco felt as if the sky had fallen in on him. There was no doubt he had something serious. His avarice was vanquished by fear, and he did not oppose the judgement of the doctor and the rest of the family. In consternation, they pinned their hopes on the prodigious knowledge of the most famous eye-doctor in Spain. They agreed not to wait a single day, nor even an hour, before consulting him.

'Ah, Golfín!' Bringas knew all about him. They told wonderful stories about the man. He restored the sight of many a blind person whom the doctors had despaired of. He had earned a fortune in the Americas, and he wasn't doing so badly in Spain either. Talk about feathering your own nest! He'd charged eighteen thousand reals for treating the Marqués de Castro's cataracts, and he'd sent such an enormous bill for curing the Cucúrbitas boy's conjunctivitis that the family had had to mortgage themselves for six years to pay it off. 'But anyway, let's hope that, God willing, we'll come out of this all right. Let Golfín come and cure me, even if he has to take everything I've got.' Then they discussed whether or not he should go to the doctor's himself, or whether they should send for the ophthalmologist, and Bringas chose the first option as being the cheaper one.

'Paquito and I can take a carriage, and then . . .'

'No, you're in no state to be out on the street. We'll have him come here.'

'He won't come, my dear. These great men of science never leave their houses except to attend royalty or really wealthy people.'

'Of course he'll come. I'll go downstairs. Her Majesty will write him a little note . . .'

'That's a brilliant idea. And if her ladyship wants to add that I'm a poor man . . . even better still. God bless you, my darling.'

So Golfín came and saw him, and in his rough and kindly way cheered him up and salvaged the hope he begun to give up. The problem was not serious, but the cure would take a long time. 'You have to be very, very patient, and follow my instructions exactly, to the letter. You have a touch of conjunctivitis, which we need to combat quickly and energetically.'

Poor, unfortunate Bringas! For the moment, bed, special diet, rest, and belladonna.

Thus began a miserable period for the wretched Thiers. It was no good him taking off his bandage, because he could hardly see a thing, and it hurt so much that he stayed in the dark, where his only consolation was the memory of Golfín's words and that divine promise he had held out as he left: 'You will see again, you'll see as you've never seen before,' which was his way of praising the plenitude of that precious faculty we prize over all the rest in our body. To see again . . . ! But when, oh Lord; when, blessed St Lucy? The poor man was not short on patience, and in his dire straits he set his mind enthusiastically to religious contemplation, and spent part of his lonely hours praying. His

wife never left his side except when obliged to by the arrival of
some inopportune visitor, or when Milagros came in with a
doleful air and called her aside to regale her with a few tears or
calculated compliments ... It was too late now to think of going
to a spa, unless Bringas got better by the beginning of August,
which did not seem very likely.

Pez was one of the respectable family's most steadfast friends
in this period of tribulation. One afternoon, when he was able
to speak to Rosalía alone in *Gasparini*, she said to him: 'We're
about to run into difficulties and I don't know how we're going
to get out of them.' To which Manuel replied with a quixotic
gesture, offering to help her out of these difficulties, whatever
they might be. This noble thought penetrated the lady's mind
like a ray of light from Heaven. Now she could rely on some
support in the storms she might find herself in later on. Now
there was a place of shelter behind her, a fall-back in case of
dire need ... Now she had an arm, a shield, near her ... Life
seemed easier, clearer, all of a sudden ... I'll do my best,' she
thought, 'to see that this friendship isn't incompatible with my
reputation.'

CHAPTER 31

Seeing her husband so dejected and woebegone brought back all
Rosalía's old feelings for him; her respect for him was purged of
all her fancied grudges, and re-emerged magnified and sincere,
almost to the point of veneration. The conceited lady experienced a sudden tenderness toward her trusty partner of so many
years, for although he had never really gratified her pride, he
had not caused her any trouble either. She set to reminiscing
about their prosaic but peaceful married life, full of petty
privations and simple pleasures, which seemed trifling on their
own but made for an agreeable set of memories if you took
them all together. With Bringas she had enjoyed none of the
things she should have had by right of her beauty and her
genuinely aristocratic rank: no comforts, distinction, pleasures,
greatness, nor luxuries; but, on the other hand, how calm and
peacefully the days flowed by, with no panic or false pretences
or creditors! The guiding principle of that pedestrian creature

was to owe nothing whatsoever, and thanks to him they were genteel, honest, hard up and happy in equal measure. No doubt, if she'd landed a man like Pez, she'd be in a more prestigious position ... 'But God knows,' she thought sensibly to herself, 'what agony they go through in those households where they're always spending more than they have. You have to see that sort of thing close up and go through it and feel it yourself to know what it's like.'

In short, after her husband's condition worsened, Rosalía became mentally and emotionally closer to him, tightening the matrimonial knot. Sympathy for his misfortune and the habit of sharing all that life dealt them, adversities and good fortune alike, worked a miracle in her. How carefully she nursed him! How gently her hands applied the medicines! How charmingly and skilfully she administered the balm of sweet words to the sick man's soul! Bringas was so grateful that he never stopped praising God for His beneficence in inspiring his helpmate with such an admirable sense of her conjugal duty. Private pleasures lightened his load, and in his mood of religious enthusiasm, he believed that his wife's attentions were the faithful expression of divine assistance. He was only downcast when she had things to do and had to leave his side; he was forever calling on her for the slightest little thing, begging her to hurrry up so that she could devote herself entirely to him.

The whole of this time, Rosalía laid aside her finery. She had no time or peace of mind to be thinking of clothes. They lay buried in her chests of drawers, awaiting a more propitious moment to emerge. It had not even occurred to her to get dressed up ... It wasn't exactly a good time to be thinking of fripperies like that! Was this truly repugnance for luxury, or was it self-sacrifice? There was something of both in it. If it was self-sacrifice, she took it to the point of appearing before Mr Pez in the most homely and graceless attire imaginable. The only shred of vanity she retained was always wearing her best corset, so her figure would not be ruined. But her hair was dressed in the most rudimentary style and from her house robe one could ascertain by induction all the episodes that had occurred during the running of a household where money is scarce. One afternoon, she had said to Manuel: 'Don't look at me. I'm a mess.'

And he had answered: 'You're beautiful like that, and you always will be, whatever you wear.' A compliment which delighted her.

Bodily weakness necessarily entails unfortunate lapses, even in the strongest of characters. A prolonged illness can resemble the effects of old age in a man, making him seem like a child, and Bringas did not escape this psychosomatic malady. His debilitated state made him burn with tenderness, and that tenderness translated into a kind of whiny rapture.

'Sweetheart, you're no ordinary woman. I tell you, you're an angel ... You know, it's been my will that's been done in this household. You've been a slave. From now on, we'll do only what you say. I'll be the slave.'

On the first day of what we shall call Golfín's reign, Francisco had the money box brought to his bed, so as to get out the housekeeping money as usual. But all of a sudden, that maudlin sentimentality, or rather puerile passivity, which I described earlier, inspired in him a trust he had never felt before. 'You don't need to bring the box over, my love. Here's the key; just go ahead and take what you think we'll need.' And so she did. Bringas was still cautious enough to ask for the keys afterwards and stow them under his pillow, because all raptures have their limits, as do senile and infantile weaknesses.

Thus Rosalía was able to explore the secret treasure. She went through the contents of the false bottom, counting and recounting it all, amazed at the amount of money there. Her husband had a lot more than she had suspected; he had quite a capital. There were five four thousand real notes, which made twenty thousand reals, and then some more in smaller denominations that came to three thousand seven hundred. The five big notes made the most elegant little sheaf the lady had ever seen in her life. As she examined the money, the resentments and complaints that had plagued her at various times in the past came back to life ... The man who possessed all that wouldn't let her wear a new dress! The master of that sum insisted on dressing his wife like a priest's housekeeper! ... What a silly old man he was! ... If she was going to be the true head of the house from then on, as he claimed, she was going to have to change her ways, be more demanding and use the family savings in a way more suited to their dignity ... Wasn't it idiotic to save money that way, without getting anything out of it? If only he had lent it out for interest or invested it in one of the organisations that share out their dividends ... !

The discovery of the treasure forced Rosalía's thinking out of the circle of humility and self-sacrifice into which it had been corralled by her husband's illness. Bringas said to her, in a fit of enthusiasm: 'When I get better, I'll buy you a grosgrain dress, and if I'm still doing all right in the winter, you'll have another made of velvet. You ought to look elegant once in a while, and not just because of presents from the Queen or your friends, but with the product of my fruits of my savings and my honest labour.'

And she started to think that although the treasure did not exactly belong to her, most of it ought to be in her hands. 'I've gone without for long enough, I've had to make do too many times to be as hard up as I am now, when really and truly I've got money. If he won't give it to me, I'll have to make him understand he owes me some respect.' One morning, Milagros caught her in this frame of mind, with so much success, that it seemed as if Providence had planned the whole thing to satisfy the fortunate Marquesa. She was still in the process of announcing, with sighs and groans, the imminence of her catastrophe, when Rosalía said to her in a determined voice: 'Will you sign an agreement promising to pay me back within a month what I lend you? Because the closer we are, the more we need to make sure we do things properly. Will you give me two per cent interest per month? Will you add on to the agreement those six hundred reals you owe me? . . . Because friendship is one thing, my dear, and business is another. I hope you don't mind . . .'

Naturally, the Marquesa said a sincere and fervent yes to everything. Not to believe her would have been like doubting the very light of day.

'Well, on those conditions, I'll lend you the four thousand reals,' said Rosalía, in the self-important tones of a moneylender.

Those who have had the privilege to see, either in reality or in rapturous visions, the gate of Heaven and flights of angels round it singing praises to the Lord, surely cannot have worn a more radiant expression than Milagros when she heard that joyful news. But . . .

CHAPTER 32

There is always a *but* lurking in every happiness, and in the Marquesa's case it was because she really needed *five* thousand to make up the sum ... Because she did: she had to pay a little bill ... Anyway, what difference did it make? As to the interest, she didn't care if it was two, or four, or six per cent. 'Believe you me, my dear, the more you make out of it, the happier I'll be.' Rosalía hesitated for a while; but in the end the two of them came to a satisfactory arrangement, and that very afternoon they made out and signed the contract in the *Furriela*, taking all the necessary precautions so that Isabel, who was hanging around, would not get wind of anything.

Milagros bid Francisco goodbye in the most affectionate and enthusiastic terms she had ever used in her life: 'You know, you've got a wonderful wife! God's gone and sent you one of his chosen angels. Don't you go complaining about your eyes, my friend, it doesn't do any good, you'll get better soon enough. You just thank God for what you've got, because those of us who have people like Rosalía around can face all sorts of calamities and bear them bravely.' A deeply moved Francisco went to shake her hand as the Marquesa covered the chosen angel with frantic, noisy kisses.

The said angel had obeyed a variety of motives in acting as she did. In the first place, the desire to do her friend a good turn was a major influence. Secondly, the notion so often voiced by Bringas that she could make all the decisions had taken charge of her mind, engendering other notions of power and authority. She had to show by her actions, even if they were rather risky ones, that she had ceased to be a slave and that she had her sovereign role to play in the distribution of the conjugal fortune. She appeased her conscience with this, as well as the fact that she was lending the money to get interest. The pipsqueak couldn't complain if the five thousand came back suitably augmented. All of the above might not, in the end, have emboldened her enough to make the loan, had she not counted on a reliable fall-back in the extreme case of Bringas finding out and disapproving; she was depending on the offer made to her the evening before by the family friend, who, as he drew her to the window at dusk to admire the melancholy beauty of the horizon, had clearly said, in terms that are faithfully rendered here, the following: 'If, for any reason, either because of *his* medical expenses, or because you can't balance your accounts; I mean it, if for any reason you find yourself in difficulties, you have only to let me know, either verbally or by sending me a note, and right away I'll ... No, no, it's nothing ... Forgive me for putting it so baldly, so bluntly, so indelicately perhaps. There's no other way of discussing these things. It's between the two of us, and Bringas will be the last to know . . . In the privacy of our honourable and pure friendship, I can offer you something I have plenty of and you can accept what you need with no offence either to your dignity or mine.'

These phrases were followed by others of a more romantic than financial nature, in which the unhappy gentleman expressed once again the comfort his bruised spirit gained from being able to breathe the atmosphere of her household and lay down the burden of his sufferings with the understanding person who had come to occupy first place in his heart and mind. Rosalía left the window with her head in a whirl. She would dearly have loved to stay there a couple more hours, listening to his rhetoric, which, to her way of thinking, constituted society's belated payment of a debt of homage it owed her.

A few days passed without Bringas perceiving any noticeable change in his condition. Golfín tortured him cruelly three times a week, painting his eyelids with a brush dipped in silver nitrate, and then another moistened with saline solution. This treatment made our friend see stars, and he needed all his strength of will and all his manly dignity not to start bawling like a baby. The application of cold compresses assuaged his pain somewhat. Not long after the cauterisation, he would experience a certain sense of well-being, which made him think he was getting better, and he would praise Golfín in fulsome terms. After ten or twelve days on this régime, the wise doctor declared that the good gentleman would see a substantial improvement throughout the month of August, and that in September, he would be completely and utterly cured. The patient had such faith in the great master's word that it never occurred to him to doubt the accuracy of the prognosis. After the twentieth, the cauterisation, which was now being done with copper sulphate, was less painful, and the patient could take off the bandage for a while in the darkest room, as long as he did not look at anything in particular for any length of time.

Francisco's extravagant praise of Golfín led him as if by the hand to another set of ideas, which made him frown and look surly. 'When I think of the bill I'm going to be sent by this St Lucy in an overcoat,' he would say, 'I begin to tremble. He'll cure my eyes, all right, but he's going to extract an eye tooth out of my wallet . . . It's not that I begrudge paying for something as precious as eyesight; I don't mind parting with all my savings, if I have to; but the fact is, love, the great man is going to leave us without a shirt on our backs.'

Both husband and wife were well aware that famous specialists always take into account the patient's income when they make out their bills. Rich men and tycoons get fleeced, it is true; but when they are dealing with a poor office worker or someone on a modest income, they become more humane and are willing to accept reality. Rosalía had heard of a family (the De la Caña ladies, as a matter of fact) whom Golfín had charged very little for a cyst removal and a long, difficult convalescence. Convinced of these ideas of distributive justice, applied to suffering humanity, the great Thiers spent all his time with Golfín badgering him with cannily planned lamentations about his situation. The good man went on so, that it seemed almost as if he were begging for alms. 'Oh, dear Dr Golfín, I'll bless you my whole life long for doing this, and I'll bless you even more for my children's sake than for my own, the poor little things won't have anything to eat if I don't have eyes to see! ... Oh, my beloved Dr Golfín ... please cure me quickly so I can get back to work, because if this lasts much longer, that'll be it for my family! ... We're horribly in debt because of this illness. At the Heritage office they've put me on half pay, and if I don't get my sight back soon ... what a future I'm going to have! ... And I'm not just saying it for myself. I don't mind if I end my days in the workhouse; but my poor children ... my poor little darlings ...'

CHAPTER 33

These ideas did not accord at all with the notion Golfín had of the Bringas's position and influence, since he had seen the happy couple so many times at the theatre, and on the boulevards and other public places, both of them very well dressed; and since he had also seen Rosalía on the Castellana* in a carriage with the Marquesa of Tellería, as well as Mrs Fúcar and Mrs Santa Bárbara, and he was even convinced he had met her at some society reception, competing in finery and hauteur with the very best of families, he had assumed, based on these social signs, that Francisco was independently wealthy, or that at least he was one of those government employees who know how to extract from politics the juice that others try in vain to squeeze out of the hard, dry substance of their work. But Golfín was a little naïve about things of this world, and since he had spent most of his life abroad, he was unfamiliar with our customs and that special facet of Madrid life which would be termed *mysteries* in other places, but which are no mystery at all to any of us here.

As Bringas started to recuperate, his wife noticed that those frenzies of conjugal affection to which he was so given in the darkest days of his illness began to abate. She observed that those exaggerated demonstrations of affection were no match for the hope of recovery, and that when the latter was winning out over discouragement, the weepy, clingy, senile child would recover the virile stamp of his real self. Naturally, all that about *her being the lady of the house and him being the slave* turned out to be a lot of hot air, the whim of a spoilt invalid. As soon as our man could manage by himself and pass the time in his armchair in *Gasparini* without any pain, even though he could not see, he began itching to inspect everything and issue orders and be told about all that went on in the house ... Rosalía would claim she was busy so as not to have to listen to him, and she left him with Paquito or Isabel most of the day, shutting herself up for long periods in the *Camón* where Emilia had started work once again amidst a sea of fabrics and ribbons, whose frothy waves reached as far as the door.

But the economist, ever impatient to demonstrate his authority, would order her to appear before him, and there, with the attitude if not the gaze of an implacable judge, he would display in public (in front of Torres or some other friend) his power as domestic sovereign.

'I can smell cooked sugar. What's going on? Our little girl told me she saw a big parcel delivered from the shop ... Why wasn't I informed?'

Rosalía answered lamely that Mr Pez was lunching with them that day, and that a guest like him could not be treated like Cándida, who was happy with half a bun and a couple of dried figs for dessert.

'But my dear, you must have spilt a sack of cinnamon on the stove ... The house reeks of it ... if I were well, things like this just wouldn't happen. You must have made enough vanilla pudding for an army ... You just don't think. If you'd only asked the Royal chef how to make this or that, he would have sent it to you right away ... And tell me, now: why have I been hearing scissors snipping away all day? ... I'd like to see what's going on, and what that good-for-nothing Emilia is up to here ... What's she doing, making dresses for the Marquesa? As if we didn't have enough on our hands without running her ladyship's fashion salon into the bargain ... And tell me something else: whatever did you make for the children to wear? They were attracting attention yesterday in the Plaza de Oriente.'

'Attracting attention!'

'Yes, attracting attention ... because they were so well dressed ... I suppose we should be grateful that's the only reason. Golfín said this morning, "I saw your children yesterday in the Prado, looking very elegant." Get that, *very elegant*! Believe you me, my dear, I was none too happy when he said it and I just can't get it out of my mind. What else is the poor man to think, when he sees our children decked out like prize lambs, as if we were one of the wealthiest families around? ... He's bound to jump to absurd conclusions. I suspected something was up yesterday, because when I had the bandage off for a while, I noticed our little girl was wearing a lovely pair of scarlet stockings. Where did she get them? ... And since she has got them, why doesn't she at least take them off as soon as she gets home ... What is all this? What's going on here? ... We'll find out just as soon as I can see properly again, without my eyes hurting, which won't be long now, God willing.'

Needless to say, all this jabber had Rosalía at her wits' end. She tried to calm him down with artful explanations; but for all her ingenuity, she could not quite achieve the desired result, for the great economist was of an exceptionally suspicious nature, and extremely well versed in household matters and arts. When she was alone, the lady would vent her oppression of spirit, silently muttering irate and resentful words: 'You stupid old skinflint, when will I ever prove to you that you don't deserve me? When will you ever learn that a wife like me should cost more than a housekeeper? You just don't get it, do you, you silly idiot, you mousey little man? Well, I'll see to it you do some day.'

She plotted how to emancipate herself gradually, and practised the phrases whereby she would declare her firm resolve to

do away with that foolish, ridiculous enslavement; but her
spirits took a dive when she considered what would befall her if
the *silly idiot* discovered her explorations in the false-bottomed
treasure chest. Mother of God, what a state he'd be in! ... She'd
made a great mistake in removing that portion of the conjugal
fortune, because even though she thought of it as hers by right,
she shouldn't have taken it without Mr Mousey's* say-so ...
But she'd made an even bigger mistake in thinking she could
play such a clever trick on a man like him. The excuses she had
thought so reasonable at the time now seemed useless and
unworthy of a thinking person. Her course of action now
seemed groundless, and her conscience began arguing loudly.
No, she couldn't simply wait for her husband to find out the
money was missing. She started to squirm at the mere thought
of him finding out; it was vital to get the ill-fated sum back in
place; it amounted in fact to six thousand reals, for she had
taken five thousand for Milagros and a thousand to redeem the
candlesticks and get a few odd bits and pieces.

The need to put the money back became so imperative that
she could think of nothing else. She was counting on the power
of the agreement they had signed and the strength of the
Marquesa's word. Milagros announced soothingly on the
twenty-second: 'It's all arranged. You can relax.' But Rosalía, in
the meantime, was going through agony, fearing a catastrophe
every second and dreaming up all sorts of devices and machi-
nations to avoid one. Up until that point, the silly idiot had kept
to the good habit of giving his wife the keys so that she could
get the money out of the savings box. But one afternoon, he
went back to his old ways all of a sudden, and taking out the
dreaded box, he opened it and started feeling around inside ...
Lord, Lord, what a ghastly moment! Rosalía turned every shade
imaginable. She was stunned, too terrified to act.

'Can't stop fiddling around, can you? ... You don't take a
blind bit of notice of Dr Golfín ... What a man! ... Give that
box here.'

'You get your hands off it, woman,' said Bringas, defending
his treasure energetically.

He counted the hundred-real pieces one by one; he fingered
the two gold pieces, the old watch which had belonged to his
father, a chain and an antique medallion ... Since nothing was
missing, there was no danger, unless he lifted the false bottom
... Rosalía was tempted to scream something outrageous like

'The house is on fire!' but she did not dare, because Paquito was there. Now the skinflint's supple hands were caressing the part where the false bottom lifted up. Rosalía called on all the saints, all the Virgins, the Holy Trinity, and we think she even made a vow to St Rita,* if only she would come to her aid in that hour of need. But just as Francisco inserted his fingernail into the groove in the wood, he miraculously changed his mind ... He withdrew his fingers, and closed the box. Rosalía's heart left her mouth and her lungs began functioning again. She had been just a hair's breadth from ... No doubt her husband had no idea, nor even the vaguest suspicion of the fraud, and even though he usually counted the notes just for the pleasure of it, this time he did not do so, the good Lord only knows why. Perhaps all the lady's invocations to the saints were heard, and some kind angel breathed in Mr Mousey's ear the idea of counting his savings another day.

CHAPTER 34

But Rosalía could not rest until she saw him put the box carefully back in its place, as if he were laying a sleeping child in a crib, and lock the drawer. Only then did she give thanks to Heaven above for the great mercy she had just been granted. But what divine intervention had prevented from happening that day could perfectly well happen another. The saints are not always in the same frame of mind. In case he decided to check the false bottom again, the industrious lady came up with a solution which, she hoped, would stave off a confrontation while she waited for the time when she could put herself out of danger for ever by replacing the money. Her solution, then, was to put some pieces of paper the size of bank notes in the box; and if she could manage to find paper that was of the same type as that used for money, so that it would not feel different to the touch, it would be easy to deceive her husband, since he could only see the notes with his fingers ... She set to work, searching out and scrutinising all the paper in the house. At last, on Paquito's desk, she found some that seemed to her very similar in consistency and pliability to the sort the Bank used for its notes. She arrived at this conclusion after a lengthy comparison of the different types of paper with a two hundred real note she had. To refine the imitation, she needed to give it the patina of use, that sticky softness notes get from being handled by so many cashiers and creditors, by spendthrifts and misers alike. Rosalía submitted the pieces of paper to a series of operations to simulate the crumpling of notes in public circulation.

'What do you want, child?' she said crossly to Isabelita, who had come to stick her little nose in as usual. 'Go and keep Papa company, he's all alone.'

She shut herself up in the *Camón* to avoid detection, and once inside she crumpled the paper into a ball. Then she straightened it out and flattened it with the palm of her hand, until repeated handling had given it the desired level of pliability. It lacked that tacky feel that real notes have; but how was she to obtain that? It seemed impossible, although in fact her hands were ideally primed for the task. She had just been making croquettes in the kitchen, and she had made sure not to wash her hands so they could imbue the paper with some of that grime at which, to my knowledge, no idealist has ever turned up his nose so far.

When she thought she had worked on it long enough, she decided to put her creation to the test. Overcome with nerves, she said to herself: 'I don't know what there is about this paper that makes it so different from anything else. I don't think I'm going to fool him.' And her fingers would do a touch test, comparing the true and the counterfeit note. 'Suppose I couldn't see ... Suppose someone gave me this one and I were trying to tell the difference between the real one and ... Oh, there's no mistaking it! You can tell at once ...' And she would heave a sigh, so disheartened that she was on the point of abandoning the whole operation. But then she thought: 'No. When you know the secret, you can tell the difference; but if you didn't know ... I'll put them in the false bottom, and God will decide. We'll just have to wait and see.'

That evening at dusk, when Bringas took out the box, the lady had the pieces of paper ready so as to be able to use them if the skinflint opened the false bottom. But he did not. Then, as if to save him the trouble of going to his desk, Rosalía took the little box from his hands and during the brief moment she was replacing it, managed to insert the false money which was to pipe up at roll call for the notes that had gone away. Needless to say, this temporary solution was very dangerous, and she needed to get the matter permanently resolved in a hurry, by asking Milagros to pay up.

The following day, which was 25 July, St James's Day, it was excruciatingly hot. Bringas was in his shirt sleeves and Rosalía, who was wearing a light cotton percale robe, fanned herself incessantly and complained all the time about the climate in Madrid and Bringas's decision to live in a west-facing apartment. And the skinflint had the nerve to proclaim that he liked the heat, that it was very good for one, and that he felt sorry for the *idiots who leave town*! That very day, the great economist had announced solemnly to the whole family that he had decided they were not going to the seaside, which had made Rosalía even more irritable than the heat. Trapped in Madrid at the hottest time of year, when all the people she saw socially had emigrated! The top layer of the Palace city was almost deserted by then. The Queen had gone to Lequeitio, accompanied by Tula, Antonia and the crème de la crème of the Royal entourage. Milagros and Mr Pez were also getting ready to leave. So poor Rosalía was going to be all alone, with only Torres, Cándida and the office staff and small fry from the third floor for company ... She was so overwrought that she could not utter one single calm word the whole day, and everything that issued from her august lips was harsh, quarrelsome and threatening. Paquito was lounging on a mat, reading novels and newspapers. Little Alfonso was running around playing as usual, impervious to the heat, but with his breeches open in front and behind, showing his rosy flesh and airing anything that wanted to peek out. Poor Isabel could not cope with the temperature as well as her brother. Pale, haggard and devoid of energy, she would slump on chairs or on the floor, febrile and lethargic, yawning and stretching constantly and seeking out cold, hard objects to rub against. She had lost interest in her dolls and had no inclination to do anything: she simply watched what went on around her in the house, which was quite memorable that day. Francisco decided they should make *gazpacho** for dinner. He made it better than anybody, and in the past he used to appear in the kitchen with his sleeves rolled up and turn out a *gazpacho* that made people scrape their plates clean as a whistle. But since he could not go to the kitchen at that point, he issued instructions from his study. Isabel was the telegraph that listlessly transmitted his orders, and she came and went constantly with culinary messages: 'He says you should chop up two onions in the salad bowl ... don't add more than one tomato, with all the seeds taken out ... He says you have to make sure you cut the bread into little pieces ... and don't put much garlic in ... You mustn't add too much water and there should be more vinegar than oil ... You should add two cucumbers if they're small, and you're to remember the pepper ... about half a thimbleful.'

By night-time, the poor child had a voracious appetite; and even though her papa said the *gazpacho* had not turned out very well, she liked it a great deal, and ate as large a helping of it as she could. When she went to bed, the deep sleep of childhood prevented her from sensing the difficulty she was having digesting the mass of things in her stomach. Her nervous system rebelled, and her brain, as if trapped between two forces, the congestive action of sleep and her overactive nerves, began to function at an extraordinary rate, reproducing all it had witnessed during the day. In a terrifying nightmare, Isabel saw Milagros come in and have a secret discussion with Mama. They went into the *Camón* and stayed there for a little while counting money and talking. Then Mr Pez arrived, a nasty man, like a devil, with saffron whiskers and green breeches. He and Papa talked politics, saying that some wicked rascals were going to cut everybody's head off, and that Madrid was going to be a blood bath. The same blood bath lapped at her mama and Mr Pez with its crimson waves as they talked in the Little Room; she was saying that they could not go to the seaside now and he that he 'couldn't delay any longer, because his girls were getting very impatient'. Then Mr Pez went all blue and flames started coming out of his eyes, and his kiss burnt the little girl. Then he picked up little Alfonso and sat him on his lap, saying, 'My boy, aren't you ashamed to be showing your ... ?' To which Alfonso responded by asking for money, as usual ...

Later, when all the guests had gone, her papa got very angry at her mother for answering back. Her papa had said: 'You're a spendthrift,' and she had gone and shut herself up in the *Camón* in a huff ... Then they had another visitor. It was Mr Vargas, head of payroll at the Administration, where her Papa worked. After talking and talking, Vargas had said to her papa: 'My dear Mr Bringas, the chief has said that as of next month you're to go on half pay.' When he heard this, her daddy had gone as white as a sheet, as white as milk, or whiter, and heaved such sighs ... ! And they talked and talked and Vargas and her papa said there was going to be a blood bath too, and the *so-called* revolution was on its way without fail. Her mama came into the study just in time to see Vargas leave; he was a little man, the size of a flea, and he had a hoppy sort of walk. Her mama and papa had started saying angry things and calling each other names again ... He kept thumping the arms of the sofa and she stalked round and round *Gasparini*. She had never seen her parents so upset.

'You're a spendthrift.'

'And you're a miser.'

'It's impossible to save any money or keep track of things with you around.'

'Well, you're impossible to live with.'

'Where would you be without me?'

'You just don't deserve me.'

Gracious me! Her mama had gone into the *Camón* in tears. She went in after her to try and comfort her: she had tried to climb up on to her lap, but she could not. Her mama was as big as the Royal Palace, or bigger. Her Mama had kissed her a lot. Then, forgetting her anger, she had taken out a dress, and then another, and another, and lots of material and ribbons. Just then her papa came in suddenly, without his bandage, and her mama had cried out in fear.

'Indeed, ma'am, I see what you're up to now,' said her papa icily. 'You've brought an entire clothes shop into my house.' And her mama got flustered and went bright red and stuttered, 'I ... I ... you see ...'

At this point, the poor child's delirium began to mount, and she felt all these foreign objects and bodies pressing on each other within her. They were all inside her, as if she had swallowed half the world. Crammed into her diminutive stomach were her papa, her mama, her mama's dresses, the *Camón*, the Palace, Mr Pez, Milagros, Alfonsito, Vargas and Torres, in a thick liquid, dyed a revolting hue, blocking and squeezing her intestines horribly ... She writhed in discomfort, seeking to dislodge the mass of things and people that was weighing her down, and all of a sudden bleeaaagh ... ! Out it all came like a torrent.

CHAPTER 35

She felt better . . . freed of that terrible seething in her brain. Her mama had wiped the sweat from her face, talking to her lovingly. Rosalía had heard her moaning, the unmistakable symptom of a nightmare, and jumped out of bed to go and help her. It was midnight. Afterwards, she made her a cup of tea and Prudencia helped her change the sheets. Half an hour later, the poor child was sleeping peacefully, and her mother went back to bed on the sofa in the study, because the bedroom was sweltering. But first she went to tell her husband what had happened.

'The usual thing?' he asked, from beneath the sheet, his sole cover.

'Yes, the usual thing, a nightmare, convulsions; this was one of the worst attacks she's had. She calmed down eventually. Poor little love! And you will go on letting her tendency for epilepsy take hold . . . when you know only too well it could be cured by sea bathing . . . !'

'Swimming in the Manzanares* would do her just as much good . . . if not more so.'

Rosalía's objections were lost in the surrounding rooms. Bringas, after coughing a little, consigned his opinion that there was better swimming to be had in the Manzanares than anywhere else in the world to the bosom of sleep.

Our friend was improving so markedly that Golfín stopped coming to the house in mid July. Francisco went to his surgery twice a week, accompanied by Paquito. Since the doctor lived on Arenal Street, they did not have far to go. Bringas wore special dark glasses and a large green visor to protect his eyes from the light. Golfín, who was always very attentive to patients referred by Her Majesty, never kept him waiting. He was very satisfied with the cure and praised the excellent constitution of his patient, who had shaken off the symptoms in just a few weeks. In the last week of July, the ophthalmologist announced to his client that he was leaving for Germany at the beginning of August. 'But you don't need to see me any more. I'm going to discharge you, but just to be on the safe side, one of my

assistants will drop in three or four times while I'm away.'
Bringas was overjoyed to be discharged by the conscientious
doctor, since it was an unequivocal sign that he was cured. Ever
honest and tactful, he prayed the doctor to send him, before he
left, 'You know . . . the bill for your services.' Golfín courteously
begged him not to worry. 'There's plenty of time . . . What's the
hurry? Very well, just as you wish.' And the great economist, as
he left with his son, weighed up in his mind the terms of that
arithmetical enigma which was soon to be revealed. What sort
of rate or fee would the doctor apply to him? Would he assess
him as a genuine poor person, a senior civil servant, a man of
modest means, or a cringing, penny-pinching bourgeois? Bringas
thought about this all the time, night and day, wishing that the
bill would arrive to put him out of his agony of doubt.

Ever since Francisco announced to his wife at the beginning
of August that they were going to have to pay the doctor, the
poor lady felt it even more urgent to replace the notes she had
removed from the savings box. Fortunately, Milagros had paid
back over half of the sum she owed her, promising to give her
the rest before she left for Biarritz.* 'Things are working out
nicely for me,' she said. 'I'm sure to have enough to pay off the
people I owe any day now, and I think I might even be able to
lend you some if you need it . . . No, no, it's nothing . . . You
see, I don't need it, and it'll be safer in your hands than in mine.'
These promises and offers made Rosalía think that the end of
her troubles was in sight. They were both happy, although
Thiers's wife was somewhat low in spirits because she could not
go to the seaside, and they had a delightful discussion about
fashion. Milagros, with that special gift of hers, adroitly managed to take back some of the little things she had given Rosalía
in those ecstasies of affection prior to the loan. 'Since you're not
going away, you really won't be needing this straw boater . . .
nor this straw base either . . . I'll see what I can do with it myself
. . . You won't be able to use the cashmere here. It's not at all
the sort of fabric for this heat. Since it can be chilly up there
sometimes, I'll take it with me. I'll bring you something nicer.
Oh yes! I'll leave you a few yards of écru linen so you can make
outfits for the little ones, and a few pieces of crêpe I have left
over.' Mrs Bringas agreed to everything. Since she herself was
doomed not to distinguish herself in the North, she wished to
revenge herself on her fate by dressing up her offspring: she had
already bought the patterns, and planned ingenuous creations

so that her Isabel and Alfonso could publicise their opulent mama's good taste in the Plaza de Oriente, amongst their republic of playmates.

'Sobrino has some summer wraps in,' said Milagros, 'that I'm very excited about. I'm not leaving without one. You know the ones . . . stoles in imitation black Chantilly, with guipure.'

'I've seen them, my dear; I saw them yesterday,' replied the other, with a great sigh.

'Don't be sad, darling,' said Milagros, hugging her. 'In Bayonne I can get you those things for half the price, and bring them in without paying any customs duty. I'll bring you one of those stoles, even nicer than the ones Sobrino has. Would you like some checked gingham, for the children, that I don't need? I'll send it over. In exchange, I'll take some of those *fichus*, they're not really the thing for Madrid . . . Will you be going to the Prado? Because all you need there is a little veil and a chemisette. It's hard to keep a hat on your head in Madrid in the summer. You really won't be needing that linen hat base I sent you. I'll use it. You can have it back in the autumn, fixed up with something really new, that hasn't been seen around here . . . Oh yes! Go and have a look at the sailor hats that have come in at Sempere's, and those little cap or beret things, for the children. They're just darling . . . And don't buy anything else: I'll send you a pair of blue stockings for both of them, and I think I have a good-size remnant of *piqué* you could use.'

In exchange for all the things she had taken back with such cheerful unconcern, she sent her a bundle composed of shapeless fragments, ribbons and remnants which were, quite frankly, useless. At least Rosalía managed to find enough there to make a cravat for Paquito and another to grace Mr Mousey's august neck.

One morning when Rosalía was alone, Thiers having gone to see the doctor, Pez called in unexpectedly. Dressed for summer, in an elegant lightweight suit of dark alpaca, he looked like a boy. Rosalía was always glad to see him, and especially so on this occasion, for he looked so glowing and youthful. The noble lady's esteem for him grew greater every day, and took an ever firmer hold in her thoughts. She was captivated, not so much by his attractive person, his manners and his self-assurance, but by his proposal to take care of her should she ever find herself in difficulties. She would have surrendered to the protector before the lover; by which I mean that if Pez had not matched his advances with material offers, the territory gained would have been much less extensive. Despite his expertise in the subject, Pez was counting on the strength of his personal charms much more than on that other weapon. But very few of us have the privilege of being acquainted with all the varieties of human fallibility. That military strategy, used as a fall-back, turned out to be more effective than Cupid's darts.

That day, Pez was so expressive, so daring and witty right from the start of the interview, that Rosalía, realising she was virtually alone in the apartment (since the children and Prudencia were all out), was greatly alarmed. All that was pure and modest in her soul, both her natural instincts and those Bringas had inculcated over years of blameless married life, rose up in self-defence. Pez acted like a lovesick youth at that critical hour: he was transformed into one of those romantics who wear their desperation like a medal and pride themselves on their death wish. His words and behaviour were in perfect keeping with the ardour of the season, and they terrified Rosalía, who was a mere novice to the agitations of such guilty friendships. It must be stressed, in her honour, that our libertine met a virtuous resistance he was not expecting, since, as I heard him say several times, he had thought that the fruit was so ripe it would fall off the tree of its own accord.

CHAPTER 36

The analysis of Rosalía's virtue yielded a peculiar result. Pez had not been skilful or lucky enough to catch her in one of those unfortunate moments when the desire to satisfy a whim or the need to discharge a financial obligation touched off in her a powerful appetite to obtain sums of money whose size varied according to the circumstances. At such moments, her passion for pretty clothes and the urge to keep up appearances and disguise her misdeeds blinded her, so that she would not have hesitated to purchase victory with the currency of her virtue . . . And there we have the reason for Pez's defeat. When he decided to storm the fortress, it was well supplied. Bringas's wife had money just then. Milagros had paid her over half of what she owed, and she had promised to give her the rest next Sunday, as well as some extra that she planned to leave with Rosalía for safe keeping. Confident she could acquit herself of her most pressing obligation, the attractive and well-preserved lady thought she was in a position to display a little firmness, a virtue less susceptible to love than to material interest. Pez described that vain character of hers, that temperament insensible to all passions except that of dressing elegantly, in a sentence that has stuck in my memory. The great observer said that she was like a bull, which goes for the cloth and not the man.

My friend pressed his suit with romantic fervour, and who knows, maybe the contest might have ended ill ... But Divine Providence intervened by sending the children home. Francisco arrived a little later, and the two gentlemen talked politics for a while, commenting on the blindness of González Bravo's poli-cies,* about which Pez, thanks to his state of mind, painted a very black picture indeed. It made Francisco's hair stand on end to listen to him. Arresting the generals and the Duke of Montpensier had been a bad move. The revolutionaries had said their *last word* in *La Iberia** a few days earlier, and the Government had issued its final ultimatum. The Army favoured the revolutionaries and it was even being said that the Navy ... 'For God's sake, Mr Pez, don't say such dreadful things!' Thiers exclaimed, clutching his head with both hands, and forgetting to remove them for quite a while.

'I wash my hands of it,' the other man said. 'I see a cataclysm on its way, and quite frankly, when I learned that the Liberal Union, which is a governmental party, a party of order, a serious party, is helping the revolutionaries, what can I say ... it doesn't seem quite such a bad thing any more.'

Thiers almost lost his temper at this, since his friend's benevolent attitude seemed like a prelude to defection. Bringas proceeded to air his disgust at the Progressives, the National Militia, Espartero, and of course, the cavalry's helmets; at that pretentious Riego Hymn, the *so-called* Democrats* and just about everything else under the sun until Pez grew weary and changed the subject to his upcoming trip. He was in no hurry to leave Madrid, nor did he think it was strictly necessary for his health; but his girls were pestering him to take them to San Sebastián as soon as possible, and he couldn't postpone the expedition any longer. The poor things were dying to show off their summer wardrobes on la Concha and la Zurriola,* and they were so eager to get away that if he didn't take them soon, it would break their hearts. Their mama was staying put,

prostrate at the All Souls' altar, swapping tittle-tattle with other
fanatics like herself. It would be a rest and a relief for the poor
girls to go up north, and thus it was undoubtedly a good thing
for their delicate health. For their papa, the trip was more of a
nuisance than a holiday, because his daughters were always
nagging him to take them to Bayonne to buy clothes and
smuggle them back illegally. And his Josefa and Rosa were not
obliged to go to the lengths some women are, wearing what
they've bought and packing their trunks with used clothes; they
had no need to don two winter coats, six pairs of stockings, two
skirts and four shawls. They were lucky enough to have a father
who was a director at the Exchequer, which exempted them
from that embarrassing method of smuggling. The head of
Customs at Irún owed his job to our Pez, and indeed had some
Pez blood himself on the maternal side, which meant that the
girls could buy up half of France and bring it back to Spain.
'This trip causes me all sorts of headaches,' said Pez finally,
'because I can't show my face in Bayonne or Biarritz without
being deluged by ladies of the upper and middle classes begging
for my card or a note to give to my cousin in Irún ... Most of
the time I can't turn them down ... It's part of life here and it
seems quixotic to worry about the treasury losing revenue. It's
so typical of the Spanish to see the State as a sanctioned thief, a
full-time thief, a time-honoured thief ... We all know that
philosophical axiom of immorality which argues that robbing
the rich to give to the poor is no crime. I always say there's just
no hope for this country ... The things one sees are enough to
make any of us turn preacher. Last year, when I refused to help
a well-heeled Marquesa smuggle in a shipment of clothes, she
almost scratched my eyes out. She was like a tigress; started
screaming for the revolution and the demagogues. And a duchess
I know, who's no fool, had the nerve to send through, right
under my nose and my cousin's too ... Get this! ... Fifty-four
trunks full of the latest fashions!'

Having said which, he took his leave, and only stopped by the
next day to say goodbye, since he was going that very afternoon.
He managed to talk to Rosalía alone for a little while, and
professed such heartache and such wounds from the cruel darts
of love, that the chaste lady could not help pitying him,
experiencing two types of vanity at once: one from virtue
triumphant, and the other at being the object of such a formi-
dable passion. Her worth and beauty must be quite considerable

if such a serious and self-possessed being could prostrate himself before her like a little boy; when a man like him was so besotted with her, saying he would *pay with his life* (I quote) for the smallest favour.

Milagros did not leave until the twenty-ninth. How busy she was those last few days, and how many trials and tribulations she had to undergo to get ready for the trip!

'My dearest,' she said to Rosalía when they were alone in the *Camón*, 'you'll have to excuse me, but I can't pay you the rest of that money before I go. I've told my solicitor to give you the sum on the fifth or sixth of next month, because by then he should have received some rental payments from Zafra. Don't you worry, he won't let you down. It's top on the list of instructions I'm leaving with Enríquez; and just so he won't forget, I remind him every time I see him. "Make sure you don't forget ... make sure now, Enríquez ... The first thing you've got to do is pay my friend that little sum I owe her."'

Rosalía was none too happy with this delay; but since the promise appeared to be such a solemn one and it was not too long to wait until 5 August, she had to bide her time. Her friend proceeded to bedazzle her with noisy demonstrations of affection, swearing that she would bring her all the very latest things from France. 'I'm assuming we'll run into Pez up there, he can spare us the bore of having to go through Customs, which is horrible, the officials are so vulgar. If they had their way, they'd open every single trunk ... and I've got a mere fourteen. And I always have three or four more on the way back. You can't imagine how exhausted I am after all I've had to arrange these last few days. Needless to say, my darling husband doesn't lift a finger to help. Everything has to be done for him. This year he didn't even bother to ask for free tickets. I had to do it myself, I sent some little notes to the president of the executive committee, and in the end they gave them to me, but it was like getting blood out of a stone. And I didn't manage to get them to give me two reserved compartments like they have done in the past, only one. It's outrageous! ... I tell Sudre that's what he gets for defending the Railway Company in the Senate the way he does, fighting to the death for them. I get so het up when I travel. I always think I've left something behind, or that we're going to miss the train, or that they're going to make me pay for the excess baggage ... Just think, fourteen trunks! It's going to be pandemonium. Leopoldo is taking his dog, María her Angora cat and Gustavo a cage of birds for a friend. Then we have to think about what all those creatures are going to eat along the way ... And all of us in a single compartment. It's going to look like Noah's Ark! Fortunately, we know the conductor and after we have dinner in Ávila, María and I are going to move to a sleeping compartment ... I'm taking Asunción ... I can't live without my maid. We'll have at least twenty-four pieces of hand luggage. I just can't sleep if I don't take my own pillows. Agustín is determined to take a wash basin so he can freshen up two or three times along the way. My toilet case is vital, because I hate arriving at stations looking a mess. Leopoldo is taking his draughts board, his bat and ball, his puzzle, his dress pistol and a notebook to write down the names of all the tunnels we go through and the time we arrive at each of the stations. Gustavo is lugging along half a dozen tomes to read along the way; and that useless husband of mine, who thinks of nothing but his own comfort, gets furious if he doesn't have his slippers, his long silk nightcap, and his inflatable cushion ... And I have to remember it all, because we can't each have our own servant. Those days are gone, I'm afraid, and I get the feeling they're not coming back.'

CHAPTER 37

The Marquesa hugged Francisco warmly and expressed her heartfelt wishes for his complete recovery; she kissed the children, and finally bid goodbye to her friend in the hallway with all kinds of loving words and embraces.

Rosalía was sad and disconsolate after she left, not only because of the absence of her closest friend, but because she could not leave herself, which made her feel as if she were in exile. A fine summer she was going to have, lonely, bored to tears, sweltering to death, putting up with the rudest and most tiresome of husbands, and undergoing, in short, the shame of staying in Madrid when even concierges and boarding-house owners were going away for the summer! To have to say 'We didn't go anywhere this summer' was a declaration of struggling gentility that the aristocratic lips of a daughter of the Pipaóns and the Calderón de la Barcas, of an illustrious scion of a whole dynasty of Palace officials, simply refused to pronounce. If only they could go to La Granja for a few days; her Majesty was sure to give them an attic or something to stay in, and they could give themselves a few airs, even if all they took with them were bags of provisions laden with lard and salt cod, like country hicks at the seaside! ... But it was not to be; the sultan of the household indignantly refused every suggestion that they leave the capital city, and ranted on about the stupid wastrels who went on holiday with borrowed funds, people who spent three months a year here on strict rations just for the pleasure of staying in hotels for a few days and showing off by criticising the food.

His severity toward Rosalía softened somewhat over time. Bringas was not totally intolerant, and even if he were, he could bring himself to sacrifice some of his economic dogma for the sake of conjugal peace. He did not find Rosalía's explanations about her improvised luxury entirely convincing, but he made an effort of goodwill and accepted some of them. His matrimonial religion demanded that he take some inexplicable things on faith, and so he did. Had Rosalía only stopped there, peace would have reigned once more in the household after that temporary upheaval; but she was incapable of containing herself any longer, and the habit of secretly flouting the rules of the Bringas Order was simply too well established in her mind. This habit afforded her an obscure pleasure, as well as satisfying her vanity. Why shouldn't she have her own way for once, after having been a slave for so long? Every one of those prohibited and clandestine actions gave her an intimate delight both before and afterwards. Her conscience could somehow produce endless sophistries to justify all she did. 'I've gone without often enough ... It's not as if I don't deserve to live better ... He'll have to get used to seeing me a bit more liberated ... And after all, I'm only doing it for the sake of the family reputation ...'

What most perturbed her those first few days of heat and loneliness was the need to put the money back in the box. Milagros had not given her the whole sum. How was she going to come up with the rest? Right away, she thought of Torres, and she brought up the matter discreetly with him at the first opportunity. 'He didn't have it; what a pity! But if he could find a friend who did ... He'd let her know the following day.' Our friend was on tenterhooks as she waited for Torres to reply, because every second she felt as if she were on the brink of a catastrophe, which would be enormous, terrible and inevitable if Bringas counted his treasure. Thank goodness, or perhaps thanks to the special intervention of the numerous saints whom Rosalía was invoking, it had not yet occurred to the good man to lift the lid of the false bottom. But if it did . . . ! It was no use relying on those crude imitation notes any longer, because Mr Mousey could see again, even though not very well, and he was not going to rely on touch alone to assess the contents of his box. The lady was on pins and needles the whole of 31 July and part of the next day, until Torres gave her some hope of a solution. He began by talking about the difficulties, stressing how hard he had worked to get his friend to see the need for the loan. The man in question was called Torquemada,* and he never lent money without a cast-iron guarantee. This time, however, as a favour to Torres, he would not demand the husband's signature on the contract, the lady's alone would be sufficient . . . He could only lend her the money for a month, with absolutely no extensions, and he wanted four thousand five hundred reals back on a loan of four thousand. Oh yes! And he charged two hundred reals for commission . . .

This news seemed to Rosalía like the answer to all her prayers, and both the interest and the commission seemed a small price to pay for the great favour he was doing her. With three thousand eight hundred reals she would have enough for her needs, and there would even be one hundred and twenty reals left over for extras. It was all arranged the next day, 2 August.

Time was running out, and she was in imminent danger, as the following accurately transcribed words of Bringas show: 'My dear, Golfín will be sending me the bill tomorrow and we'll have to pay it the day after, on the third. He told me today that he's leaving on the fourth. I shudder to think that he may take me for a man of means. How much will he charge, do you think? I've been thinking about it all night, and I've been having nightmares just like Isabel . . . today Golfín said something that sent a chill up my spine . . . I'm always saying you're ruining me with all your extravagant ways . . . Imagine how I felt . . . Just as I'm worrying about making the right impression on the doctor, he comes out with this . . . in that irritating tone of voice he has sometimes . . . "By the way, Mr Bringas, I saw your wife coming out of Mass yesterday at San Ginés . . . She always looks so elegant!" The man's going to use that wretched elegance of yours to slit my throat with.'

At ten thirty the next day, while Francisco and the little ones were out walking on the Cuesta de la Vega, the operation was performed. Torres and Torquemada appeared at exactly the appointed hour, with usurious punctuality. The latter was a middle-aged man with greying hair, a sallow complexion, a four-o'clock shadow and a vague resemblance to a priest. He inevitably asked after the family whenever he greeted people and when he spoke, he would pause between each word and gasp asthmatically between paragraphs, so that his listeners always felt contaminated by his respiratory difficulties. As he made his wearisome speeches, he would raise his right arm slowly and form a sort of doughnut with his thumb and forefinger, which he would place before his interlocutor's eyes like an object of veneration. The visit was a short one. The only objection Rosalía raised to the contract concerned the repayment date, since one month seemed too short a time to her; but Torquemada assured her that it could not be extended. 'At the beginning of September he had to . . . come up with a deposit for the Provincial . . . Government, because he was putting in a bid to be . . . meat supplier to the workhouses. Madam should think . . . hard about it, because if she thought she would not *have the wherewithall* to . . . pay him back on the agreed . . . date, he would not sign the loan agreement.' The lady agreed to everything, intent only on getting out of her immediate predicament; she took the money, signed, and the two friends took their leave, sending their regards to the head of the household, whom one of them had never met. Rosalía was delighted, and could only think of how to put the money back in the savings box. A small difficulty had arisen, namely that since she did not have a four hundred escudo note,* but only various smaller ones, she had to get hold of one from somewhere. If the notes were different, even though the quantity was the same, the skinflint would be alerted to the deception. On the pretext of going to call on someone, she went out that afternoon, in terror, constantly thinking that her husband would suddenly decide to check the treasury while she was out. But a guardian angel was watching over her; nothing happened while she was doing the unusual thing of changing small notes for a larger one. The teller in Carmen Street looked at her rather strangely. That night, the delicate operation of replacing the stolen sum was successfully carried out.

My friend Bringas had rarely felt so nervous as he did just

before Golfín's bill arrived. At around ten on the third, he sent
Paquito over with a verbal message, begging the doctor to send
him his medical bill without delay, and at eleven thirty the youth
returned home bearing a letter. Bringas could hardly breathe as
he tore open the envelope with trembling fingers and unfolded
the paper. Rosalía was hovering at his side in anxious curiosity
. . . Eight thousand reals! When he saw the figure, Bringas was
perplexed, torn between joy and grief, for although it seemed
too high a sum, on the other hand his fear that it would be
utterly exorbitant was dissipated by the sight of the actual
amount. He had sometimes thought that the bill would be as
high as twelve or sixteen thousand reals, and this suspicion
drove him to distraction; at other times, he was sure that it
would not be more than four thousand. Reality had split the
difference between these two imaginary amounts, and finally the
economist had to console himself with Hermogenes' argument,*
saying that although eight thousand reals was a lot in comparison to four thousand, it was relatively little in comparison to
sixteen . . . And another thought which was more characteristi-
cally his own than Hermogenes' came to dominate the tumult
of arithmetic that seethed in his brain at that moment; that
Golfín really should not have charged him anything at all, since
Bringas had been referred to him by the Queen . . .

CHAPTER 38

'But at any rate, I can't complain. I haven't done too badly out
of this, since I've got my eyesight back at least. Health's the
number one thing, and the most important part of your health
is your eyes. And the truth is, that murderous creature did in
fact cure me. Eight thousand reals! You know, it's quite likely,'
he added, giving a sigh and getting a little upset, 'that if you
hadn't been going around looking so elegant, he might have
only shot me with four thousand . . .'

He took out the money; dictated a pleasant and courteous
letter, and put the whole lot, the letters and those banknotes
that were so very dear to his heart, into a magnificent envelope,
one of the ones from the office. Paquito was dispatched on this
second errand. Although Bringas was sad to see the emigration

of his beloved banknotes, he nevertheless experienced the deep and exquisite satisfaction of paying on time. This pleasure is only given to people who are very orderly, who save their money and thereby economise on the sensations it produces, of which they savour only the most pure and spiritual kind.

After that, the remainder of the month of August slipped by slowly and tediously; that month in which Madrid is not Madrid, but a deserted frying pan. Those days the only summer entertainment to be had was Price's Circus, with its dreadful little horses and those clowns who go through the same comic routine every day. The historic avenues of the Prado* was the only source of solace, and there in the shady gloom, lovers and groups of friends passed the time in more or less boring conversations, warding off the heat by fanning themselves vigorously and and sipping cold water. Those inhabitants of Madrid who spend their summer in the city suffer a truc banishment, like outlaws, and their only consolation is to claim that they drink the best water in the world.

In the midst of this dreadful tedium, Rosalía did not enjoy going to the Prado, because it was equivalent to parading around her poverty and her social pretensions. She had already explained her banishment with the embarrassing formula: 'We had rented a house in San Sebastián, but what with Bringas's illness . . .'; but she was tired of it and avoided situations where she would have to use it again. At night-time, the Bringases and some of the few people left in the city would take their chairs out on to the terrace, and there on the north side of the Palace they made a tolerably animated group. Cándida was always there. The party was completed by various wives – of a caretaker of the royal bedchamber, two Palace office managers, one of the Queen's private secretaries, the Head of the Royal Pantries, and the King's chief valet. The handful of the masculine sex that were in Madrid were present, and they were all of the lowest rank; but the summer is a great social leveller, and the good Bringases, anxious for company, were not about to turn up their noses at an open-air gathering with some Palace concierges, the caretaker of the royal furniture warehouse, the silversmith's apprentice, and two Palace cleaners, all of them on salaries of six thousand reals a year or under. They were occasionally joined by a chef's assistant, who made fourteen thousand, and a royal usher from the Little Room, who earned nine thousand. In these gatherings, they discussed how hot it had been that day;

the whereabouts of the Court, which had left La Granja now for Lequeitio, and other gossip about the staff and the Palace. On the third floor, in the spaces like little town squares that punctuate the length of the passageways or streets, there would be other gatherings of messenger boys, ladies' maids, sweepers and grooms who came up from the Royal Stables. At the level of the great iron railings that look out over the Plaza de Oriente, above the cornice, there was loud merrymaking all night, as those assembled laughed and played guitars and partook of libations of fermented grape juice. Cándida was hopping mad about these disorderly affairs, since they prevented her from getting a wink of sleep at night, and she was always threatening to report the perpetrators to the Head of Security.

In the mornings, the whole family would go down to the Manzanares, where little Isabel and Alfonso would go for a swim. Their papa had unpacked his cotton nankeen suit again, and what with that and his Panama hat, he looked as if he had just landed from Havana. His eyes, which were protected from the light by strong dark glasses, were improving rapidly, thanks to his careful observance of Golfín's treatment plan. The morning air and the holiday atmosphere at the bathing spot put him in a very good mood, and he was forever announcing that if *those idiots who leave town* knew about the St Jerome, Cypress, Rainbow, Emerald and Andalusian* beaches, they would not feel the need to emigrate. Even Paquito would hurl himself courageously into the waves of those dirty, roped-off little seas, and swim beautifully with one foot on the bottom. They had to spank Alfonso to make him come out of the water, but the little girl would only get in if forced to. The five of them would walk home slowly, the little ones with ravenous appetites, and Francisco in a contented state, determined to do full justice to his lunch. His wife had to overcome the greatest repugnance in order to go down to the river at all. Only her love for her children was strong enough to bring her to such a sacrifice. She found the water and the bathers all rather disgusting and common. The canvas bathing huts, which were more properly an attack on their users' decency than a protection, inspired her with horror, and the screeching of so many vulgar children grated on her nerves.

In the evenings, just before sunset, she would go out into town to visit a friend or to have a look at the most famous shops. There were very few customers inside. The stores had been rigged with long curtains which kept them somewhat less hot than the street, and the semi-darkness inside as well as the lack of clientele tended to make the assistants nod off over their bolts of fabric. From time to time, she would encounter some other lady left behind like herself, another exile. She would re-issue the famous phrase: 'We had rented a house in San Sebastián, but . . .' Her companion would usually declare with refreshing frankness: 'We're waiting till September for the cheap train fares.'

Since the shopkeepers were standing about twiddling their thumbs the whole time, they would entertain themselves by showing the lady various fabrics and little novelties. 'A lot of people will be wearing these this autumn . . . We've ordered a great deal, because they will be the season's fashion.' These phrases seemed to issue from the very folds of the garments themselves as they were unwrapped. The manager, who was just getting ready to leave on his usual trip to Paris, urged her to buy things, and she would fall into the temptation, sometimes because it was a real bargain, and other times because the merchandise cried out to her, rekindling all the fires of her passion for clothes and causing her real suffering if she did not satisfy her desire to acquire them. Oh! She had every intention of compensating for the tortures of that summer by dressing properly the following autumn, whether her husband liked it or not. She was planning to make herself a new velvet dress for the winter, and a beautiful, new, elegant bonnet. She was going to dress her little boy and girl like royalty. The silly idiot would soon see who he was up against . . . Turning these and other plans over in her mind, she would wander slowly home, stopping now and then to look at the windows of fashion and jewellers' shops, and mulling endlessly over the more or less remote possibilities of owning some of the many expensive and valuable things she saw. Madrid was such a melancholy place at that hour that it deepened her own melancholia. The emptiness of the streets at the hottest time of day, the mournful bellows of the *horchata** and lemonade vendors, the slow clopping hooves of panting horses, the shop doors hooded in long canvas screens, are more depressing than uplifting to one whose epidermis is experiencing the effects of the high temperatures and whose spirit is wistful for the beach. The thunderstorms, which were preceded by high winds and dirty clouds of whirling dust, grated on her nerves horribly, and the only pleasure she took from

them was seeing Bringas's weather forecast proved wrong; for
every time the sky clouded over, he would say: 'It'll get cooler
this evening, you'll see.' Cool down, stuff and nonsense! . . . On
the contrary, it would get twice as hot.

On the occasions when she went out at night, the heavy,
suffocating atmosphere would put her in a foul mood, exacerbated by the thought of people strolling happily up and down
on the Zurriola at that very moment. The whole of Madrid
seemed common and uncouth, a horrible place inhabited by the
crudest, filthiest people in the world. When she looked at the
people in the lower-class neighbourhoods who had taken to the
streets, the men in their shirt sleeves and the women scantily
clad, with their half naked brats playing in the gutters, she
thought to herself that she might as well be in a Moorish town,
for such was the image she had of African cities. She would get
up early and take a bath in her own home, since she had no
desire to become a naiad in such a vulgar and pedestrian river
as the Manzanares. In the early hours of the day, with the west-
facing balcony windows thrown wide, a little cool air would
come in, and the lady's body and mind received some relief.
When she went out to the shops, she was assaulted by the smells
that would issue from doors on the most populous streets, the
smell of humankind and things stewing. The barred windows of
the basement apartments sometimes gave off wafts of cool air
that made her want to stand there; but from the basements
where there were kitchens came a stench so repugnant that it
made her veer into the gutter. She would look longingly at the
water hoses, wishing she could receive their shower on her own
flesh; but afterwards the ground would give off a suffocating
vapour, mixed with emanations that were far from aromatic
and which forced her to quicken her pace. The dogs would lap
at the grimy puddles formed by the jets of the hose, and then
they would take refuge in the shade, like the street vendors,
weary of hawking their goatskin shoes, tubes for a real a piece,
tacks, railway timetables, whistles and *special energy-saving
saucepans* . . . At such times, in that acutely uncomfortable
season, only the flies and Bringas were happy.

CHAPTER 39

It was, I believe, St Lawrence's Day,* when they received a letter
that left the pair of them bewildered and slightly dazed. Which
of us has not had the occasional encounter with the fantastic,
that aspect of life which the ancients represented by the apparition of angels, gods and genies? The fantastic exists in our own
age just as in the past; the angels have merely changed their
name and shape, and they no longer come in through the
keyhole. The extraordinary event that was sprung on my friends
in their solitude was a letter from Agustín Caballero. Each of
them had a sudden vision of the generous *émigré*. Speaking in
the plural, he told them they had rented a house in Arcachon,*
and thinking that some fresh sea breezes would do Bringas and
the children good, they invited them to come and spend a month
there. The offer was both kind and explicit. The house was very
large, with a garden and every modern convenience. The Bringas
would be lodged in style and treated like royalty, and they
would not be expected to pay for a single thing ... 'Amparo
and I,' said the letter finally, 'would be delighted if you would
accept.' Rosalía's first reaction was hatred and scorn ... How
dare they invite a respectable family ... !

'It's just so they can look better by associating with us. It's so
that they can pass for respectable folks, by being seen with us.
In a word: they want us to be the respectable-looking cover for
their contraband goods. Doesn't it make you furious? It's a
downright insult.'

Francisco was so busy trying to sort out the frightful tangle of
ideas the letter produced in his mind, that he had not yet had
time to become indignant. His wife carried on chewing the cud
of her spite, but amidst the dark storm clouds unleashed in her
brain gleamed flashes of lightning that said: 'Arcachon!' The
impressive sound of this word, which sounded even better and
more *chic* if pronounced through the nose, unleashed visions of
a whole world of elegant pleasures. Oh, to be able to go to
France, and run into a few Spanish families they knew in the
train station at San Sebastián or St Jean de Luz* and to say
to them, after the initial greetings: 'I'm going to Arcachon'; it

would be tantamount to admitting one was a relative of the Almighty Father himself. When she thought of this, a puff of aromatic incense issued from the lady's heart, filled her entire chest cavity and continued on up to her nose, making it sting and puff up considerably. At long last, Bringas's brain, after an extremely protracted labour, gave birth to the following notion: 'Do you think they're married?'

'Married! ... not them ... They would have broadcast it to the whole world if they had ... No, they live like animals ... It's disgusting that they're inviting us to come and live with them. Don't they think there are any distinctions to be made between people, is there no such thing as morality any more? They think we're as shameless as they are!'

'What a pity they're not married!' muttered the economist, staring at his motionless thumbs, which seemed hesitant to join together. 'Because if they were leading a respectable life ... it would have been a wonderful opportunity. Free tickets, free lodgings, free food!'

The idea of humbling herself to Amparo and being her guest and owing her a huge favour made Rosalía's pride rebel. 'You might be capable of accepting,' she said. 'I couldn't stoop to such a thing.'

'No, I didn't ... I was just saying ... I was only thinking...' stammered Bringas, more perplexed than ever. 'But we have no reason to suspect that they haven't got married.'

'Even if they have ... do you think it's right ... ? That silly little thing who used to eat our leftovers!'

'Oh, goodness me, woman, never mind about that; who cares any more? People forget these things soon enough. No one asks wealthy folk if they've ever lived off charity. Look, in Arcachon nobody will know either them or us ... I'm not saying I want to go. On the contrary, I'll write back saying thank you, but ...'

This negative made the ideal vision of a trip to a famous resort reappear before the lady's eyes. 'Arcachon!' What exquis-ite music that would make in her social calls in the autumn, when she could use a phrase that was so blue-blooded it seemed to carry a rustle of silk with it: 'We've been in Arcachon.' This spark was enough to touch off another storm in that swollen head, while Bringas, meanwhile, was simmering with financial calculations: 'We could have a little holiday in France without spending a thing!' Husband and wife sat there a long time wrapt in wordless contemplation, mulling over their thoughts, but without voicing them. From time to time, they would look at each other in silence. No doubt each of them was waiting for the other to say something, to propose some conciliatory formula ... They talked about it again that afternoon; but Rosalía, puffed up with pride, went on claiming repugnance and running Agustín and Amparo down. That night, the prospect of the trip gained so much ground in her mind, that she ventured to ask herself a question inspired by her sense of right and wrong: 'And what do I care whether they're married or not, or whether she's no better than she should be?' Tolerance flooded her soul; but she was reluctant to give in and admit defeat, so she waited for her husband to give way first, so that she could follow suit, affecting obedience and resignation. The great Thiers, meanwhile, having thought over the advantages of the trip, watched his wife as if wishing she would make some overture of reconciliation. They acted like a couple who have fallen out, when neither one wants to be the first to break the ice and talk of making up.

Rosalía went to bed convinced that the following morning Bringas would wake up disposed to accept their cousin's invitation. She already knew what she would say. First of all, outrage, a great fuss about her dignity, a lot of harsh words for Amparo and Agustín; then a series of modulations marking a transition. She, Rosalía, always tried to stifle her own inclinations, and to sacrifice her wishes to others ... She was prepared to make all kinds of sacrifices and to undergo all kinds of embarrassment and humiliation for the sake of her children. It was clear that Isabel needed some sea bathing, and little Alfonso too ... In the face of that need, her wishes, her scruples were meaningless. In short: if Bringas thought they should go, she would close her eyes and ...

But contrary to her expectations, the skinflint said not a word about the trip the following day. He got up humming, and seemed to have forgotten all about the matter. Rosalía tried to get him to react, by complaining bitterly about the St Jerome beach and the atrocious heat, but to no avail. All he would say was: 'It won't be long now ... After the fifteenth, it will start to get cooler again.' This drove Rosalía to distraction.

She waited impatiently until the afternoon, consumed by anxiety: and seeing that Mr Mousey was not going to breathe a word about Arcachon, she ventured to ask: 'Well, what are you going to say to Agustín? I confess that as far as I'm concerned, even though I find the idea of living with them revolting ... for the children's sake, I ...'

'The children, stuff and nonsense! They're fine,' exclaimed Bringas, waving his Panama hat as if he were about to shout a hurrah. 'The swimming in the Manzanares is the best in the world ... Look what rosy cheeks our little girl has. And little Alfonso is looking wonderfully sturdy ... When I think of the *idiots who leave town*, it makes me laugh ... And anyway, I've been thinking ... Whatever they say, there are always expenses. We would have free tickets as far as the frontier, but what about after that?'

'It's only two hundred and thirty kilometres,' burst out Rosalía, who had been feeding her fantasy by reading the railway guide.

'Well, whatever it is, those kilometres are bound to be expensive. And anyway, how can we show up without a present for them? Do you think we're going to look good arriving empty-handed? ... And then there would be other expenses ... No, my mind's made up, we're not going. After the fifteenth it'll get cooler. You can see the days getting shorter. Last night it was a little more comfortable ... We're not leaving, my dear, we're doing just fine in Madrid.'

Rosalía heard him in intense vexation, but her pride forbade her to protest. She said nothing, and the serpents of her vanished fantasy writhed in her bosom. She had become accustomed to the idea of running into friends in San Sebastián station and thrusting Arcachon down their throats; writing an Arcachon address on her letters, and Arcachonising away to her heart's content the whole of the following autumn and winter.

CHAPTER 40

In her lonely exile, the unhappy lady had only one consolation, namely, that her children were in marvellous health. Over the summer, little Isabel, whose fits always worried her mama to death, had not suffered a single one of those attacks that were blighting her childhood. Whether or not the St Jerome bathing spot was any good, the fact is that the little girl was plumper and rosier, and had developed an excellent appetite. As to the little boy, I need not say that he was quite bursting with health, thanks to the waters of the Manzanares. He was so robust that he was forever trying to prove his strength and straining to be bigger and more powerful. His developing instincts spurred him incessantly to physical activity, to test himself and learn new feats that required great expenditures of energy. Climbing as high as he could, shinning up posts, capering around, lifting heavy things, dragging furniture all over the place, digging trenches and pouring water into them, playing with fire, and if possible with gunpowder, were the activities he loved most. He showed no signs of having inherited his father's mechanical skills. He was a skilful destroyer of everything that fell into his hands. While he was exerting himself in this way, his tender little mouth would be uttering blasphemous oaths he had picked up on the street. When his prim little sister heard him, dear me! She would run straight to her father and tell tales. 'Papa, Alfonsito is saying things . . .' And Francisco, who detested bad language, would shout: 'You come here this instant, my boy. Bring me a hot pepper from the kitchen!' And with the pepper in one hand and the criminal by the neck, he would threaten to scrub his tongue with it; but then he would scowl fiercely at him and say: 'All right, this time, I'll let it go; but if I ever hear you using that foul language again, I'll burn your mouth and your tongue will drop out and instead of talking like a human being, you'll bray like a donkey.'

Young Alfonso was obsessed with removal vans. He was in seventh heaven every time he saw one on the street. He found the whole spectacle exciting: the massive carthorses, that huge container where the contents of a whole house went, with the mirrors slung underneath, and last of all the louts in blue overalls perched on top, dozing off to the gentle swaying of the contraption. His dream was to be like those lads: to drive a van, to load and unload it, and he fantasised about a cart so enormous that it could carry all the furniture in the Palace. He would pass hours at a time in an ecstasy of imitation, exercising his mind and his muscles in reproducing this fantasy as authentically as possible. Just as Don Quixote dreamed of adventures and then carried them out as far as he was able, so Alfonso imagined Herculean moves and tried to perform them. Francisco, who was in *Gasparini* with Isabel, would hear furniture being pushed around, cracks of the whip, and these terrible words: 'Garn . . . git on wi' ye . . . git . . . giddy up . . . gee up there, git, horse!' In the middle of the room he would have piled up chairs, between whose legs were the crockery and utensils, the stone for pounding meat, the pestle, dusters, brooms and everything else he could lay his hands on. The cat would be crouched on top. Then he would start cracking his whip over the whole lot, and if anything fell off, he would start shouting and stamping his foot. Redfaced and sweaty, the pugnacious infant would not stop until Isabel came in with a message from her papa, wanting to know what all the noise was about.

'Oh Papa, you should see him,' she would report, giggling helplessly. 'He's gone and put the chairs on top of each other, and he's cracking the whip and saying funny things . . .'

'Tell that Galician brute that if I have to go in there, I'll have his hide . . .' (Bringas was in the unfortunate habit of identifying all Galicians as brutes, a custom only too widespread in Madrid, and one which betrays both ill manners and ignorance.)

Isabel's tastes and pastimes were quite different from her brother's. The reason they always played apart had more to do with their difference in temperament than their sex. We should not be indifferent to the sprouting of personality in these rough drafts of human beings we call children. They are our premises; and we are merely the consequences of them.

Isabel, as I was saying, did play with dolls from time to time, but was much more interested in finding, collecting and keeping things. All sorts of useless bits and pieces, every unclaimed object she came across in the house, would find its way into the little boxes she kept in a corner at the foot of her bed. And woe betide anyone who touched that sacred cache of hers! If Alfonso ever dared to put his sacrilegious paws on it, she would moan and groan for a week. These magpie traits of hers seemed to get worse when her health was more delicate. Her only happiness at such times was going through her treasure, sorting and replacing the objects, which came in an extraordinary variety and were, generally, entirely useless. Scraps of embroidery thread, silk and material filled one box. Buttons, toiletry bottle labels, cigarette ribbons, postage stamps, used fountain pens, empty matchboxes; they formed an incalculable mass of nondescript things, meaningless fragments with no possible use. But her favourite pile was one of French prints that were handed out as prizes in school, little vignettes of the Sacred Heart, the Wondrous Love, of María Alacoque and Bernadette,* those little cards from Paris that represent the sacred in the same style as a fashion plate. She also had what she called lace paper, which was in fact printed wraps from cigar boxes. Those were from Agustín's cigars, and had been given to her by Felipe. I shall not list the empty packs of needles, old gloves, screws, artificial flowers, San Isidro* whistles, puppets, the remains of a crèche, and endless other trivialities she had stacked away. She also had a money-box, carefully stashed elsewhere, which gave off a delightful jingle of coins when you shook it. It was so full, it weighed a ton. She had her work cut out guarding it and keeping it away from the covetous eyes and greedy hands of young Alfonso, who, given half the chance, would have broken it open and spent all the money on firecrackers ... or on a removal van with real live horses.

Isabelita was so in love with her hoard of trinkets that she hid it from everyone, even her mama; for Rosalía would mess it up and muddle things around and seemed not to care for it very much, since she had once said: 'Don't be such a skinflint, love. What possible use is there in keeping all that rubbish?' The only person she allowed to touch the treasure was her papa; for he admired the little girl's patience, and praised her habit of saving things.

On those long summer days, Francisco, who was not allowed to read or do close work or concentrate on anything, would have been mightily bored had he not been able to play with his daughter at going through her things and sorting them out and setting them in order. 'Sweetheart,' he would say after his siesta, 'bring me your boxes and let's amuse ourselves.' The two of them spent the whole afternoon unobserved in *Gasparini*, sitting on the ground, taking the things out and classifying them, and then putting them back again with loving care. 'You know, these things might still come in handy,' the economist would say. 'Let's put the apricot stones right here. Let's see: there are twenty-three of them. Now put a piece of paper over them, like this. But first you have to put the little box of pens and beads in between, so the apricot stones won't roll around ... There we go! Let's have another piece of paper. Why don't you start giving me the matchboxes: we'll stack them in twos, like this. See? If you cover everything up, it won't slide around. Now then, give me some more things ... We shouldn't put the bone buttons next to the metal ones; and let's separate the bone ones from the wood ones too, so they don't fight. There are classes everywhere, my child ... That's it ... Now let's put these scraps of fabric on one side, so they don't get mixed up with the artificial flowers, we don't want them getting jealous of them and arguing. There's all kinds of bad behaviour in the world ... The art works should go separately. This is a museum where the English tourists go, they can be these whistles ... Carry on giving me things ...'

Often, after they had put everything away, they would get it all out again to rearrange it a different way. Both of them played with the dolls, dressing and undressing them, receiving and paying calls. Meanwhile, the little brute Alfonso shouted to his horses and loaded his cart until he dropped. Whenever he could not get his own way, the little boy would seek refuge at his mother's side, just as his sister always ran to Francisco to be petted or to demand justice in disputes with her brother. Alfonso knew exactly how to butter his mother up with shrewd caresses; whenever he wanted to extract her small change from her, he would cajole her and cover her with kisses.

'I want to tell you a secret, Mama,' he would say, climbing on to her lap, nestling up to her and whispering in her ear. 'A secret ...'

'Oh really, oh, what a sweet little thing! What you want is a penny, is that it, my darling?' And the knowing little rascal would breathe into his mother's ear the following words, softer than the beat of a fly's wings: 'Papa says I'm turning out just like you, that I'm a wild one.'

CHAPTER 41

The ingenious lady watched the second half of August go by in mounting terror, because by all indications, each day that passed brought the beginning of September closer. When she hinted at an extension to Torres, he paled and said that Torquemada could not wait because of this and that and the other ... They had spelled it out very clearly to her the day they drew up the agreement. It was the main clause, and Mr Torquemada was bound to be counting on her ...

When she heard this, the lady weighed up the difficulties of the situation in her mind, and found them more serious than in previous cases. It goes without saying. of course that Milagros's attorney did not bring her the sum she had promised on the fourth or the fifth, or any other day in August. She could hope for nothing from Cándida but make-believe. To whom could she turn? Bringas had his sight back, and it was insane to think of removing anything further from the household treasury. Perhaps the best course was to be frank with her husband and confess her lapse to him, but it was also the most difficult one. He would throw a fit! ... People would be lining up to listen to him. And once he found out about her deceptions, he would impose a period of such repression that the thought of it terrified Rosalía more than her present distress. Her plan was to emancipate herself gradually, not to bind herself even tighter to authority ... She would work things out herself, as best she could. God would not forsake her, He had always come to her aid in the past.

After the twenty-fifth, she could barely contain her feverish anxiety, and the taste of bitter gall was continually on her lips. She could not forget for a moment the impasse she was heading for, and try as she might, she could not come up with an expedient solution ... If only Pez would come back soon! ... He had offered so many times! ... But when she remembered how prickly she had been on the previous occasion, it occurred to her that her worthy friend might not be so disposed to be generous on his return to Madrid. 'Oh, no!' she told herself. 'He's devoted to me. He'll do whatever I say.' At that point, she recalled the scene that day, and ended up concluding that she was too prudish by far ... If only she hadn't been so ... so stupid, she wouldn't be having to borrow money from that beast Torquemada. And to think that a woman of her rank could find herself in such straits! ... And all for what? A trivial sum ... She could dispose of thousands if she so wished. Eight years before, the Marqués de Fúcar, whom she often met at Milagros's house, had tried to court her. And how had she reacted? Just like a porcupine. And the Marqués wasn't her only admirer. There were many others, all of them wealthy, whose insistent attentions had signalled that they would do anything for her. But she had kept her distance and maintained a rigidly respectable appearance. She had never suspected that her unshakeable pillar of respectability would one day totter on its foundations, and she found her present thoughts so strange that it seemed as if she had become a different person altogether. 'It's necessity that makes us who we are,' she told herself. Necessity leads to many evils, and we should not be too hard on those who stray from the straight and narrow. Before judging them, we should say: 'Here, take what you need; buy yourself enough to eat, cover your nakedness ... Are you well fed and well dressed? Well then ... now let's talk about morality.'

When she began thinking along these lines, Rosalía was filled with admiration for her earlier self, for the Rosalía of the period before the sleights of hand that now had her at her wits' end; and while on the one hand she blushed to think of the airs and graces she had given herself in the past, on the other she was proud of having been so faithful to her husband and so resigned to her life of poverty. The palatial fortress of that happiness was still standing, but the bomb that was to blow it up was already set and primed. Before lighting the fuse, she who was still spotless, at least in deed, gazed mournfully at the castle so she would be able to remember what it had been like when she sat amongst its ruins.

The last few nights in August she went to the avenues of the Prado once in a while to meet up with the Cucúrbitas ladies, and even though she was tortured by the imminence of the due date, she took part in the small talk. They formed quite an animated group, and were joined by a few gentlemen. Bringas's wife reviewed them all in her mind, examining the financial situation of each. 'This one's poorer than we are,' she thought. 'He's just a sham, all show, and beneath that flashy exterior all he makes is twenty thousand reals. Heaven knows how he manages to maintain that huge family of his ... That one is nothing but lies and hot air ... Oh, now there's a man for you: he's supposed to make two hundred and forty thousand reals a year, but they say he doesn't like women ... Now this one's a real ladies' man; but he likes them to foot the bill ... and he's really beginning to look his age ... This one hasn't got a thing to his name ... he's a vulgar Don Juan who only runs around with prostitutes ... This one must like me a lot, judging by the way he looks at me and the things he say ... but Torres told me that Torquemada had to lend him two thousand reals so he could take his wife to the seaside, she's a cripple, poor thing.' From this inspection, it turned out that almost all of them were shamefully broke to a greater or lesser extent; they hid their poverty beneath frock-coats purchased after a thousand sacri-fices, and the few who did have money were chilly, sensible types ... The lady was well and truly imprisoned behind a double wall: poverty and respectability. If she jumped both of them, where would she end up? ... As she sat there in the gloom of the Prado, observing the tide of people strolling up and down, she saw some passers-by, just a few, who drew the attention of her distracted mind. The nearest street lamp shed just enough light to recognise their faces by, before they were lost to view among the dusty shadows. She saw the Marqués de Fúcar, back from Biarritz, pompous, crass, and loaded with bank notes; Onésimo, who treated the Treasury as if it were his own account; Trujillo the banker; Mompous, Buenaventura de Lantigua the stockbroker and others. Some of these powerful men knew her, others not; the odd one had cast her glances that were clearly amorous. Others behaved impeccably both in and out of the home ...

Rosalía retired to her own abode with her head full of all these Madrid characters, and watched them parading back and forth through the most well-lit part of her brain as if they were in the Prado. First the poor, then the rich, then the respectable ... and back to the beginning again. To add to her distress, Bringas was more pleasant and affectionate with her of late; but as far as spending was concerned, he was more rigid than ever.

'My darling,' he remarked at bedtime, 'I'm going back to the office on the first of September. I have to work and we absolutely have to cut back. We've got terribly behind, and we have to make up the lost ground by doing without. I'm counting on you, as always; I'm counting on you to be thrifty, obedient and sensible. If we're to get ahead, we have to resolve not to spend a single penny on fripperies. With the clothes you have now, you could look elegant for at least six years. And if you were to sell something so that I could have a suit made, these old bones of mine would be really grateful ... I'm sorry if I came down a little too hard on those bad habits you were developing ... I rather got the impression you were letting our usual regime slide. But bearing in mind your good qualities, I'm prepared to forget that absurdly ostentatious way you were behaving, and I hope you'll do likewise and go back to your modest ways and not force me to take extreme measures. That way our children will have food on the table and shoes on their feet, and I can count on a peaceful old age.'

These severe but reasonable words both moved and terrified her. It was utterly impossible for her to go back now to their time-honoured system of *make do and mend*, and the infinite metamorphoses of the peach-coloured dress; but it made her unhappy to think of deceiving that poor soul. In this dilemma she commended herself to Providence, thinking: 'God will come to my rescue. I'll wait and see what happens before I decide what to do.'

If only the great Pez would return soon, he would get her out of that morass in no time. She began to think of how to exploit his generosity without selling herself. If she could manage that, she would be the cleverest woman on earth ... But in order for that to happen, Manuel had to come back from that tiresome resort. Carolina had said he was coming back at the beginning of September, but not when exactly. How nerve-racking! And to think that on the second ... !

The first thing the harassed lady needed to do was to stop the moneylender from descending, or at least to put him off for a few days, until Pez got back. Despite Torres's pessimistic predictions, she hoped for some success if she visited Torquemada in person, and on the thirty-first she ventured to go to his house; a disagreeable but necessary step which she was confident would yield good results. The said gentleman lived on the Travesía de Moriana, in a huge, dusty, gloomy apartment, crammed with furniture and huge old paintings, all of different styles and value, the spoils from his enormous clientele. It was a museum of impossible luxuries, of excess, of short-lived splendours, a house of sobs and sorrows. Rosalía was overcome with secret terror as she went in; and when Torquemada appeared from amidst the junk in a fez and a corduroy smoking jacket of a peculiarly nondescript colour, she began to feel like crying.

CHAPTER 42

'And how's the family?' asked Torquemada by way of greeting.

'Quite well, thank you,' the lady replied, taking a seat in the proffered chair.

She proceeded to lay out her request for an extension, employing winning smiles and the sweetest words she could think of. But Torquemada heard her out with frosty severity, and then, making a doughnut with his thumb and forefinger and holding it up to her gaze as if it were the Blessed Sacrament being offered for the adoration of the faithful, he uttered the following fateful words: 'Ma'am, I have already told you that I . . . cannot, I simply cannot help you. It is quite im . . . possible.'

And seeing that the victim refused to credit such cruelty, he added the clinching argument.

'If my own father were to beg me for . . . this extension, I wouldn't grant it to him. You have no idea how pressed I am. I absolutely must make a . . . downpayment. My honour is at stake.'

Endless repetitions of her plea made no dint on his stony heart.

'Just ten days,' she said, transfixed by the thought of the agreement she had signed.

'Not even ten minutes, ma'am; it just cannot . . . be. I'm very . . . sorry; but if by the second . . .'

'For God's sake, sir; think of your own mother . . .'

'I shall be obliged to present . . . the agreement to Mr Bringas, who according to my sources . . . has sufficient funds.'

Despite this, the poor woman, having spent the night tormented by insomnia and anxiety, went back to visit her creditor the following day.

'And how's the family?' he asked her after they had exchanged greetings.

Rosalía begged and pleaded with more vehemence than the day before, and Torquemada refused and refused and refused, underlining his cruelty with the terrifying apparition of the doughnut in the space between the two interlocutors' eyes.

Since sighs were not having the desired effect, Rosalía essayed tears. The moneylender thought she was about to faint and rang for a glass of water, which she refused to drink because she could not bear the thought of it. The power of a woman's tears was proven on that occasion; for the flinty Torquemada softened at last, and the extension was granted.

'But I swear to you, ma'am, that if by the seventh . . .'

'Not the seventh, the tenth . . .'

'The eighth. But then the eighth is a holiday, the Virgin of . . . September. Let's say the ninth, you see how understanding I'm prepared to be. But if the money isn't paid back on the ninth, I shall have no choice . . . Mr Bringas has sufficient funds, according to my sources.'

'Oh, thank Heavens! Until the tenth.'

Rosalía thought herself a lucky woman now she had a few

days' breathing space in front of her. That would give Pez time to return. Would to God he came soon.

Bringas went back to the office again on 1 September, although he did very little work, and spent the whole time talking to the deputy head of the department. They had played a dirty trick on him, cutting his pay in August like that, and just as soon as Her Majesty got back he was going to bring it to her attention, she'd soon see about such a pointless absurdity. While Thiers was at the office, his wife spent the day virtually alone. People rarely came to call, since most of her friends, except for the Cucúrbitas ladies, were still at the seaside. Refugio came to see her two or three times, and they chatted about fashions and the things Refugio had been sent from Bordeaux. Rosalía no longer treated her so superciliously, although she was always careful to establish the difference between a respectable lady and a woman whose conduct is mysterious and shady.

Ever since she found herself up to her neck in financial problems, Rosalía had got into the habit of calculating, every time she talked to someone, how much money that person possessed. 'That bitch has got money,' she said to herself one day, as she looked at the Sánchez girl and listened to her fulsome description of the business she was setting up.

As she watched Refugio leave, it occurred to Rosalía that she could always ask her for help. Horrors! This daring notion was immediately rejected as ignominious. No; she would much rather have a huge scene with her husband and put up with all he would have to say, than humiliate herself and swallow her pride like that ... That Refugio was a right little baggage! Our friend blushed for shame at the very thought of lowering herself to ask for favours of a certain sort. Only the day before, Torres had told her that the girl was the talk of the neighbourhood, and that she was involved with three or four men at once.

On the fifth, a clerk from Sobrino Brothers came to tell Rosalía that the new season's fashions were beginning to come in from Paris. There were some wonderful things. Sobrino invited his distinguished client to come and take a look and give him her opinion on some brand new fabrics that were rather eye-catching. She accepted the invitation; but even the sight of all those new, luxurious articles was not enough to take her mind off her sufferings. She would have liked to have bought them all, or at least some of them; but – Heaven help her! – how could she possibly do so in her current dire situation, with a grave domestic catastrophe hanging over her head? 'I ordered this with you in mind,' Sobrino kept saying, with devilish amiability. But she only looked anguished and complained of a headache, and refused to buy anything, even though she could not take her eyes off those original fabrics, especially the wonderful outfits being modelled on the tailor's dummies. All those fichus, laces, shawls, chemisettes and pelisses made a *Thousand and One Nights* of clothes. On the sixth, feeling the noose tightening around her neck, dejected and almost despairing, on the verge of tears, and feeling a secret urge to confess all to her husband, Rosalía went back to Sobrino Brothers. She only meant to pass the time and tear her thoughts away from the terrible image of Torquemada for a while. But as she was going down Arenal Street, she ran across young Joaquín Pez, who joyfully announced: 'We've received a telegram; they get back tomorrow.' When Rosalía heard this, she felt all at once as though the heavens began to smile and the lowering storm clouds in her mind dispersed; the business of the ninth was solved, the world greatly improved, and mankind redeemed of its age-old sufferings. She continued down the street fresh-faced and radiating affability; and when she got to Sobrino's, she began looking at things and giving her opinion on all of them, praising some, pouring scorn on others, avid to see and comment on everything. 'Have this sent to my house ... You see, Mr Sobrino, you've got your way in the end; I'm going to take that fichu.' Her delirious babble that day was seasoned with many such phrases, all of which had to do with purchases.

CHAPTER 43

The great man arrived at last. Rosalía rightly supposed that his first port of call, once he had freshened up after the journey, would be his friends' at the Palace. As soon as Bringas left for the office, she set to work on her toilette to receive the gentleman who had occupied such a place in her thoughts when she was feeling low. For Manuel was sure to come back from the seaside even more witty, gallant and generous than ever. The lady recognised his footsteps as he came up to the door, and began to tremble ... and was overcome with shame ... Don't give up, now! She gave herself an appraising glance in the mirror and rated her appearance impeccable. Then, having made him wait a little while, she went into the Ambassadors' Room ... She must have been overcome with emotion as they exchanged greetings, for she was a little awkward. She scarcely noticed that she was muddling words up and that she began to stammer when she talked about Bringas's complete recovery. Pez was looking wonderful! He seemed ten years younger, and was in fine pisciform* fettle. His affability and distinguished air had not changed a bit; but right from the start of the interview Rosalía noticed something that she found as strange as it was discouraging. She had thought that Pez would be just as forthcoming with her as the last time they met, and in this she was thoroughly disappointed. My friend behaved with great prudence and restraint, and addressed himself to her only in the proper and polite terms one is supposed to use to a lady. Had his feelings for her undergone a radical change? It couldn't be because she wasn't looking her best, because she'd surpassed herself that day ... Time passed, and our Rosalía could not get over her shock, which began resolving itself into rancour as Pez gradually worked his way through all the usual topics of polite conversation: the weather, the heat in Madrid, the health of all and sundry, the conspiracies, without once broaching what in her eyes was the appropriate subject. The shortness of her replies and the tense way she fanned herself signalled her vexation. Pez acted cooler by the minute, with a slightly superior air as if he were above human frailties, and he continued talking about innocuous subjects with astounding ease, never once stumbling, or saying anything that betrayed a torn conscience or an imperilled virtue. The northern breezes had transformed him into an exemplary gentleman, a model of rectitude and restraint. His similarity to Our Lord's father seemed more striking to Rosalía than ever, but she now found his blond good looks the most insipid kind of perfection. All he needed was the staff of lilies and he could have featured on those cheap cards of the saints they sell on the streets. Rosalía began to find all this caution repugnant, and she was just gathering up all her scorn to bestow it on him, when she was assailed by the memory of her obligations on the ninth. Pez read her face, and remarked, 'You're looking rather pale.'

Rosalía did not answer. She was sunk in despondency, thinking, 'Sin, your real name is necessity, and that's the honest truth ... What woman would be stupid enough not to spurn all these despicable men, unless she had no other choice?'

Pez became a little more tender, and said that she seemed strange that day, as if she were sad or very worried about something. She took this as a favourable juncture to mention her problem. She would test Pez to see if he was the same flirtatious and generous gentleman he had always been, or if he had become a hard-headed egotist. She too assumed an air of gracious reserve, and replied: 'Oh, it's nothing. Anyway, who cares what happens to me?'

My friend slowly descended from his teetering heights of virtue. He moved closer and told her she was ungrateful, in the tone of a reproachful lover. Rosalía glimpsed a hope of salvation which shed a weak light upon the gloom of that fateful day, the ninth, which was so dreadfully close. But the doorbell rang all of a sudden announcing the return of the children, so she could not be more explicit, and neither could Pez. She had time to say only one thing: 'I couldn't wait for you to get back ... I need to talk to you ...'

This gratifying exchange, which was going quite according to plan, was interrupted by the children bursting in and much kissing all round. But later, after Bringas had come home and spent a long time deep in discussion with Pez about politics, Rosalía found a moment to exchange a few more words with her gentleman friend in the Little Room, in secret, upon which he concluded his visit and took his leave.

Rosalía was more sad than happy all that afternoon and evening. Her husband found her so laconic as to be almost mute, but as usual he did nothing to correct her. A reserved woman is to be preferred in any household over a loquacious one, and Thiers was not anxious to make exceptions to this rule. On the morning of the eighth, Rosalía, clad in a neat and simple outfit, said goodbye to her husband. She was off to Mass, as the mother-of-pearl prayerbook in her hands proclaimed ... Her husband should not worry if she was a little late back, because she was off to see Cucúrbitas's sister, who was prostrate on her bed and close to death.

'I heard she was due for the Last Rites today,' said Bringas, who was genuinely concerned about the lady in question.

She left after giving out instructions for luncheon, on the assumption she might be rather late, and left Thiers to the attentions of the barber, for he no longer trusted himself to shave, after his eyesight had been damaged. Paquito was there too, being reprimanded by his papa for various things, one of which was the boy's youthful failure to avoid being contaminated in the University by those plaguey sympathisers of the *so-called* revolution. When he was with his friends, he made a point of proclaiming himself an obscurantist; but of late, he had started betraying certain reservations, certain concessions, a certain weakness . . . in short, his angel had developed a mild case of the virus . . . 'Of the revolutionary virus,' said Bringas two or three times as he was being shaved, 'and it's vital to root it out. You'll soon see what a mess we'll have on our hands if that rabble win. All the horrors of the French Revolution will seem a farce compared to the tragedies that will happen here.' The lad had developed another trait that Francisco found intensely annoying, and that was the noxious effect on his mind of a perverse and accursed doctrine called Krausism.* Bringas had heard a friend of his, a very knowledgeable priest, call it *pestilent*, no less. Recently, Paquito had been spouting some complicated gobbledygook about the I, the Not I, the Other and who knows what else, which the good Francisco found quite maddening. He told his son roundly that if he did not get all that philosophising out of his head, he would take him out of the University and put him to work in a shop.

The whole morning went by, and finally they sat down to lunch, tired of waiting for Rosalía. She arrived around one, somewhat hot and bothered. 'She's looking really bad, poor thing,' she said, taking the question out of her husband's mouth before he had a chance to ask after Cucúrbitas's sister. And she shut herself up in the *Camón* to take off her veil and change her dress. That afternoon, they all went out for a stroll in their Sunday best, in quasi-military formation, with the little ones beautifully turned out, and Mama and Papa as grave and solemn as ever. It is not inappropriate to mention that Rosalía Pipaón de la Barca had never, ever, looked up to her husband more than she did that day . . . She watched and listened to him with a certain veneration, feeling herself extraordinarily inferior to him; so inferior, that she was almost unworthy to meet his gaze. She behaved in a dazed and absentminded way while they were out, and this became even more pronounced at home that night. Her attention was divided from the simple scenes of domestic life and all that was being said and done around her, and was somewhere else altogether, dwelling on faraway things that no one but she could know of.

'Goodness, you're miles away tonight,' said Bringas, in some irritation, when he noticed her make a mistake for the third or fourth time.

She dared not say anything to this. Afterwards, while the children were playing lotto with their father, she shut herself up in the *Camón*. Sitting there with her arms crossed and her chin on her chest, she surrendered herself to meditations which were to consume her mind as flames consume dry chaff.

CHAPTER 44

'Oh, his face when I said it! ... Even though he tried to hide it, I could see he was put out ... *This last trip has ruined me ... The girls wanted everything they saw in Bayonne ... I've spent a whole year's income ... But anyway, I'll see what I can do ... I may be able to come up with something* ... Holy Mother of God! It's dreadful to sell yourself and not get your asking price ... No; he'll make every effort not to lose face and end up looking a fool in front of me ... [*She sighs three times, as if saying a rosary of anguish.*] We'll just have to wait and see what happens tomorrow. Tomorrow at ten I'll get the definitive reply as to what he can do ... Oh, surely he'd rather die than look ridiculous ... If he hasn't got it, he'll just have to go out and look for it. That's his duty. Aren't I worth that and more? A lot more? Aren't I giving him a treasure in exchange for a trifle? And what is this in comparison to the fortunes other women have gone through? I'd be ashamed to name such a sum to a real gentleman ... This is the bitterest gall that ever a woman did taste.'

She spent the night racked with painful uncertainty, waking every other minute goaded by the red-hot stab of her obsession. Her body slept but her obsession lay wakeful. The wife looked enviously on the sweet peace of the conscience that lay at her side. Francisco was sleeping the sleep of a delivery boy who has worked hard all day long and who shrugs off all loads on his mind the moment he closes his eyes. Lucky man! He had no needs, he was happy with his cotton suit. He couldn't see beyond his cheap and dowdy tie, purchased from one of those street stalls outside the central Post Office. 'Tell me what you need, and I'll tell you whether you're honest or not.' This saying floated into Rosalía's mind; she had unwittingly become a mistress of popular philosophy.

'Look at the saints, what were they?' she thought to herself. 'People who didn't give a hoot if they went about looking like tramps. There's no doubt that I just don't have that disinterested nature which is the basis of virtue. No matter what they say, you're born a saint. You don't become one by sheer willpower, you have to come into the world that way. My husband was born to be a nobody and he'll die in the odour of sanctity.' This did not stop her from envying him, for she was beginning to realise how hard it was and how much it cost to want not to be a nobody. The poor woman lay there besieged by dangers, full of anxiety and remorse, while her husband slept peacefully at the edge of the abyss.

He slept as if the shame that hung over them were in fact a long way off. However much the vain woman tried to placate her conscience with fallacious arguments, her conscience refused to let itself be whitewashed and struggled fitfully. Rosalía was not aware of its terribly accusing gaze because she had other things before her eyes: firstly, the dilemma of the ninth, which demanded great sacrifices, including even her honour; and second, certain cobwebs made of silk that enveloped her face. In the feverish restlessness of that night, all her ideas, even her feelings of remorse, were filtered through confused images of the finery and falderols of the autumn season.

The following morning, when she took Bringas his hot chocolate, she found him in a jovial and chatty mood, humming snatches of songs. She, on the other hand, was sorely troubled. Later, Cándida, who had been commissioned to bring back her purchases from Sobrino's to avoid arousing Mr Mousey's suspicions, brought various things over. The lady was so sunk in considerations of the perils of that day that she did not have the heart to look at the organdy and chenille for more than a few minutes before bundling it all into a drawer ... She was expecting to hear from Pez at eleven. Bringas invariably left for the office at ten thirty. That day, he was less punctual than usual, and all his good humour of earlier vanished over breakfast because Paquito read out loud some clandestine circulars which were going around Madrid, which threatened the Queen and guaranteed her speedy overthrow. 'If you bring any more of those filthy papers here,' said Thiers in a rage, 'I'll take you out of the University and put you to work in a shop on Toledo Street.'

He left in high dudgeon, and shortly afterwards Rosalía received the letter she had been awaiting with such anxiety. 'It's not very thick,' she thought, in unbearable suspense, as she went into the *Camón* to open the envelope alone, for Cándida was hovering in the vicinity and her eyes were as sharp as a hawk's. 'It's not very thick,' she repeated, taking a sheet of paper out of the envelope. 'There's nothing in it.' And indeed, it was only a letter, written in the Head of the Exchequer's neat, conventional handwriting. She could not read because of the fury that overwhelmed her when she saw the letter was unaccompanied by other papers. The missive, which was less than a page long, trembled in her hands. She glanced through it, looking for clear, categorical statements. It took her only a few seconds to skim the whole thing ... Every sentence in it tore at her heart as if the words were meathooks ... 'He was most terribly, dreadfully sorry not to be able to help her that day ... It was quite impossible ... He had found the family finances horribly behind, with a huge backlog of debts to be paid ... Despite all appearances to the contrary, he was in deep financial straits ... He must state quite frankly, in the bosom of confidence, that the grandiose appearance of his household was nothing more than show ... Nevertheless, he would have been only too anxious to help his lady friend, if he had not unfortunately had to pay a bill that very day ... But some other time ...'

Rosalía could not finish. She was blinded by rage and shame. She tore up the letter and crumpled the pieces. If only she could do the same to that despicable creature! ... Yes, he was utterly despicable, because she'd told him clearly that her honour and her family's stability were at stake ... What creatures men were! She had been foolish enough to imagine some of them had some gentlemanly qualities ... What a mistake, what a disappointment! And for that she had degraded herself the way she had! She deserved to be beaten and thrown out of her respectable home by her husband ... It was ignominious enough to sell oneself; but to do it for free! ... At this point, tears of rage and pain ran down her cheeks. They were the first she had shed since her marriage, for those she had cried for her children when they were ill were of another kind altogether.

And worse was yet to come, for all was lost ... If by three o'clock that afternoon she wasn't in the inquisitor's* house with the money in hand ... He would wait for her until three, not a minute more. When she thought of this, Rosalía's head felt like a volcano. To whom, Holy Virgin, to whom could she turn? ... She could not gather her wits even to commend herself to all the saints and all the virgins. She was overcome by desperation ... But just as she was giving in to it, a ray of hope shone through the stormy skies of that brain ... Refugio ...

Yes; Torres had said just a few days earlier that Refugio had been to Trujillo to cash ten thousand reals which her sister had sent her to help set up her business.

CHAPTER 45

Time was running short; the situation would admit no delay. Without pausing to consider whether or not it was an appropriate step, she ventured to take it anyway. It was twelve o'clock. 'I'd go through anything rather than have Bringas find out,' she said, putting on her lace mantilla in a hurry. 'I prefer to lower myself to ask this favour from a ...'

Refugio lived on Bordadores Street, opposite the little Plaza de San Ginés, in a perfectly respectable-looking house. Rosalía was surprised at how nice the stairway was. She had been expecting to find a filthy hall and shady tenants, and it was quite the contrary. The occupants could not be more respectable: on the ground floor was a shop that sold religious objects made of bronze; on the mezzanine was a Béjar woollens business, with a copper nameplate on the screen; and the first floor housed the offices of a religious paper. This gave Rosalía some encouragement, which the poor woman sorely needed, for she felt as if she were off to the slaughterhouse when she contemplated the degrading step she was taking. 'The things one will do in a pinch!' she thought, as she rang the bell of the second floor flat. 'Who would have thought I'd find myself doing a thing like this. Now all I need is for her to send me packing to make me even more ashamed and complete my punishment.'

Refugio herself opened the door and was very surprised to see her. Rosalía, who was very flustered, hovered between laughter and seriousness; she did not know whether to be familiar or formal with the Sánchez girl. It was a curious situation, which presented a tricky problem of social conduct. Between the door and the drawing room, they exchanged only odd words, short phrases, and monosyllables.

'This way, if you please,' said Refugio to Mrs Bringas, showing her into the sitting room. 'Celestina, come and help me clear off these chairs.'

Celestina must be the maid. Or at least, so our friend thought at first; but then she had to amend this conclusion. Celestina looked as odd as Refugio, and at the same time so very much like her, that it was not easy to tell which of them was the mistress. 'Probably,' thought Rosalía as she sat down in the first vacated chair, 'neither of them is.'

The Sánchez girl was very dishevelled. She had not done her hair yet. She wore only a light chemise on top, so poorly fastened that it showed part of her ample bosom. She was shuffling around in a pair of buckled shoes which she wore as if they were mules, and the heels clattered noisily on the tiled floor.

'I was going to throw on a robe,' said Refugio, after rifling through a pile of clothes on the sofa; 'but since we know each other so well . . .'

'Oh, there's no need to bother, my dear,' replied Mrs Bringas, determined to be pleasant at all costs. 'It's so very hot . . .'

As she said this, she looked around the room. She had never seen such disorder nor such an extraordinary mix of good and bad things. The door on to the drawing room was open, and it looked like the store room of a shop. All the chairs were draped with hats in various stages of composition, bits of ribbon, pieces of material, and threads. Cardboard boxes gaped open, revealing handfuls of beautiful fabric flowers, all jumbled and withered, if one can say such a thing of artificial blooms. The truth is that some of them were crying out for a bit of water. There were fichus trimmed with jet and chenille, linen chemisettes and some lengths of lace. This chaotic mass of fashionable objects reached as far as the sitting room, where it had overtaken some of the chairs and part of the sofa, and got mixed up with Refugio's own clothes, as if a revolutionary hand had done its best to avoid even the possibility of putting things in order. Two or three of the Sánchez girl's dresses gaped open from the armchairs, showing their linings, with the bodices and sleeves tugged inside out. There was a bronze leather boot under the table, and its twin was up on top of the console. There was an account book from the laundress open on a side-table with some jottings in a feminine hand: *Chemises, 6; petticoats, 14*, etc. . . . The side-table was made of wrought iron, painted black, with flowers. On the mantlepiece above the fireplace stood a magnificent bronze clock, indecorously flanked by two appallingly tasteless gilded porcelain dogs with chipped ears. The prints on the walls were crooked, and one of the curtains was torn; the floor was covered in stains; the glass mantle of the lamp was covered in soot. The bedroom door was ajar, and she glimpsed a huge bed with gold Empire bedsteads, rumpled and unmade, as if someone had just got up.

Refugio assumed Mrs Bringas had heeded her requests and was coming to see the articles she had to sell.

'You've come a bit late,' she told her. 'Did you know that I'm selling the whole lot off? I'm not cut out for this. I don't know what my sister was thinking of when she decided I should go into business . . . To give you an idea . . . I've done nothing but lose money from the beginning: not many people pay up, and I'm not the sort of person to plead with them . . . So the sooner I get rid of all this stuff, the better. I've had a lot of ladies coming over to buy what little I have left.'

'All the same,' remarked Rosalía, taking out some marabou feathers and aigrettes from one box, and ribbons and braid from another, 'there are still a lot of very pretty things here.'

'Do you like those aigrettes?' asked Refugio, delighted to be magnanimous with her. 'You can have them . . . a present from me.'

'Oh no . . . I couldn't possibly.'

'Oh, go on, take them; I'd love you to have them . . . I'd rather you had them than some woman who's going to buy them without paying me . . . And look,' she added, going through to the living room, 'you can have this hat too; it's not made up yet, but you can take whatever ribbon you like to go with it.'

Rosalía, stunned by this generosity, and somewhat more inclined to look favourably on Refugio, insisted on declining the gifts.

'Are you snubbing me because I'm poor?' remonstrated the other in a steely voice.

If Rosalía had not gone to see her for the purpose we all

know, and if her need for money had not been so great that it made her prepared to put up with anything, she would certainly have refused the kindnesses by which the other woman, who was so very inferior to her in all respects, was attempting to put herself on Rosalía's own elevated level; but she did not want to seem stand-offish just when she needed to ask a favour . . . And what a dreadful one! When she tried to imagine formulating her request, her whole being was drenched in revulsion, as if some bitter, foul liquid were filtering through her pores, coursing through her veins and up into her mouth. She tried various times to come out with her demand, but could not muster the courage. She even thought of saying nothing and fleeing the place. But the merciless logic of her need held her fast; and since she could see no other way out of her obligation, she was forced to lift that bitter cup to her lips. 'Now that I've made myself come this far,' she thought, 'I'm not leaving without trying my luck.' Time was running out; it had already struck one . . . Two or three times she had the words ready in her head and got ready to say them, but they would get choked on her lips by the bitter gall of her saliva. 'What a fool I am,' she thought, 'to be worrying about a little slip of a girl like this.' Finally, she struggled so hard that the words came stumbling out. The poor woman fanned herself, feigning indifference, and did her best to look calm and to banish the roiling blood in her cheeks.

'Now then, Refugio, there's something I wanted to talk to you about. I've come to ask you a favour.'

'A favour?' said the other, intensely curious.

'Yes, a favour,' said Mrs Bringas, somewhat disconcerted by that curiosity. 'I mean, if you can; if not, it's no matter.'

'And what might that be?'

'Well . . . if you can, now,' the lady went on, swallowing the gall which deadened her tongue. 'I'm in need of a certain sum. I know that you have . . . I know that you cashed an amount at Trujillo's . . . So then: if you wouldn't mind lending me five thousand reals for a few days, I'd be very grateful . . . That is, if you can; if you can't, it's no matter.'

She felt tremendously relieved having said it. The great weight on her chest seemed to lift somewhat. Refugio heard her out calmly, and did not appear to be surprised. Then she pursed her mouth judiciously for a while before replying.

'I'll tell you this much . . . I do have the money; but I don't know if I should lend it out. I'm expecting some very big bills tomorrow . . .'

She gazed impudently at Rosalía, who would have preferred her not to stare so much and to hurry up and give her the money. After a pause, during which Refugio appeared to be doing calculations on Mrs Bringas's brow, she came back with the following: 'As for the money . . . I do have it: look.'

She rummaged around in a container that looked like a sewing-box, and emerged with a handful of things from the bottom. There were scraps of material, loose thread and bank notes, all mixed up in an untidy ball.

'You see . . . I've got plenty. But . . .'

Rosalía's eyes lit up when she saw the notes. But then they darkened again when the wretched creature shoved the money back down in the box, shaking her head, and said: 'I'm sorry, ma'am, I can't do it, I just can't.'

Rosalía thought to herself: 'That sly minx wants me to humiliate myself even further, she wants me to beg and plead and snivel in front of her . . . she wants me to throw myself at her feet so she can trample all over me . . . Oh, you little hussy, if I weren't in this state, do you know what I'd do with you? Lift up that skirt of yours and give you a good hard spanking with a broom on your great big *derrière* . . . Lending money to a person like me would be a great honour for you, you silly little fool.'

Naturally, the lady did not voice any of these thoughts. On the contrary, she employed sweet words, more suited to the purpose of her visit.

'Well, think it over, my dear. You might find that you could . . . Perhaps you could postpone paying your bills for a few days, whereas mine . . .'

'I only wish I could,' said the other, with affected sympathy. 'I feel so sorry for you, having to leave empty-handed like this . . .'

The patronising tone of this last remark was even more galling. Rosalía would have loved to seize her by that mane of hair and rub her face on the ground.

'Couldn't you make a special effort?' she stammered, drawing valour from the deepest part of her soul.

'If only I could! . . . It makes me so sad not to be able to help you. Believe me, I'm really sorry. I'd do anything to be of service to you and Mr Bringas . . .'

'No,' said Rosalía sharply, alarmed at hearing her husband's name used. 'This is my business, and mine alone. You are not to mention it to Bringas. It's got nothing to do with him.'

'Oh! . . . I see,' murmured Refugio, gazing once again at Rosalía's brow.

Rosalía noted that after staring at her, the dreadful woman started rummaging around again in her sewing box . . . Had she softened at last, was she taking out the notes? No . . . She made the gesture of a person who is determined not to give in to weakness, and repeated: 'I can't, I just can't . . . You're the only person I would even be considering lending it to right now. For you or Mr Bringas I'd do all I could, I'd go hungry for you if I had to. But you know, I'm afraid I'm as weak as water; I'm such a fool that if you came crying to me I might be silly enough to feel sorry for you and lend you the money; and that would be really silly, because I need it myself.'

'That's it,' thought Rosalía, beside herself with rage. 'The little slut wants me to go down on my knees to her . . . Well, I won't do it.'

And out loud, feigning a serenity she was far from feeling, she said: 'If it's such a nuisance, let's just forget it.'

'I can't, I just can't. I signed a solemn agreement . . .' declared the Sánchez girl, decisively.

'Oh well, in that case, don't worry.'

'So . . . Why didn't you go to the seaside with the family?'

This complete change of subject was torture to Rosalía. They were moving on; the subject of the loan was closed. She answered the silly question about their summer holidays with the first idiotic thing that came into her head. She felt so hot that she would willingly have dived headfirst into a bath to prevent herself from bursting into flames.

'It's dreadfully hot and stuffy in here.'

'Just a minute then, I'll close the shutters to keep out the sunlight.'

Rosalía sat there for a while with her soul hanging in the balance, staring at the prints of bullfighters on the wall. She saw them through a haze of anguish. She was so driven she did not hesitate to degrade herself a little further. She tapped Refugio on the knee and uttered the following words, trying hard to make them sound casual and friendly.

'Oh, go on, lend me that money, there's a dear.'

'What?' said Refugio, in surprise. 'Oh yes! The money. Do you know, I'd forgotten all about it ... Do you need it that badly, then? Are you under that much pressure? To be honest, I thought you were a lender yourself, not a borrower.'

Rosalía would have liked to counter this malicious observation by tearing out the woman's tousled locks. But what could she do? She had to swallow her bitterness and submit to whatever was necessary.

'Yes, my dear; I am in rather a pickle. If you want, I can pay you interest ... whatever you prefer.'

'Oh, good heavens, no! What do you take me for? If I were to lend you the sum you want, and I very much regret that I can't do that, I wouldn't charge any interest. Not for members of the family.'

When Rosalía heard that the little baggage considered herself one of the family, she almost flew off the handle ... It was torture to have to put up with her remarks without exploding. She gritted her teeth and did her best to grimace in imitation of a smile. 'I must be foaming at the mouth,' she thought. 'If I don't get out of here soon, I shall have a fit.'

Refugio put her hand back in the box and drew out the bundle of notes. Merciful Heavens! Things were going to resolve themselves at last ... ! Mrs Bringas concealed her tension as she watched the young woman flatten and finger the notes as if she were counting them. But the little ... shook her head disconsolately and said: 'I just don't have enough left ... I'm sorry, ma'am, it's just not possible, not possible.'

But instead of putting the bundle back where it had come from, she left it on the mantelpiece. This stoked Rosalía's dying hopes.

'You know,' remarked the other woman, stretching out in the armchair as if it were a bed, so that her feet almost brushed the lady's knees, 'I'm ruined; it's as simple as that. I went and got myself into a business I knew nothing about, and since I'm not the hard-nosed type, they've all taken advantage of the fact that I can't say boo to a goose to get what they can. Everything went fine at the beginning; the whole world was at my disposal. The stock would come in and the ladies would come and see me and leave with quantities of it. I had only the very best stuff, and I wasn't charging much for it, either. But when it came time for them to pay ... they weren't to be found. "I'll be round next week ..." "I'll stop by ..." "Come back another day ..." "I don't have it right now ..." One excuse after another, and when all's said and done, there was nothing there but poverty and pretence. Lord, Madrid's all show, you know. A gentleman I know says that this place is a sort of ongoing carnival, where the poor dress as rich people. In this city, everyone's poor, barring the odd few. It's all sham, ma'am, pure sham. People here don't live comfortably at home. They live in the street; there are families who survive all year round on nothing but potato omelettes just so they can dress well and go to the theatre ... I know women whose husbands are civil servants who are out of work half the year, and you wouldn't believe how beautifully turned out they are. They look like duchesses and their children like royalty. How do they do it? I have no idea. A gentleman I know says that Madrid is full of mysteries like that. There's plenty of women go without at mealtimes so as to buy clothes, and others who find a different way. I could tell you a few stories, oh, I've seen it all, I have ... they find ways to get money, they buy their clothes with whatever they can, and then they go badmouthing other women as if they weren't just as bad themselves ... Anyway, they haven't paid me for half of what I've sold; the other half is out there somewhere, and there's not a soul alive who could get it back. Stuck-up, lying hypocrites! And then they come round here putting on airs ... "You great so and sos – I say to myself – don't deceive anyone; I live off my own work. But you lot are swindling half the world, you'd take the bread out of poor people's mouths to make silk dresses." You should just hear them going on, criticising and finding fault with other poor women. There's one who's always been snooty to me and who's gone to any lengths to avoid paying me, and then she comes round here asking for money ... What for, I'd like to know? Maybe it's to give her lover.'

She delivered this tirade with an energy and feeling that

showed her well acquainted with her subject, bestowing fiery glances on the unhappy petitioner the whole while. Rosalía listened with her nostrils enormously distended, her eyes fixed on the ground, her breathing laboured, and her lips clamped shut to contain her furious desire to say or do something unseemly.

CHAPTER 47

This is what she would have said, had she been able: 'For that brazen, cynical way of talking about ladies whose shoes you're not fit to remove, I'll have that viper's tongue of yours plucked out and I'll have you whipped through the streets, naked from the waist up, like that, and that, and that . . .'

In her mind, she lashed Refugio until she bled. By this stage, Mrs Bringas was so furious and was having to make such an effort to hold her tongue that she would have preferred any domestic calamity over the horrendous torture to which she was being subjected. 'I'm going to have to leave,' she thought. 'I can't bear it any longer. I'd rather have my husband despise me and order me about like a slave than have this wretch spit in my face a moment longer.'

But when she thought this, she imagined Mr Torquemada, doughnut in hand, explaining to Francisco that he was obliged to pay the debt; then she pictured the outraged husband . . . No: no effort of the imagination could suffice to conjure up the noble wrath of that saintly man, who so hated dishonesty. 'Anything, anything but that,' she thought, finally. 'Even having this forward little hussy walk all over me . . . At least this way I can bear the shame alone; no one knows about it, no one's going to reproach me with it.'

'A gentleman friend of mine,' said Refugio, switching from lecture mode to a friendly, offhand manner, 'says that there's nothing but shabbiness all round; that there are no real aristocrats here, and that almost all the so-called rich people, the high society types, are nobodies . . . For example, where else in the world does a lady with a title like the Tellerías' go around asking for a thousand real loan, like she did to me? There have been men who have shot themselves because they lost six hundred reals on cards. And when a young man squanders twenty thousand reals on a woman, they say he's ruined the family. And then there's all those folks that live off other people, I know plenty like that, who go to the theatre with free tickets and travel for nothing, and even wear secondhand clothes . . . All for the sake of appearances! When I see people like that, I feel quite proud of myself, because I don't owe anyone anything, and if I do, I pay up; I work for my living, and no one can tell me what to do, and most of all I'm not trying to pull the wool over anyone's eyes; if people don't like me the way I am, they can lump it, know what I mean? Because I earn what I have . . . Celestina, go down to the Levante café and ask them to send us up some coffee. Would you like a cup?'

'No, thank you,' said Rosalía shortly, at the end of her tether.

She got up to leave. She found the woman so disgusting and so hurtful to her pride, with her vulgar words and her vile thoughts, that she refused to be degraded any more. Refugio burst out laughing and caught her by the arm, saying: 'Are you sure you won't have coffee with us? Do wait a bit, I'm thinking of giving you the money.'

Rosalía sat down, feeling more cheerful at these words. The devil before her eyes, winking and leering at her, suddenly became human and even pleasant.

'It's a quarter past two,' sighed Mrs Bringas, unable to repress a smile, and finding Refugio's wide, gap-toothed mouth peculiarly attractive.

'When do you have to pay the money by?'

'Three o'clock,' said the other, spontaneously.

'Oh, then you've got plenty of time yet.'

The door banged as Celestina went out to fetch the coffee. She of the missing tooth lolled on the chair in a position that verged on the indecent, not merely lazy, and said, laughing rudely: 'If *Madam* were here, you wouldn't be going through all this trouble, you could throw yourself at her feet and shed a few tears . . . They say *Madam* always comes to the aid of her friends who go to her with their troubles and who have tight-fisted or good-for-nothing husbands. Of course, if I had the nation's purse-strings in my hand, like her, I'd do the same thing. But never you mind, they'll soon sort her out. A gentleman who comes here says we're really going to see some heads roll this time.'

'And how many gentlemen do you know, you little slut?'

Rosalía would have liked to say, had she been in a position to reprimand her. 'You seem to be friends with all the gentlemen of the species. Couldn't one of them give you a good punch in the face and knock out all the rest of those pretty teeth of yours?'

'Things are going to change around here pretty soon,' said Refugio carelessly. 'And that'll take care of the whole lot of them. We'll all be free, completely free.'

This lack of respect, this way of talking about Her Majesty, made the lady so angry that she was on the verge of throwing all her circumspection to the winds and scratching the odious creature's face and saying: 'Take that, maybe it'll teach you some manners.'

But she had to make do with uttering a few reproving monosyllables. Her face was beetroot colour. As she waved her arms about, the Sánchez girl knocked over a little basket on the mantelpiece, out of which fell a packet of cigarettes.

'Oh, so you smoke, too, do you, you filthy wench?' Rosalía wanted to ask, if she could have spoken freely; but she watched the girl pick the packet up off the ground and said nothing.

Shortly afterwards, a waiter brought in the coffee, and left the tray on the side-table. They had to move a lot of things to make room for it. Refugio and Celestina, after reiterating their invitation to Mrs Bringas, served themselves. They treated each other as equals, and were on an easy, familiar footing with one another. As I mentioned earlier, it was impossible to tell which of them was the maid and which the mistress, although Celestina did look somewhat shabbier than Refugio.

'Holy Mother of God!' Rosalía exclaimed to herself. 'A right pair I've gone and landed myself with, to be sure! If the good Lord gets me out of here safe and sound, I will never, ever, do anything like this again.'

'Celestina,' said the gap-toothed girl, in a friendly voice, 'don't I get my hair done today?'

The other explained that she had a lot to do, which was why she was running late. The place was a mess still: the sitting room was all topsy-turvy, and so was the bedroom ... When Refugio had finished her coffee and Celestina had begun to clean up the room, Rosalía, unable to curb her impatience any longer, closed her fan with a snap.

'It must be very late. Maybe a quarter to three.'

'The awful thing is,' said Refugio, toying with her victim,

'that . . . now that I think of it . . . You know, I can't give you the money after all. I'd forgotten that today, this afternoon in fact, I have to pay someone over two thousand reals.'

Rosalía was convinced there was a boa constrictor wrapped round her chest, squeezing the breath out of her. She sat speechless. She would have happily thrown herself on the vile creature and sunk all ten fingernails deep into her devilish face. But the things we think and desire, we rarely do. She got up . . . All that came out was a guttural sound, a feeble sign of her rage, muffled by dignity.

'She's playing with me like a cat with a paper ball,' she thought. 'I have to leave before I strangle her.'

'Wait,' said Refugio. 'I've just thought of something. I promised to help you, and I'm not about to go back on that promise. A Sánchez Emperador's word is the word of an emperor . . . Especially for a member of the family.'

'Get the family out of your filthy mouth,' thought Rosalía.

'I've just thought, I could borrow it from a friend.'

'Do you have any idea how late it is?' said Mrs Bringas, regaining hope.

'She lives quite close, on Sal Street.'

'But how can you take your time at a moment like this?'

'Nah . . . I've got time to do my hair. Celestina!'

'My dear . . . you don't have time.'

Refugio got up. Rosalía moved towards her, picked up the dress and made as if to put it on her.

'Put this dress on . . . and a shawl, and a headscarf . . .'

Refugio went into the bedroom. She called out 'My corset,' and Mrs Bringas hurriedly took it in to her and helped her fasten it. While she was doing this, the cunning girl remarked casually: 'Mr Pez might well be able to get you out of this fix . . . But he's not always flush. In fact, right now, the poor man's stony broke . . .'

Rosalía said nothing. Her face flamed and her heart constricted with embarrassment. Instead, she held the sides of the corset together and tugged furiously on the drawstrings, as if she were trying to cut the she-devil in two.

'Good heavens, ma'am, you're pulling me apart . . . I don't lace myself this tight. I leave that to those stout women who want sylph-like figures . . . What do you think, should I do my hair up?'

'No . . . just tie it back in a chignon with a ribbon and a net

... You'll look fine like that ... in fact, you look better ...
with your hair a bit wild ... You look like that portrait of
Herodias* that's in the Palace ... Come on, hurry up and get
ready ... put your hair up ... it's getting very late, you know
... Look, I'll help you.'

Refugio sat down, and Mrs Bringas arranged her voluminous
hair in a jiffy.

'I've got myself quite the maid here!' said the Sánchez girl,
laughing. 'What an honour!'

And then, just as she looked ready to go out, she began to
sing and pace around the room. Rosalía was horrified to see her
sit down again quite calmly.

'But, my dear!' she exclaimed in vexation.

Her brain was whirring like a clock about to strike. The other
woman said, with serene refinement: 'It's very hot; I don't feel
like going out just now.'

'But you ... are you playing with me ... or what ... ?'

'Now just you calm down, ma'am, and don't go getting cross
or hoity-toity with me,' said the Sánchez girl. 'I won't stand for
any temper tantrums, and there's no need to get on your high
horse with me. You go back where you belong and leave me in
peace. As to the five thousand reals, here they are: I'm going to
give them to you now to save myself the bother of having to go
out. I'll borrow what I need later.'

CHAPTER 48

Despite having said this, she still had not given Rosalía the
money, which left her in agony.

'I'm going to give you a piece of advice,' said the vile woman.
'It's good advice, because you see I care about the family. It is:
don't get involved with Milagros; she can run rings around the
sharpest woman on earth. Go back to your corner next to that
namby-pamby husband of yours, and stay out of trouble ...
And don't go to Sobrino's any more. Madrid's no easy place to
live, I tell you. And don't trust that Milagros when she flatters
you, she's a sly, slippery customer.'

Rosalía nodded sagely to all to this. Finally, the Sánchez girl
put the notes in her hand ... Oh! What relief the unhappy lady

experienced! In case the she-devil decided to take them back again, she resolved to leave at once.

'Oh, are you leaving?'

'It's very late. There's not a moment to be lost. Naturally, I'm most grateful to you. Oh yes! . . . Would you like me to make you out a receipt?'

'There's no need,' said Refugio, gallantly, striking a noble and disinterested pose. 'Not between members of the family . . . Oh yes! I'll send the hat and the other things over this afternoon.'

'As you wish.'

'But just one moment, I have to tell you something.'

'What?' asked Rosalía, petrified again.

'I'm going to tell you what the Marquesa de Tellería said about you.'

'About me?'

'Yes, you . . . she was sitting right there, in the same armchair as you, the day before she went to the seaside. She came to buy some artificial flowers from me. She talked about you and she said . . . oh, this is so funny! . . . she said you were a vulgar social climber!'

Rosalía sat stock still for a moment. The phrase struck home in the most sensitive part of her. She had never been so deeply hurt in her life. And as she rushed hastily down the stairs, she felt the pain of that wound to her self-esteem more than those she had sustained to her rank. *A vulgar social climber!* The frightful verdict was fixed in her mind, where it would remain like an inscription permanently branded on her flesh.

'My Lord, the things I've been through today, only You alone know . . . I think I've gone white,' she thought as she took a carriage to Torquemada's house. 'What agonies I've suffered . . .'

She arrived at the house and went up in a panic, because it was gone three. But she was fortunate, and found the inquisitor at home, though impatient and getting ready to go over to the Palace. He greeted her with a smile and asked after the family. She did not find the adoration of the doughnut made by his fingers quite as mortifying as before. The pleasure of averting that great peril and freeing herself from such a disagreeable creature prevented her from concentrating on such superficial matters, even if they were tiresome. She made the meeting as brief as possible and took her leave. She was in such a tizzy after all she had been though that day . . . !

'I can't believe Milagros really said that about me,' she thought, on her way back to the Palace, tortured by that horrible inscription burning into her forehead. 'That little vixen made it up ... What a day! When I get home, the first thing I'm going to do is see if I've gone white. I've certainly had cause enough.'

And the first thing she did was look at herself in the mirror. We may as well say, for the peace of mind of any ladies who might find themselves in a similar situation, that she did not have a single white hair. Or if she did, they did not show. And if they had shown, she would have found some way to cover them up.

It is, however, an indisputable fact that as a result of the many contretemps she had suffered over the previous few days, the lady was so worn and dispirited that her husband began to suspect she was ill. 'There's something the matter with you, don't deny it. Shall we send for the doctor? ... You see, if you'd gone swimming in the Manzanares, you'd be another woman.' But she declared there was nothing wrong, and though she did not refuse to have the doctor come, she could not name any very concrete symptoms to him. It was all in her nerves, those little devils that love to plague great ladies, when they are not helping them to conceal something. The facts of Mrs Bringas's case were that she found herself weepy and frightened of the slightest thing, that her appetite was gone, and principally that she saw her husband in a peculiar new light. Although her esteem for him had lowered considerably, the external forms of respect she paid him betrayed a certain studied refinement. This lent itself to different interpretations; but given the impossibility of determining the causes of such extravagant demonstrations of affection, we have to turn to hypothesis, and see them as a phenomenon similar to sweet-talking a Customs officer when you want to smuggle contraband goods through. Rosalía was trying the non-violent, venal method for unloading her clothes. She started wearing them one by one. Every day, Francisco would notice some new thing and an argument would ensue. She would attempt to appease him with charming fibs, hugs and loving words. But she did not always succeed, and the respectable gentleman began to grow seriously worried about those luxuries that kept materialising out of trap doors, like theatrical surprises. Several times he insisted on an explanation, to which he would listen whilst arraying himself with a veritable arsenal of logic, at whose appearance his wife trembled like a criminal when proof is produced. But she was slowly hardening, or rather, learning to shield herself from his officious rebukes. She began not to take them to heart so, not to worry much whether Mr Mousey believed her or not. She was just about resolved to explain these irregularities with the irrefutable argument *because I do*, when a terrible thing happened which freed her of the trouble, because the Customs man was so dazed by it that he forgot all about his accounts. This mental and emotional disorder of Bringas's came about as follows.

One morning, he went to the office as calm as ever, but his elbows had not touched the desk before one of his colleagues, Mr Vargas, came up to him and whispered in his ear: 'The Navy has declared for the revolutionaries.' This struck Bringas as so absurd that he burst out laughing. But Vargas persisted, giving details, reciting the texts of the telegrams ... Francisco was stunned, as if he had been hit on the head by a stone. He could hardly breathe ... To add to his distress, the other added some even more foreboding remarks. '*Après nous, le déluge*, my dear Bringas ... It's really happening this time.' Once our economist had recovered his wits somewhat, he and his friend and some other officials went to the Deputy Head of the Department's office (the Head was in Santander), where he met up with other staff members, all in the greatest consternation. 'This is really serious ... How disgraceful! ... The Spanish Navy! ... How can this have come about? Well, as soon as they had ships ... I can't believe this is real ... And what will the Government do? ... Send the army in right away ... Absurd, this is a landslide ... Cádiz and Seville have risen; the whole of Andalucía is in flames ... Poor *Madam* ... They did try to tell her, but she wouldn't listen ... And what about the generals who were in the Canaries? They're in Cádiz. And Prim?* Sailing for Barcelona ... That's it then, it's all over.'

This happened on the nineteenth. Bringas went back home more dead than alive. The whole of that day and those that followed, his brain seemed addled: he would not eat or sleep and did nothing but beg for news. He would embrace anyone who brought good news and irascibly dismiss those whose news was adverse. The poor man was so beside himself that he even forgot about the running of his own household. If his wife had dressed up as the empress of Golconda,* he would not have batted an eyelid.

His loss of appetite affected his whole system. Frankly, he

was behaving as if he might be seriously ill. He was having difficulty walking, stumbled over words, and his eyes began playing up again, deforming objects and turning them strange colours. What a pity to take such a turn for the worse, just when his eyesight was doing so well and when he depended on it to be able to finish the hair work, which was almost complete! 'There's nothing for it,' he would say. 'If this disgraceful situation prevails, I shall die.'

Rosalía and Paquito de Asís were very down at the mouth too, although at times Rosalía's curiosity was stronger than her grief.

The revolution was a bad thing, or so they all said; but it also represented the unknown, and the unknown attracts those with vivid imaginations and seduces those who have formed irregular arrangements. There was change on the way, a different way of life, something new and awe-inspiring which might prove to be fun. 'Well now,' she thought, 'we'll just wait and see how it turns out.'

Pez continued coming to the house; but she had taken such a dislike to him that she barely spoke to him. On that score, the proud lady's thoughts were so numerous and varied that I am incapable of reproducing them. She vowed never again to fish for such small fry, and pictured herself casting her nets on the high open seas, whose waters were traversed by elegant sharks, pompous whales and fish of real consequence. In her dreams, she saw herself the following winter waging a social campaign that would be as pleasant as it was productive. She would have no more dealings with the Pez family and the Tellerías and other such petty folk, but would seek out more solid and reliable support amongst the Fúcars, the Trujillos, the Cimarras and other genuinely aristocratic families.

CHAPTER 49

It was the end of the world ... Francisco groaned as he heard that Béjar, Santoña, Santander and other towns had risen. Mr Pez, with unspeakable cruelty, told his friend not to think that such a collapse could be remedied, that there was no hope for the Queen and that she had no choice but to take refuge in

France ... Oh, he had warned them, he had said so, he had foreseen and prophesied what was happening!

Cándida, on the other hand, brought good news ... 'Noval-iches* has gone off with a tremendous army, just tremendous ... He'll send them packing in no time, you'll see ... They say that some of the towns in Andalucía have resisted the rebels ... There are a lot of folk around here who like to make a fuss and paint too black a picture. I've been told it's not as bad as they say.'

Bringas hugged her. 'And that Prim, what's he up to?' he asked.

'I heard someone had shot him ... Or else that they're going to shoot him ... I'm convinced that if the Queen roused herself and came down here and showed herself to the people and gave them a piece of her mind and said, "You are my children, all of you," all this would be over before we knew where we were.'

Bringas thought so too; but he would have preferred Narváez to come back to life, a somewhat more difficult undertaking. 'Oh! If only the General were still alive ... If this doesn't sort itself out soon, there's going to be a bloodbath in Madrid, because there aren't many soldiers left here and those democrats or demagogues will take to the streets. We'll have a guillotine in every square.' The poor man got worse every day. He was amazed at the tranquillity of his colleagues, who were taking the catastrophe very philosophically, and did not rule out the possibility of getting other jobs in different offices somehow, if the revolution did away with the Royal Heritage. He found the notion of defecting so repugnant that he swore he would go begging on the streets rather than plead for a job from those revolutionaries, as they called themselves.

'Don't you fret, my dear,' said his wife. 'You can always go back to the Holy Places office.'

'But, you silly woman, do you really think there will be any holy places left? There'll be nothing but unholy places. You won't believe what a frightful mess we'll have on our hands: guillotines, blood, atheism, promiscuity, and all the other nations ... they may be on their way already, for all I know ... will come to the Queen's rescue; they'll come in and divide up poor Spain between them.'

The good man almost had an apoplectic fit on the twenty-ninth when news of the battle of Alcolea* reached Madrid. The news was brought by Paquito, who had been down at the Puerta del Sol and had seen a big crowd . . . There had been a general there haranguing the mob, and another who had torn his epaulettes off. After this, people ran through the streets looking more jubilant than panic-stricken. Various groups were going around shouting hurrahs for the revolution, for the Army and the Navy, and saying that Isabel II was no longer Queen. Some of them carried banners with various mottoes, and others were busy taking the Royal coat of arms down off the shops. Paquito de Asís told his father all this, toning down the more unpalatable parts. The poor lad had to disguise his feelings, for even though his thinking was cast in the same mould as his father's, he was still a boy and he could not help being fascinated by the notion of liberty, which casts its spell over every enquiring mind that starts toying with historical and social concepts. As he recounted what he had seen, in a tone of distress and consternation, a strange, incomprehensible joy pulsed through his whole body. He did not know where it came from; but doubtless it was because his mind was not prepared to resist the explosive excitement of the city; he had inhaled it as one inhales the air that others breathe.

'There's no hope now,' said Bringas, making an effort to rise above his utter dejection. 'We must prepare ourselves. God's will be done. Resign yourselves. The mob will soon be here to sack the Palace . . . They won't spare anyone. We must be dignified, and accept martyrdom.'

He choked . . . They fell silent, listening to the sounds out on the passageways and down in the courtyard below. There was great alarm all over the Palace. The inhabitants stood in their doorways asking for news and exchanging impressions. Some of them went downstairs, anxious for news; but silence reigned in the courtyard, and even though the gates were open, not a soul came in. Just when they were least expecting her, Cándida appeared in a great state, and announced amidst stifled groans: 'They're here, they're here . . .'

'Who, ma'am, what's happening?'

'The looters . . . Oh, my dear Mr Bringas! . . . We saw the mob go down Lepanto Street. You should have seen them, with their gallows-bird faces, their unshaven beards, their grimy hands! . . . They're coming to cut our throats, for sure.'

'But what about the Palace guard . . . the Royal Halbardiers?'

'They must have mutinied too. They're all on the same side. Oh, the good Lord save and keep us!'

There was panic in the house for a while; but it did not last long, because when they went out into the passageway, they saw people out there chatting calmly, as if nothing were amiss.

'Whatever's happening?'

'Oh, nothing much: just a few urchins kicking up a rumpus in the gateway; nothing to worry about. They've sent over some guards from the City Hall.'

Paquito de Asís went down, against the wishes of his father, who feared some unforeseen catastrophe, and came back half an hour later with further news: 'There's a bunch of civilians on guard down below.'

'Are they armed?'

'Yes: they've got what they could pick up yesterday in the Park ... But they're harmless sorts. Some of them are in hats, others in caps, others in hunting caps and the rest in berets. They look like clowns.'

'A fine time for tomfoolery this is ... And what about the soldiers?'

'They've taken refuge in the barracks.'

'Great Heavens, man, in other words we're at the mercy of the mob, the rabble, the masses as they call them ...'

'They've put up a sign that says: *National Palace, guarded by the People.*'

'Yes, they'll take fine care of it, they will,' said Bringas bitterly. 'There won't be a scrap left in the Palace. At least, they'll have had plenty to get their hands on before they get as far as us. By the time they get up here, they'll have had their fill of looting, and ...'

They passed the night in painful uncertainty. Bringas and many of the other men stayed up and laid in provisions for many days. They expected to be set on by the mob at any moment. But, to their great surprise, not a sound disturbed the august silence of the Palace. It seemed as if the institution of the monarchy slumbered on there, tranquil and serene, as it had done in the good old days.

On the morning of the thirtieth, Cándida came rushing in.

'Do you realise what's happening?' she enquired without preamble.

'What is it, ma'am, what's happened?' they chorused anxiously, thinking something earth-shattering had occurred.

'Those poor men who are guarding the Palace went without dinner last night. They've been here since mid-afternoon yesterday, and no one has thought to send them anything to eat. I don't know what the City Hall or the Junta are thinking of, because, by the way, they've formed something they call a revolutionary junta. They're in a sorry state, those men, I can tell you. I went down this morning to talk to them. You wouldn't believe this, Mr Bringas, sir: but the poor things are as kind-hearted as they come ... If those are the only revolutionaries we see around here, we can all sleep soundly in our beds. Some of them went up to the Royal apartments, and they've been wandering around in a daze, gawping at the ceilings. The others were asking where the kitchens are. My dear, I felt awful, I felt so bad, when I saw they were just dying of hunger! You can't imagine how sorry I felt for them. My neighbours and lots of other people from the third floor have been down to bring them food, and they're sitting around in the main gateway. They were trying to split a tortilla between thirty and a bottle of wine between fifty. What a laugh. Come down and see for yourself. There's nothing to be afraid of; they wouldn't hurt a fly. They haven't stolen a single thing. And all they've killed is the odd pigeon. Two or three of them were trying to shoot our innocent neighbours; but they haven't had much luck. The revolutionaries are very bad shots.'

'Poor pigeons! ... Come to think of it,' said Bringas, 'I did hear shots this morning.'

'They didn't get many. They gave me three nice fat ones ... I tell you, those poor men are the salt of the earth.'

'Now that I don't believe,' said Bringas sharply. 'I can't accept that, it's sheer nonsense. There must be a catch. And if it's true what you say, then they're not rabble, I'll say it again, they're not rabble: they're gentlemen in disguise.'

CHAPTER 50

When things had settled down and law and order were restored – although they had barely been disturbed – the Junta officially took over the Palace, appointing someone to take charge of it and sending over a detachment of soldiers to act as guards. The inhabitants of the Palace no longer feared for their personal safety, but they were seized by another kind of worry: namely, that they would soon be expelled from what had now become the National Palace. Many of them started manoeuvring to be able to stay. Others, like Bringas, wanted to show their scorn for the revolution by vacating the rooms that no longer belonged to them as soon as possible. I had occasion to learn and evaluate the feelings of each of the inhabitants of the city on this matter, because, as luck or misfortune would have it, I was the one the Junta designated to take charge of the colossus and administer all the former possessions of the Crown. The moment I was installed in office, I was besieged by anguished residents of the city. I had no choice but to leave some of them where they were, because of the nature of their job; they alone knew all the ins and outs of some indispensable aspect of the running of the place. This was the case for the people who took care of the furniture and the wardrobes. Others would come up with complicated arguments as to why they should be allowed to stay, and not a few claimed revolutionary sympathies so as to become tenants of the Nation as they had been previously of the Monarchy. All of them came with letters of recommendation from various personages, fallen or falling, newly risen or on the rise, requesting permanent lodgings or else an extension before they had to move out. García Grande's widow brought me such an appalling stack of cards and letters that I let her stay where she was as long as she liked, in order to avoid having to read them.

I knew that Bringas wished to leave right away. But his wife came to see me to beg me to let them stay another month in the Palace, while they looked for a house, to which I willingly agreed. The distinguished lady told me, whilst we were on the subject of the extraordinary, unprecedented events of the day, that she was not so implacably opposed to the revolution as her husband; that she was convinced the Queen would come back, because the country could not do without her, and that, in the meantime, she was going to wait and see what happened before passing judgement. Clearly, there was a new era on the way, a different mentality, different customs; wealth would move from one quarter to another; there would be great upheavals, sudden falls and rises, surprises, extraordinary events and all the disorderly, blind commotion of a society that has been chafing for change for a long time. From what Mrs Bringas told me, in those very words or others that I do not recall, I came to realise that the worthy lady was excited at the prospect of the unknown.

I wished to pay Bringas the courtesy of notifying him in person that he could stay in the apartment as long as he liked. He thanked me, but declared that he did not wish to owe the so-called Nation any favours and that he could not wait to get out of the place. Pez was there, and between us we discussed recent events, including the recent formation of the Junta and the Provisional Government. Bringas was greatly put out to find that Pez was not as indignant about the situation as one might have expected, given his record. But Pez defended himself with calm and well-chosen words, brandishing the theory of the *fait accompli*, the key to Politics and History. 'What are we supposed to do, shed rivers of blood?' he said. 'What's happened? Just what I said, just what I prophesied, just what I predicted. We have to bow to the circumstances and wait patiently to see what these gentlemen come up with.' Besides, the great Pez thought that the fact that the Liberal Union had joined the revolution was a guarantee that it would not get dangerously out of control. He was just going to sit tight, without a job for a moment, and he had told the September revolutionaries: 'We'll just see how you do. I foresee you'll do just the same as we did, because the country isn't going to help you out . . .' And what a lucky coincidence! Almost all the people on the Junta were friends of his. Some of them were distant relatives, that is, they had some Pez blood in them. He had plenty of friends and relations on the Provisional Government too. In fact, he was surrounded by pisciform faces on every side. Rather than calling this coincidence, let us call it a lesson in the Philosophy of History.

Bringas took no heed of my pleas to stay in the apartment. His wife, who came to my office to thank me the day they moved, said they had taken a very small house; but that they would soon take a more spacious one, for she could not live in a cramped little hovel that was more storeys up than the Santa Cruz tower. Both Bringas and Paquito out of work! This was truly a catastrophe for the Bringas family economy and was not conducive to the contemplation of great things. But somehow or other, the family had to do its best to live up to its customary reputation and continue to live in a seemly fashion. 'At this crucial juncture,' she said, after a long conversation during which she had bestowed some rather incendiary glances on me, 'the family's future depends on me. I shall save them.'

The story of how she achieved this does not belong in this narrative. We know nothing of the lady's later self. But it can be said that subsequently, according to reliable sources, Mrs Bringas managed to triumph easily and with a certain flourish over the awkward situations into which her irregularities led her. It is an incontrovertible fact that, in order to pay off her debt to Refugio and rid herself of that hateful gadfly, she did not have to struggle as she had on other, similar occasions, described in this book. For those incidents, events, tame melodramas or whatever you want to call them, were merely the preludes to her moral metamorphosis, and must have caught her while she was yet an inexperienced novice.

To tell the truth, of course,* I was sad to see them go. The day they left, the top floor of the Palace city looked like a town under threat of shelling. Everyone was moving; there was a mêlée of people and a colossal transfer of all kinds of furniture and household effects in process. It was impossible to get through those dark streets. Little Alfonso Bringas was thrilled at the spectacle, and would have liked to take charge of transporting all those items in his very own vans.

Mr Mousey was a sorry sight. He walked slowly, clinging to his wife's arm, seeing double and speaking indistinctly. Rosalía, who was serene and somewhat majestic, said not a word all the way between their apartment and the Plaza de Oriente; but her eyes shone with proud conviction, for she was conscious of her role as linchpin of the family in such dire circumstances.

She told me as much, in those very words, later on, in a private interview. By that time, we were well into the revolutionary period. She attempted to renew the tokens of her ruinous affection; but I hurried to put a stop to that, for although it seemed natural that she should be the breadwinner, now that the family found itself made redundant, I was not prepared to go against all the laws of morality and domestic economy, and fulfil that role myself.

NOTES

p. 3 the Vignola school: Giacomo da Vignola (1507–73) was an important Italian architect, a disciple of Michelangelo. He designed buildings with stern but elegant façades and wrote a classic treatise on architecture, the *Regola delli cinque ordini d'architettura* (1562), which helped to disseminate the revival of the Roman classical style.

p. 3 Gothic ... Plateresque: The Gothic style in architecture corresponds to the medieval period (*c*. 1150–1500), and sought to create an impression of weightlessness, light and space by slender columns, flying buttresses and spacious naves with pointed arches and arched ceilings, as seen in the great medieval cathedrals. The Plateresque was a Renaissance style characteristic of early sixteenth-century Spanish architecture, typified by elaborate but delicate stone ornamentation covering the walls of buildings. The two styles would not be seen together, especially not in combination with the classical designs of Vignola. The description is a pastiche of nineteenth-century bourgeois taste.

p. 3 buskins: open-toed shoes that laced up round the calf, as used by ancient Greek and Roman actors.

p. 5 our dear Thiers: Adolphe Thiers was a famous French statesman and political and economic theorist of the nineteenth century. Galdós uses the same ironic nickname for the unprepossessing Francisco Bringas in the preceding novel, *Torment*.

p. 5 Paquito: the Bringas's eldest son Francisco de Asís, always referred to by this diminutive nickname.

p. 5 five thousand reals: one real was worth twenty-five céntimos and four reals was equivalent to one peseta, although the peseta was not made the official unit of currency until after the 1868 Revolution. For ease of reading I have standardised the monetary references given in different units into reals wherever possible.

p. 9 *Saint Helena*: small remote island in the South Atlantic where Napoleon Bonaparte died in 1821 after a six-year captivity at the hands of the English. He was buried by a stream with two weeping willows, and the English forbade any decoration of his tomb, which bore only the words '*Ci-gît*' (here lies). The subject was a popular one with Romantic painters.

p. 9 El Escorial: monastery in a town of the same name, near Madrid, where Spanish royalty are buried in state in a huge pantheon.

p. 9 Lamartine: Alphonse de Lamartine, French Romantic poet, 1790–1816. Galdós makes many satirical attacks on Romanticism in his novels.

p. 9 Pipaón: Pipaón is Rosalía's maiden name. In Spain, married women may use either their maiden names or their husband's name, prefaced by the possessive 'de'. Notably, though, Rosalía is referred to both here and in the novel's title by the familiar and even slightly pejorative article 'la', as in 'la de Bringas' and, here, 'la Pipaón'.

p. 9 capillatory artist: mocking neologism devised by the author to refer to a maker of hair pictures.

p. 10 Campo del Moro: area of parkland behind the Royal Palace.

p. 11 a cerberus with a tricorned hat: Cerberus is the three-headed dog guarding the entrance to the underworld in Greek mythology; this is a humorous reference to a member of the Civil Guard, part of whose uniform includes a curious three-pointed hat.

p. 12 Bayeu's angels: Francisco Bayeu y Subías (1734–95) was a Spanish painter, Goya's brother-in-law, and court painter to King Charles III. He did various frescoes in palaces and cathedrals throughout the country. The one of angels referred to here is probably *The Fall of the Giants*, which dates from 1764.

p. 13 Plaza de Oriente: a square in Madrid in front of the Royal Palace.

p. 13 Philip IV's horse: King of Spain from 1605–65, during the great age of empire. There is a statue of him on a horse, commissioned by Isabel II, in the Plaza de Oriente.

p. 15 García Grande's widow: Cándida, the Condesa de García Grande, who has appeared in previous novels by Galdós, such as *Torment* and *Our Friend Manso*.

p. 15 Raphael: Raffaello Sanzio (1483–1520), an Italian Renaissance painter and architect, best known for his Madonnas and frescoes in the Vatican.

p. 15 Tristán: Luis Tristán de Escamilla (1586–1640), a Spanish Baroque artist who studied with El Greco and was known for his paintings on religious subjects.

p. 16 Máximo Manso: philosophy teacher who is the protagonist of *Our Friend Manso*.

p. 17 Simancas archives: the important Royal Archives, founded in 1563 in Simancas, in the province of Valladolid.

p. 17 *Gasparini*: an Italian painter who lived in Spain for much of his life. The Bringas family name their room after the attractive rococo Gasparini Room in the Royal Palace.

p. 17 *Furriela*: old name for the Palace housekeeper, who kept the keys and oversaw the cleaning and maintenance of the building.

p. 18 I had auctioned off a couple of plots of timber and hay in Riofrío: Riofrío, near Segovia, is the site of some ancient common lands and also of one of the Royal Palaces. The narrator's illegal sale must therefore involve property that is not his, and that either belongs to the townspeople or to the Crown, necessitating the intervention of a high Palace official like Bringas to stop court proceedings against him.

p. 18 the five years O'Donnell was in power: Leopoldo O'Donnell (1809–67), a general and politician, was prime minister for five years (1858–63) at the head of an uneasy coalition of all the liberal parties, known as the Liberal Union. These were the boom years of Isabel II's reign, characterised by economic expansion, easy prosperity, moral relaxation, and extravagant life in high-society circles in Madrid.

p. 20 the Marquesa de Tellería: Milagros, one of Galdós's many recurring characters, who also appears in *León Roch's Family*, *Our Friend Manso*, *Torment*, *The Forbidden*, *Fortunata and Jacinta* and *Torquemada in the Fire*. Milagros, as a Marquesa, has a higher rank than her sister Tula, the Condesa.

p. 20 Alejandro Sánchez Botín: rich, vulgar and tyrannical character who was Isidora Rufete's lover in *The Disinherited*. Also appears in *The Forbidden*, *Fortunata and Jacinta* and *Torquemada in Purgatory*.

p. 20 Santa Barbara ... official salutes: St Barbara is the patron saint of artillerymen. Galdós is ironising here on the colonel's utter lack of battle experience.

p. 20 first civil war: the First Carlist War, 1833–9, arose from a quarrel over Isabel II's right to accede to the throne, which was disputed by her uncle, Carlos de Borbón. Don Carlos and his son and grandson continued to be a dynastic threat until the end of the century.

p. 20 *sword of Demosthenes . . . Garibaldi's soul*: Colonel Minio, in his ignorance, mistakes the names. He means to refer to the sword of Damocles, Penelope's veil, and Garibay's soul.

p. 22 **María**: María Egipcíaca is the beautiful, spoilt heroine of *León Roch's Family* who becomes a religious fanatic under the noxious influence of her brother Luis.

p. 22 **Gloria . . . Lantigua**: Gloria is the tragic heroine of *Gloria* (1876). She dies at the end of that novel. Her father, the lawyer, reappears later as a minor character in *Fortunata and Jacinta*.

p. 22 **the wish to be someone**: Galdós is alluding here to the motto associated with struggling middle classes in Madrid at the time, whom he frequently satirised for aspiring to a higher station in life than they could afford.

p. 23 **Agustín Caballero**: Rosalía's wealthy cousin, one of the main characters in *Torment*. At the end of that novel he causes a great scandal by going to live in Bordeaux with Amparo Sánchez Emperador without marrying her.

p. 23 **traditional Madrid costume**: the *maja* popularised by the artist Goya, who often portrayed the brazen, flamboyant lower-class women of the eighteenth century with their dark lace mantillas.

p. 24 **María Sudre**: also known as María Egipcíaca, Tula's niece.

p. 24 **León . . . the de Horro boy**: all three are characters who have already appeared as their adult selves in earlier novels. León Roch becomes María Egipcíaca's husband and Federico Cimarra marries León's great love, Pepa Fúcar, in *León Roch's Family* (1878). Rafael de Horro is one of Gloria's suitors in *Gloria*.

p. 24 **two extinguished candles**: the office being said is the Tenebrae, celebrated on Wednesday, Thursday and Frid..y of Holy Week, at which the Crucifixion is commemorated by gradually extinguishing the fifteen candles on a high triangular candelabra.

p. 24 **Washing of the Feet**: ceremony commemorating the washing of the disciples' feet by Christ on Easter Thursday. High Church and sometimes civil authorities washed the feet of twelve poor people, a procedure being copied here, with characteristic self-publicisation, by Queen Isabel II.

p. 28 blue and red ... tricorned hats: soldiers, officers, and constables from the Civil Guard.

p. 29 the sad story of her son-in-law: León Roch, who has a disastrous marriage to María Egipcíaca in *León Roch's Family*.

p. 31 *casaque*: fitting jacket with wide open sleeves, which flares out over the hips into an overskirt, often worn looped up at the sides.

p. 32 chemisette: underbodice, with or without sleeves, made of very lightweight fabric and trimmed with lace at the wrist and sleeves, worn by women in the nineteenth century as extra cover and decoration at the neck and sleeveline.

p. 33 Sobrino Brothers: famous department store in Madrid at the time, where Rosalía goes to buy the latest fashions and fabrics.

p. 34 polkas: short jacket with loose sleeves made of cashmere or velvet and lined with silk.

p. 35 canezou: muslin jacket or sleeveless bodice worn over dress.

p. 36 Gonzalo Torres: loan-shark who also appears in *Torment, The Forbidden* and the *Torquemada* cycle.

p. 37 *Las Toscanas*: famous hat store of the day.

p. 37 aigrette: spray of feathers used to trim a hat.

p. 39 Rubens ... Van Loo: Peter Paul Rubens (1577–1640), Flemish painter, known for his large, sensuous, fleshy models. Galdós likens Rosalía to a Rubens model on various occasions. Paolo Veronese (1528–88), Italian painter, who did vast canvases depicting allegorical, biblical and historical subjects. Charles-André Van Loo (1705–65), French painter, who specialised in elegant portraits of European royalty and high society in the mid-eighteenth century.

p. 40 Murillo's ... St Joseph: Bartolomé Murillo (1617–82), Spanish painter famous for his religious subjects.

p. 40 flowering staff: according to legend, Joseph's staff burst into flower as a sign that God had selected him as the Virgin Mary's husband. In iconographic tradition, the flowers usually shown were lilies, as a symbol of his purity.

p. 41 generals ... banished: the arrest of the generals was the prelude to the September Revolution that dethroned Queen Isabel. On 7 July 1868, the hard-line prime minister Luis González Bravo, the last prime minister under Isabel II, banished all the Liberal Union generals

(Serrano, Dulce, Zabala, Córdoba and Echagüe) to the Canary Islands for plotting against the Queen.

p. 43 *Atheneum*: intellectual club, to which Galdós and most of the politicians and male writers of his day belonged. It held lectures and debates and had a good library.

p. 43 *Mahabharata*: ancient epic poem from India, containing the Bhagavadgita, the most important religious text of Hinduism.

p. 44 Francisco Cucúrbitas: minor character who appears in *León Roch's Family* and *Miau*.

p. 44 going swimmingly for poor Pez: play on Pez's name, which means fish, and the Spanish phrase *estar como un pez en el agua*, to be in one's element, to be happy.

p. 44 Moderates: Conservative political party, founded in the 1830s, which represented the interests of the upper classes.

p. 45 *Et in Arcadia ego*: Latin phrase, meaning 'And I, too, have lived in Arcadia.' It was a popular Renaissance theme of nostalgia for a lost, bucolic past. Galdós ironises the notion here by putting it into the mouth of this self-seeking, complacent bureaucrat, complaining about his wife.

p. 47 Scropp's: famous contemporary toyshop on Madrid's Montera Street.

p. 49 mozambique: lightweight dress fabric of cotton and mohair, in fashion that year.

p. 51 Worth: Charles Frederick Worth, the famous English couturier of the nineteenth century, who worked in Vienna and Paris from the 1830s on, and designed clothes for Empress Eugenie, wife of Napoleon III of France, during the Second Empire (1852–70).

p. 51 González Bravo: Prime Minister Luis González Bravo (1811–71), formerly Minister of the Interior under the dictatorial Narváez, whom he replaced on the latter's death in the spring of 1868.

p. 52 Rotondo and Sons: major fabric store in Madrid at the time.

p. 52 barege: semi-transparent silk and wool mix, from Barèges in south-west France, where it was originally made.

p. 52 Marabou feathers: plumes from the wing or tail of the West African Marabou stork were often used for trimming hats.

p. 52 Moreno Rubio: physician whose clients are mainly the rich and famous. He appears in various Galdós novels.

p. 52 Poor Man's Cottage ... Artificial Mountain: attractions in the Retiro, a large park in the middle of Madrid, built in 1630 as a complex of Palace and pleasure gardens for the Royal Family but subsequently modified and gradually opened to the public.

p. 53 Ferdinand VII: despotic king who reigned from 1814–33, during the Romantic period.

p. 54 Newton: Isaac Newton (1642–1727), English mathematician.

p. 55 'gallant gesture': expression made famous by Emilio Castelar, Rector of Madrid University, who used it ironically to criticise Isabel II in an 1865 article in which he attacked her proposal to sell off property belonging to the Royal Heritage in order to bolster the Treasury funds. This caused an outcry, because she had no authority to sell off Crown property as if it were her own, and also because she proposed keeping twenty-five per cent of the profit for herself. Castelar was dismissed for publishing the article, which led to student demonstrations. These were brutally repressed by the government on 10 April 1865, known as St Daniel's Night, in which Galdós participated.

p. 58 Archena: pretty spa town in the southern province of Murcia, famous for its sulphurous hot springs, which have been used for medicinal purposes since Roman times.

p. 59 novena: Catholic devotion consisting of nine days of prayers, or services divided into nine parts.

p. 60 Bonelli ... Trouchín: owners of famous restaurants in Madrid during the nineteenth century.

p. 61 Tobacconist Order: non-existent religious order. Milagros is punning rather cattily on the fact that the woman's dress is tobacco-coloured and that tobacco is sold in *estancos* (tobacconist's).

p. 63 Money that's left idle ... problems: Milagros is parroting a version of Adolphe Thiers's financial theories about the importance of investment for the capitalist system.

p. 67 Montpensier: Antonio of Orleans, Duke of Montpensier and son of Louis-Philippe, who was the former king of France until 1848. The Duke married Isabel II's sister, Luisa Fernanda. He was the Liberal Unionist conspirators' candidate to replace Isabel II on the throne in the event of an uprising, and he was officially requested to leave the country in early July 1868, as the threat of revolution grew clearer.

p. 72 St Lucy: patron saint of eyesight and the blind.

p. 75 Watteau: Jean Antoine Watteau (1684–1721), French painter at the court of Versailles. The Watteau style in jackets and coats usually referred to a loose, sack back.

p. 79 St Anthony's Day: 13 June.

p. 79 belladonna and laudanum: belladonna is a drug made from extracts of the nightshade plant, used to relieve pain, among other things. Laudanum is tincture of opium, also used as an analgesic and to soothe the mind and produce well-being.

p. 79 *Ainda mais*: Portuguese and Galician for 'besides'.

p. 81 Feast of St John: 24 June.

p. 90 Cestona: northern spa town in a mountainous and picturesque area of the Basque Country, which people visited to enjoy the tranquillity and take the spring waters.

p. 90 Balsaín: forest belonging to the Crown.

p. 91 La Granja: Royal Palace and gardens near Madrid.

p. 91 Grimaldi ... Ursins: Jerónimo Grimaldi (1720–86) was a famous diplomat from the powerful Genovese Grimaldi family; Marie-Anne de la Trémoille, Princess of the Ursins, was a French noblewoman who became confidante and lady-in-waiting to Philip V's wife and exercised great influence in Spanish affairs of state between 1701–14.

p. 94 Refugio Sánchez Emperador: poor relation of Rosalía's. Her sister Amparo was the heroine of a previous novel involving the Bringas family, *Torment*, at the end of which Amparo unexpectedly eloped to Bordeaux to live in sin with Agustín Caballero. Refugio has since become a kept woman herself.

p. 98 generals had arrived in the Canary Islands ... Lequeitio: the three allusions to contemporary events here would place the date in the last week of July. The exiled generals sailed to the Canary Islands on 13 July. General Juan Prim, leader of the conspiracy movement, was in exile in London, but obtained permission in late July from the French government to go to Vichy to take the waters for his liver complaint. In the process, he obtained Emperor Napoleon III's agreement not to oppose the uprising, as long as Prim guaranteed he would not put the Duke of Montpensier on the Spanish throne. The Queen was about to move to her summer palace in La Granja, just outside Madrid, and then on to a northern spa town, Lequeitio, in the Basque country.

p. 98 Cabrera had been to visit Don Carlos: Ramón Cabrera (1806–77) was a diehard Carlist general; Don Carlos de Borbón was the latest Carlist pretender to the Spanish throne. Don Carlos, aware that Isabel's reign was tottering, summoned a general meeting of his followers in London on 20 July 1868, to discuss what to do in the event of the Queen's fall. This allusion is another indication of the instability of the monarchy and of the forces of opposition massing abroad, about to move in for the kill.

p. 98 *non possumus*: Latin, 'we cannot'.

p. 103 Pawnsville: Galdós is punning here on the idiom *llevar a Peñaranda*, 'to take to Peñaranda', which meant to take to a pawnshop, based on a sound similarity between *empeñar* (to pawn) and *Peñaranda* (the name of a town in Salamanca province).

p. 104 Navalcarnero: small, poor town near Madrid.

p. 108 Ibrahim Clarete: mocking nickname for González Bravo, prime minister at the time. Ibrahim was an Arabic name and Clarete refers to claret, meaning that he was a drinker.

p. 116 the Castellana: central boulevard that leads north from the Paseo del Prado. Constructed in 1860, it was frequented by the aristocracy and haute bourgeoisie who paraded along it in their carriages.

p. 119 Mr Mousey: Rosalía diminishes her husband's manliness by likening him to the legendary character *ratoncito Pérez* (the Pérez mouse), the subject of an ancient Hispanic folk-tale for children about the marriage of a timid, foolish and submissive mouse to an attractive and authoritative ant. The comparison is comic and insulting; in Rosalía's mind, Francisco, compared to Manuel Pez, is as pedestrian and ineffectual as a shy little mouse and as nondescript as someone called Pérez (one of the most common surnames in Spanish, and, incidentally, Galdós's own first surname).

p. 120 St Rita: saint to whom Spaniards pray for the impossible.

p. 122 gazpacho: cold vegetable soup.

p. 125 Manzanares: the river that runs through Madrid. It is notoriously small and polluted.

p. 126 Biarritz: fashionable resort in Southern France.

p. 129 González Bravo's policies: a reference to the hardline policies of the prime minister, which precipitated the revolution.

p. 129 La Iberia: left-wing newspaper in Madrid at the time.

p. 129 the Progressives ... Democrats: Bringas is showing his Conservative colours in this list of dislikes. The Progressives and the Democrats were parliamentary parties which represented the urban working classes; the National Militia was a body organised by the left-wing liberals; Espartero was a Progressive general who represented the left in the Liberal Union coalition; the Riego Hymn was an anthem sung by Spanish liberals and republicans, named after General Rafael de Riego, executed in 1823 by the despotic Ferdinand VII.

p. 129 la Concha and la Zurriola: a beach and an esplanade in San Sebastián.

p. 134 Torquemada: one of Galdós's most terrifying recurring characters, a pitiless moneylender. It is a sign of Rosalía's ignorance of the terrain of finance that she does not recognise his name.

p. 135 a four hundred escudo note: a Portuguese note equivalent to four thousand reals.

p. 136 Hermogenes: comic character in a play entitled *The New Comedy* (1792) by the Spanish author Leandro Fernández Moratín.

p. 137 Prado: referred in the nineteenth century to an attractive area of tree-lined avenues and fountains, not, as it does now, to the famous art museum of the same name. The Prado was the favourite area for strolling around in summer because of the shade of its trees, and it was frequented by all the most illustrious members of society who went there to see and be seen.

p. 138 St Jerome ... Andalusian: popular bathing spots along the Manzanares river in Madrid.

p. 139 horchata: popular cold drink sold in Spain in the summers, made from ground tiger nuts.

p. 141 St Lawrence's Day: 10 August.

p. 141 Arcachon: fashionable seaside resort in southern France.

p. 141 St Jean de Luz: small village on the French Atlantic coast.

p. 146 María Alacoque and Bernadette: Catholic visionaries, subsequently made saints.

p. 147 San Isidro: patron saint of Madrid, whose feast day is celebrated on 15 May with dancing and fireworks.

p. 156 pisciform: another punning allusion to Pez's name.

p. 158 Krausism: school of thought based on the works of the early nineteenth-century philosopher German Karl Christian von Krause, which became very popular among left-wing intellectuals in Spain in the latter half of the century. Krausism offered, amongst other things, a way to reconcile spiritual faith with rationality, which made it highly suspect to right-wing Conservatives and neo-Catholics.

p. 162 the inquisitor: reference to Torquemada, the moneylender, who shares his name with the first Inquisitor General.

p. 174 Herodias: second wife of Herod Antipas and mother of Salome. It was she who told Salome to ask for the head of John the Baptist on a plate.

p. 177 Prim: General Juan Prim (1814–70), Catalan general and statesman who masterminded the revolution and persuaded Admiral Topete of the Navy to declare against the Queen. Prim was to become prime minister under the Republic.

p. 177 Golconda: ruined city in Southern India, once the capital of a famous Muslim kingdom, famous for its diamond cutting and synonymous with great wealth.

p. 179 Novaliches: General Pavía, the Marqués de Novaliches, commander of the Loyalist forces of Isabel II.

p. 179 Alcolea: village near Córdoba and site of a strategic bridge over the river Guadalquivir where the revolutionary forces, commanded by General Caballero de Rodas, won a decisive victory over the Loyalist army on 28 September 1868.

p. 185 To tell the truth, of course: these words are one of the verbal tics of another Galdós character, the inveterate storyteller José Ido del Sagrario, from the previous novel, *Torment*. They add another unsettling query as to the narrator's identity and reliability, raising the possibility that he could be a demented hack novelist.

This section aims to provide a glimpse of some of the polemics to which this novel has given rise. Because it was one of the first Realist novels to be published in Spain, contemporary responses to *That Bringas Woman* were polarised around the issue of whether Realism itself was an exciting innovation or a waste of readers' time. After his death in 1920, Galdós virtually disappeared from critical view for some decades, partly because the tide in Spanish letters had turned in favour of modernism instead, and partly because Galdós's left-wing sympathies made him suspicious to the Franco dictatorship that ruled the country from 1939 on. By the time he was rediscovered, the value of Realism and of this novel were taken for granted. Twentieth-century critics have devoted considerable effort to debating instead the precise nature of the moral and political vision of the novel, focusing on the representation of Rosalía and the role of the narrator. Rosalía is clearly satirised both as an individual and as a representative of her society: but was Galdós's portrayal of her meant to arouse contempt or sympathy? On this issue critics have drawn diametrically opposed conclusions; the move has been largely one of moral condemnation beginning with Joaquín Casalduero until the mid 1970s, when more sympathetic voices began to be heard.

Since 1980, criticism has been largely historical, narratological, feminist and poststructuralist. An important line of criticism pioneered by Peter Bly uncovered and interpreted the complex layer of historical allusions which structure the novel. Of late, critics such as Paul Julian Smith, Akiko Tsuchiya and Elena Delgado have begun applying poststructural models of analysis to *That Bringas Woman*, arguing that it unsettles rather than reinforces readers' notion of objectivity or reality; these critics sidestep their predecessors' urge to determine the author's moral stance, since for postmodern thinkers ambiguity is precisely the point of the novel.

Since *That Bringas Woman* has become part of the vast and

growing Galdós critical industry, I cannot hope to do justice to the large number of valuable studies that exist. The following passages are intended merely to give a flavour of some of the arguments that have been made, while the bibliography that follows gives further references to Galdós scholarship written in English.

Luis Alfonso, *That Bringas Woman, La Epoca,* año 36, número 11502 (2 July 1884), p. 3. Objects to the style and subject matter of *That Bringas Woman*, which he attributes to the influence of the French naturalist Zola; claims popular response to the novel is entirely hostile.

I have talked to many different people, especially to booksellers, before printing these words, and having consulted public opinion and noted the widespread consensus on this point, I write that 'people do not like *[That Bringas Woman]*', instead of simply saying that 'I did not like it' ... I am convinced that Pérez Galdós's Contemporary Novels started to go awry with *The Disinherited*. Until then ... he had followed the beautiful lines of the English novel, and his works revealed the fruitful influence of Dickens, Thackeray and others. But in the interval between the publication of *León Roch's Family* and *The Disinherited*, the works of Zola caused a great stir and acquired universal fame; no doubt our writer became captivated by them, and, unfortunately, the results of this influence soon began to show.

Details overwhelm the whole; design, plot, and dramatic interest have given way to analysis, description and inventory; form drowns out content; the whore has supplanted the lady, the rabble has replaced urbane society, and vices have taken the place of passions ...

[T]he mania for the minute and the trivial, the delight of the naturalist school, began to wreak havoc in Pérez Galdós, and was followed by puerile sophism, a reliable indicator of decadent art. Thus we see the veiled use of ugly and lewd colloquial language ... the mixing of recent political events and great living personages into the fiction; and, finally, the habit of linking one novel to others, making a series; but not as in the Comédie Humaine, for these characters appear and disappear, in a way that confuses the reader who does not have access to all the previous novels or does not wish to reread them ...

Galdós should not have given way to financial interests

improper of such a famous and highly respected gentleman, by filling page after page without action or motive as he does in *That Bringas Woman*, just to print 'one more volume', before going on his summer holiday ... He should not have twice brought a little girl into the novel (as he does in *That Bringas Woman*) merely to describe an attack of indigestion, which twice ends in vomiting ...

In my opinion, Galdós simply has to persuade himself that, despite Zola and the Goncourt brothers, the novel is not a 'study', nor a 'human document', nor a 'physiological analysis,' nor any other such nonsense (even though many such things belong in it); it is first and foremost a novel.

Jacinto Octavio Picón, 'That Bringas Woman', El Imparcial, año 18, número 6145 (14 July 1884), p. 1. A novelist himself, Picón was enthusiastic about the work, which he considers a feat of realistic description by a master writer, and argues that it also provides a moral lesson.

Galdós's latest social study [is] crammed with detail and alive with bourgeois characters of the ignorant, small-minded and pretentious variety, whose little flaws lead them into great wrongdoing; amongst them you often see sly friends, blind husbands and women who find themselves sinning not because they love sin, but because they lie awake at night dreaming of temptation, which appears clad in silk garments in the latest fashions and bearing a noose of every kind of lace to strangle virtue ...

I shall say nothing of how Galdós paints the Bringas household, where the pennypinching thrift of the husband and the foolish vanity of his wife are locked in perpetual silent struggle ... many episodes ... enrich the book, making it a mirror where the myriad scenes of real life are reproduced ... it is not possible to condense in one article all the treasures of observation which have been lavished on the pages of this book ... I am one of those who ... considers Galdós a master, and my benevolence might appear to be favouritism. Let me simply say that thanks to him, the public is becoming accustomed to the notion that the novel could be something more than mere entertainment, and that in its pages the novelist should paint social customs honestly, so that mankind can recognise its defects and attempt to remedy them, or at least be made ashamed of them.

And if anyone thinks that it is disagreeable to see the squalid

side of society reflected, let him recall that it is not the mirror's
fault if the face it reflects is an ugly one.

Orlando, 'Spanish Novels of the Year in Literature', *Revista de
España* vol. 100 (October 1884), pp. 430–48. This reviewer is
favourable to Galdós's work as a whole, but violently critical of
That Bringas Woman as a subject unworthy of the author and
incompetently executed.

Rarely has public opinion on literary matters been so unanimous
as in the case of Pérez Galdós's latest production. Some readers
never found their way out of the labyrinth which Pez and his
companion enter to seek out Francisco Bringas; others could not
stomach the hair picture Bringas makes in payment for favours
received from the Pez family; many people of both sexes felt half-
stifled by all those ribbons and bows and materials, and confused
by all the hustle and bustle and toing and froing of the main
character, always intent on the same goal and pursuing the same
end; all agree that this novel is a flimsy thing for such a famous
author. And those who have issued such a harsh verdict are well
within their rights, for *That Bringas Woman* is unworthy of
comparison to the previous publications of this outstanding
genius, both in its subject matter and characterisation.

When one lays down this book, one is full of questions. Why
did he try to make a novel out of such base and shoddy materials?
Why, since the theme and the characters are the same [as in the
previous novel], does he insist on trotting them out once again,
when in fact the whole lot should have been condensed into a few
pages and added on at the end of *Torment*, which would have
sufficed to show what a flippertigibbet that Pipaón de la Barca
woman was. I do not exaggerate; if the descriptions of the upper
floors of the Royal Palace and the religious ceremony of the
Washing of the Feet, both of which are entirely extraneous to the
novel, were cut out, the rest could occupy no more than half a
dozen chapters if it is not to fall from the reader's hands ... The
events repeat themselves with crushing monotony, since there are
no new characters; Mrs Bringas's creditors merely pursue her ever
more hotly until they drive her to give herself to Pez, according to
the author's preconceived plan. Her plot to remove poor Bringas's
money is too artificial and childish to be amusing, nor does her
affair with Pez arouse our curiosity, for not only is it uninteresting,

but one can see it coming from the beginning, which makes it lose what little charm it had to offer.

Only at the end is there one scene in which ... one finds a certain novelty of form, and it is the one where Rosalía, who has said the most terrible things about Amparo and Refugio, goes to the latter's house ... to ask her for money ... She goes through unbelievable torments, because Refugio uses the occasion to humiliate her; but the masterly way she tramples on Rosalía's pride does not fit her character, and it would have been preferable if her speech had been designed to fit her personality better.

Cristóbal Botella, *El Noticiero* año 2, número 321 (13 October 1884), p. 3. Hostile to naturalism, which he believes has corrupted Galdós's talents.

We already know that literary realism, in its proper, true sense, has been around for a long time; it is something we encounter within our own country, from Cervantes to the present day, in the best works of our writers, with the exception of those who fell into the errors and exaggerations of romanticism.

Pérez Galdós seems to have become the latest Spanish writer to fall victim to French models. He used to be an idealist by aesthetic inclination, and thanks to that, he won his first and greatest triumphs. But then he fell in love with realism, which led him to commit some great mistakes, his only failures. *Doctor Centeno*, *Torment* and *That Bringas Woman* are the products of the ugly laws of artistic naturalism working on Galdós's powerful intelligence ... Meanwhile, the masters of the idealist school ... have fallen utterly silent, and some suppose they have retired from the field for ever.

Leopoldo Alas (Clarín). *Obras Completas* vol. 1, *Galdós* (Madrid: Renacimiento, 1912), pp. 135–6. This eminent novelist and critic praises *That Bringas Woman* in passing in a review of another work by Galdós, and explains that critical reaction was so overwhelmingly negative on its publication that he could not find a publisher for a positive review.

As bad luck would have it, I myself could find nowhere to put in a good word about *That Bringas Woman*, even though I have reviewed every other novel Galdós has ever written.

I must say in passing that I agree with the French critic [Léo Quesnel, who had praised the novel]; and even though I think

That Bringas Woman has some flaws, notably a lack of structure, I believe it is a National Episode of Contemporary Life, that is to say, a masterpiece of observation and perspicacity.

Joaquín Casalduero, *Vida y obra de Galdós (1843–1920)* (Madrid: Gredos, 4th edition, 1974), pp. 81–2. This work was first published in Buenos Aires, in 1943, during the Franco dictatorship, which was generally hostile to Galdós's work. Casalduero was the first critic to point to the link between Rosalía, Queen Isabel II, and Spain, a reading of the heroine as historical allegory which was to prove a powerful influence on generations of critics to come.

The novel is a portrait of the social environment in Madrid in the last years of Isabel II's reign. Mrs Bringas's life is the life of an individual and a nation at the same time, not only because it reflects the cultural, historical and social characteristics of her country, which is only to be expected, but because the narrow, sordid, vulgar and empty circles in which Bringas's wife moves are developed to coincide with those of Isabel II's reign. Rosalía's husband is called Francisco: they live in an upper apartment in the Palace. The same melody is playing in her dreams in the upper floors of the Palace as in Their Royal Highnesses's rooms, albeit in a different key, both as regards their marital life and their economic and social life . . .

Poor Francisco Bringas, that pusillanimous and unprepossessing character, is based on the king. His temporary loss of vision hints at another form of blindness, whose significance Galdós needlessly underlines by making it coincide with Rosalía's adultery . . . She neglects all her duties as a mother and wife, and yet her imagination goes no further than buying a piece of fabric or doing up an old dress.

José Montesinos, *Galdós*, 3 vols. (Madrid: Castalia, 1969). Extracts from vol. 2, pp. 98–130. A panoramic study in Spanish of all the Contemporary Novels. Montesinos reads Galdós as a moral humourist, a canonical literary figure, and continues Casalduero's negative response to Rosalía.

Rosalía is a hateful woman, perhaps the most hateful character Galdós ever invented, but one of the truest . . .

That Bringas Woman begins with some of the most humorous pages Galdós ever wrote. One of the Pez daughters has died, and

Francisco, who owes them some favours, has come up with a grandiose scheme to stay in the parents' good graces and which will only cost him fifty reals [sic]: to use the hair of the dead girl and other members of the family, in chestnut, various shades of blond, and white hair belonging to the mother, to create a cenotaph, a representation of a romantic cemetery made up of motifs taken from various vignettes which are described with great skill ... The cenotaph is never finished, but not through the artist's fault, for it costs him very dear. Galdós's creativity here reaches incredible heights. It is a stroke of pure genius to begin the narrative with this unimaginable piece of stupidity on Bringas's part ...

The theme is a familiar one: the problems of a social climber, married to a genuinely humble man, with no ambitions, whose virtues stem from an incurable miserliness ...

Galdós portrayed Rosalía with great venom, and for that same reason with implacable veracity. Rosalía Pipaón, product of that degenerate society of Palace servants, is a woman of little intelligence and even less education, both of which are dwarfed by an immense pride which remains largely inexplicable, unless we attribute it to the pestiferous atmosphere in the Palace.

Peter Bly, 'The Use of Distance in Galdós's *La de Bringas*', *Modern Language Review* vol. 69 (1974): 88–97. Extracts from pp. 88–9 and 97. In this important article, Bly identifies the importance of disorder and distortion as features of narrative technique in the novel and argues that they expose the disordered and distorted moral vision of the characters.

In general, literary historians have [described] Galdós's *novelas contemporáneas* as accurately observed pictures of nineteenth-century Madrid ... However, a careful examination of the use of physical space and distance in *La de Bringas*, supposedly one of the most representative novels of this Realist style, will show ... that Galdós goes beyond a simple objective photograph of the material world. He is constantly breaking down what one would expect to be the normal spatial relationships ... to produce a picture of disorder, confusion and repulsion. He even disrupts the normal literary 'distance' between the novel and its reader. The conscious manipulation will appear inevitable, if he is to expose without ambiguity the true moral fibre of his characters ...

The [servants'] quarters [in the Royal Palace] are ... a disordered collection of different structures and spaces, but Galdós's words go beyond an impartial relation of detail to express his deep feelings about the area: it is a chaotic jumble, where the normal perspectives of the physical world are broken down ... [His] images increase the impression of confusion and disorder, to the point of distortion and inversion. The locality is like a city with its own streets or districts, or a subterranean labyrinth, comparable to that of Hades, or of the Cretan Minotaur ... Selecting the Bringas family as his particular example of [its] deranged inhabitants, he is at pains to indicate that their dwelling is representative of the outer macrocosm of the Palace, just as the Palace itself is a microcosm of the greater entity, Madrid ...

[T]hroughout the novel ... the author subtly disrupts the normal physical spaces between buildings and places, either shortening or elongating them, pushing them out of their normal perspective ... The resultant close-up pictures are dehumanised, distorted: people seem like marionettes, events and material objects repulsive and vulgar ... Galdós uses the disruption of normal perspectives to expose the real truth about this period in Spanish history. The artist has to use a special, deformed technique to capture accurately a special, deformed society. Normal perspectives and visions do not suffice. To ensure that his reader does not lose the importance of his special technique, Galdós disrupts those traditional literary distances which join the reader to the book: the narrator is to a certain extent unreliable, and the book itself seems to fit awkwardly into the chronological sequence of the series thitherto published, as if it were 'odd man out'. Indeed, *La de Bringas* is an exception amongst Galdós's novels, for it is surprising to note that the reader hardly sympathises with any of the characters: Refugio, to a certain extent, but she is a minor character, and hardly a tragic victim of society's ways ... The distance between the reader and the novel is so distorted that he cannot identify with any character. And that is Galdós's intention ... He allows the reader to think for a while that he is in a normal world, but only to undermine this impression further on.

Stephen Gilman, *Galdós and the Art of the European Novel: 1867–1887* (Princeton University Press, 1981), pp. 140–1. Gilman reads *That Bringas Woman* as part of a number of novels about the morally bankrupt and infected nature of the up-and-coming Spanish bourgeoisie.

The display of painfully diseased minds in these novels ... is remarkable for its diversity and perversity, but perhaps the sickest mind of all is that of Rosalía Pipaón de la Barca, otherwise known as '*la de Bringas*'. A middle-aged and emphatically corseted avatar of Isidora [protagonist of *The Disinherited*] ... she has none of the redeeming charm and youthful spontaneity of her predecessor. On the contrary, her ingrained bourgeois money-consciousness is accompanied by a hypocrisy so tawdry that we actually enjoy her final series of humiliations. As a result, when the lady, following the representational symbol of Isidora, converts herself into a symbol of national degeneration by surrendering to Pez *père* a few days before the collapse of the Monarchy, the reader feels no personal involvement. Late nineteenth-century Spain may, indeed, be represented not unfairly by a presumptuous, surreptitious, and, worst of all, morally self-righteous whore, but the *reader* has never sympathised with her. Nor has Galdós tricked him into identifying with her. He can share in the satirical denunciation and avoid personal responsibility, a comforting situation ...

At the very end, however, if Galdós's supposedly complacent and scandalised reader reads closely enough, he is due for a shock. The hitherto more or less invisible narrator openly confesses that he, too, secretly has been a client of the fallen bourgeoise, a client all the more despicable when he refuses, for ostensibly moral reasons, to continue to assist her financially[.]

Alda Blanco and Carlos Blanco Aguinaga, Introduction to their critical edition of the novel in Spanish, *La de Bringas* (Madrid: Castalia, 1985). Extracts from pp. 28–37. The editors apply a Marxist reading to demystify the economic system that produces Rosalía's adultery, until then seen by critics in moral terms only.

[T]he novel is specifically about the crisis and disappearance of ... a whole way of life ... The conflict is clearly announced: instead of always paying in cash, there now exists the possibility of buying on credit; two very different and mutually exclusive economies ... Now it could be argued that our analysis of *That Bringas Woman* does violence to the novel ... one could insist that, on a much more simple and obvious level, this story is *really* about the vagaries of a particular lady who is dazzled by the world of appearances and the wish to 'be someone', something her social position does not permit, and who falls inevitably into the precarious lifestyle of a world of hoaxers. According to this

reading, it would be an ironic version of a sad, old human story
repeated over and over again at different times and in different
countries ... But the most profound critique in *That Bringas
Woman* lies ... in the fact that Galdós provides an analysis of the
foundations of the new bourgeois society, which is based on
commodities, and of the position of women in that society ...

It is clear ... that the higher her position on the social scale, the
greater a woman's 'credit' was, whether it derived from her own
income or on money coming from her husband. But except for
women with their own fortunes – as well as for prostitutes – it is
always the case that commodities had to pass directly or symboli-
cally through men, those who controlled the money supply, in
order to reach women. Thus we could posit the following diagram:

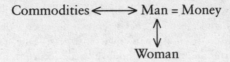

Since women are thus excluded from a direct relationship to
commodities, they can only acquire them via men, by establishing
a credit relationship. The establishment of this relationship, much
more precarious than paying in cash, suggests the following
diagram, in which the dotted line is the alternative to the direct
control over commodities usually exercised by men:

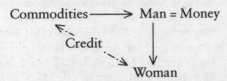

This is exactly the situation in the novel ... When Rosalía finally
realises that her relationship to commodities places her irremediably outside the traditional circuit of commodities to women via
male mediation [because of Bringas's meanness], she begins to see
that that circuit, on which she cannot act directly, is the basis for
her lack of liberty ...

However, if she does not work and has none of her own capital,
how is Rosalía to manage? ... [W]hat can Rosalía offer in
exchange for what she owes? Since she does not own anything
except herself, since her own person is the only thing that can be
emancipated, that can circulate freely, her only alternative is to
become a commodity herself.

Bridget Aldaraca, 'La de Bringas: The Myth of Private and Public Spheres', chapter 6 of El ángel del hogar: Galdós and the Ideology of Domesticity in Spain (North Carolina Studies in the Romance Languages and Literatures, 1991). Extracts from pp. 169–75. This critic objects to the moral condemnation of Rosalía as a character and argues that her actions are not only understandable but defensible in terms of a search for personal autonomy within a patriarchal society.

> The critics have tended to interpret La de Bringas as a novel about 'Rosalía's moral degradation', even imposing upon her the burden of symbolising the Isabeline monarchy and by extension, the entire spectrum of Spanish society ... The narrator explains Rosalía's passion for clothes in accordance with the folklore of the period, that most women are born with an instinct for adornment that necessitates some form of social repression, since women are not capable of controlling their own instincts. One taste of the forbidden fruit and they say goodbye to all decorum. But Rosalía's feelings towards her finery ... are much more complex. Her wardrobe receives the care and enthusiasm she cannot feel for her husband who has given her four children without ever inspiring in her sexual desire ... But Rosalía's dresses are even more than a substitute for sexual fulfilment. Her finery is also a visible manifestation of a new, precarious and secret autonomy ... Unlike Emma Bovary, or Rosamond Vincy in Middlemarch, who are capable of destroying their husbands with a terrifying cynicism, Rosalía Bringas oscillates between a desire to satisfy her own ambitions and the guilty realisation that her husband has provided for her and her children to the best of his ability. When Bringas suffers a relapse, Rosalía feels pity and concern ...
>
> At this point, Galdós moves definitively away from what might have been a Zolaesque treatment of women's fascination for luxury goods. The image of the consuming woman out of control (like the sexually insatiable woman) is the diabolical other of the angel in the house. At one extreme we have Zola's Nana, at the other, Dickens's Little Dorrit. Galdós breaks with the literary stereotype, because Rosalía is capable, like a man, of regaining her lost self-control ...
>
> Unlike the purchase of the luxurious Parisian cape, Rosalía's loan to the Marquesa fulfils a different need, although both acts demonstrate her longing to exercise control over her life. But the loan is connected with a desire to earn money, not to spend it,

with an ambition of entrepreneurship. She wishes to enter the public sphere through the male entrance that opens on to the world of finances, rather than entering through the lady's side door that opens into a sphere restricted to consumption. Prevented, however, by both her sex and her economic circumstances from entering directly into the creation of wealth, Rosalía has developed the characteristics of the ambitious but insecure social climber. What provides the comic element in *La de Bringas* is Galdós's caustic depiction of the Madrid society which Rosalía has set out to conquer.

Hazel Gold, 'Narrative Beginnings in *La de Bringas*', *The Reframing of Realism: Galdós and the Discourses of the Nineteenth-century Spanish Novel* (Durham and London, Duke University Press, 1993), pp. 30–1. Gold explains the hair picture as highly unusual kind of 'frame' for the novel, one that satirises the misuse of Realism as the meaningless agglomeration of physical details. Galdós's technique, she argues, purposefully disorients and estranges the reader *vis-à-vis* the objects under contemplation, in a way that anticipates the Russian Formalists' goal of *defamiliarisation*. She points to the fetishistic overtones of the hair cenotaph and to the burlesquing of the 'museological impulse, the compulsion to collect and view for one's private enjoyment' (p. 42) seen both in Bringas's and other characters' behaviour.

[In the choice of the hair picture as the opening], Galdós lays as the foundation for his novel a triad of closely related concepts: the miser's compulsion to hoard capital, the artist-collector's impulse to assemble museums for private enjoyment, and the fetishist's drive to eroticise a fragmented and highly personalised object. In each instance, there occurs a deracination of an object from its quotidian context. Money is removed from circulation; the art work is divested of any and all utilitarian functions and is instead enshrined in the gallery; the whole person as erotic stimulus is discounted in favour of the isolated part. In each case, too, an air of covertness or the clandestine accompanies the activities of seeing and possessing. The miser's furtive hiding and counting of his or her treasure is comparable to the private viewing of art in a personal collection or the shameful and secretive contemplation of the fetish. Naturally enough, when the object is removed from its natural environment and its prestige disproportionately exaggerated in relation to its raw worth, the result is an actual or figurative distortion of the fields of perception and representation. Examples of such distortion in *La de Bringas* include the disruptive effects of radical myopia (microscopic effect), extreme tunnel vision (telescopic effect), and a generalised breakdown of optic structures that takes place as highlights and relief outlines are submerged and disappear into a sea of minutiae (a sort of reverse pointillism).

In this way, *La de Bringas* sets up a system of interlocking activities – seeing, possessing, displaying – engaged in by the protagonists and others in their circle. *La de Bringas* is in the final analysis a novel about perception and acquisition, voyeurism and exhibitionism. That these complementary activities are shown to be self-defeating stands as one of Galdós's more scathing indictments of the Spanish middle class, poised for a revolution which would effect no real and lasting transformation of society, a revolution that was itself all show or empty display.

SUGGESTIONS FOR FURTHER READING

English translations of Galdós's novels

The Shadow (1870), trans. Karen Austin (Athens: Ohio University Press, 1980).

The Golden Fountain Café (1871), trans. Walter Rubin (New York: Latin American Literary Review Press, 1989).

Our Friend Manso (1882), trans. Robert Russell (New York: Columbia University Press, 1987).

Fortunata and Jacinta (1887), trans. Agnes Moncy (London: Penguin Books, 1988).

The Unknown (1888–9), trans. Karen Austin (Lewiston: Edwin Mellen, 1991).

Reality (1889), trans. Karen Austin (Lewiston: Edwin Mellen, 1992).

Torquemada in the Fire (1889), trans. Nicholas Round (Glasgow: University of Glasgow, 1985).

Angel Guerra (1890–91), trans. Karen Austin (Lewiston: Edwin Mellen, 1990).

Torquemada (1893–5), trans. Frances López-Morillas (New York: Columbia University Press, 1986).

Nazarín (1895), trans. Jo Labanyi (Oxford and New York: Oxford University Press, 1993).

Galdós's Life

Berkowitz, H. Chonon, *Perez Galdós: Spanish Liberal Crusader* (Madison: University of Wisconsin Press, 1948). The only English-language biography.

General Studies of Galdós

Bly, Peter, *Galdós's Novel of the Historical Imagination: A Study of the Contemporary Novels* (Liverpool: Francis Cairns, 1983). Overview of all the important Contemporary Novels and the historical background needed to interpret them.

Engler, Kay, *The Structure of Realism: The 'Novelas Contemporáneas' of Benito Pérez Galdós* (Chapel Hill: North Carolina Studies in the Romance Languages and Literatures, 1977). Introduction to Galdós's literary techniques.

Jagoe, Catherine, *Ambiguous Angels: Gender in the Novels of Galdós* (Berkeley and London: University of California Press, 1994). On social context and gender issues in Galdós's Contemporary Novels.

Labanyi, Jo, *Galdós* (London: Longman, 1993). Anthology containing samples of Galdós's theories of the novel and a collection of recent critical articles.

Pattison, Walter T., *Benito Pérez Galdós* (Boston: Twayne, 1975). Introduction to the author's life and works.

Urey, Diane F., *Galdós and the Irony of Language* (Cambridge: Cambridge University Press, 1982). Textual readings demonstrating mechanisms of irony and humour in Galdós.

Studies of That Bringas Woman

Bly, Peter, 'Galdós, the Madrid Royal Palace and the September 1868 Revolution', *Revista Canadiense de Estudios Hispánicos* 5 (1980), pp. 1–17. Galdós's attitudes to the September Revolution. *Pérez Galdós: La de Bringas* (London: Grant and Cutler/Tamesis Books, 1981). Critical guide which explicates all central facets of the novel.

Charnon-Deutsch, Lou, *Gender and Representation: Women in Spanish Realist Fiction* (Amsterdam: John Benjamins, 1990), pp. 125–35. Feminist reading of *That Bringas Woman* as a meditation on distorted family power-relations.

Hemingway, Maurice, 'Narrative Ambiguity and Situational Ethics in *La de Bringas*', *Galdós' House of Fiction: Papers Given at the Birmingham Galdós Colloquium*, eds. A. H. Clarke and E. J. Rodgers (Llandysul, Wales: Dolphin Book Co., 1991), pp. 15–27. The moral indeterminacy of Rosalía as a character.

Labanyi, Jo, 'The Problem of Framing in *La de Bringas*', *Anales Galdosianos* vol. 25 (1990), pp. 25–34. Studies transgressive behaviours in the novel, relating the bourgeoisie's preoccupation with adultery and overspending to the peculiar behaviour of the narrator.

Lowe, Jennifer, 'Galdós's Presentation of Rosalía in *La de Bringas*', *Hispanófila* vol. 50 (1974), pp. 49–65. Discusses the complex and contradictory narrative presentation of Rosalía. 'Galdós's Use of Time in *La de Bringas*', *Anales Galdosianos* vol. 15 (1980), pp. 83–88. Explains the historical significance of the time frame in which the novel develops.

Miller, Stephen, '*La de Bringas* as *Bildungsroman*: A Feminist Reading', *Romance Quarterly* vol. 34.2 (1987), pp. 189–99. Defends Rosalía from numerous critical attacks.

Ramírez, Arthur, 'The Heraldic Emblematic Image in Galdós *La de Bringas*', *Revista de Estudios Hispánicos* vol. 14.1 (1980), pp. 65–74. Explanation of various levels of meaning of the hair picture.

Round, Nicholas G., 'Rosalía Bringas's Children', *Anales Galdosianos* vol. 6 (1671), pp. 43–50. On ironic doubling in the family milieu.

Smith, Paul Julian, *The Body Hispanic: Gender and Sexuality in Spanish and Spanish American Literature* (Oxford: Clarendon Press, 1992), pp. 69–82. Lacanian reading of Rosalía's desire for clothes.

Tsuchiya, Akiko, 'The Construction of the Female Body in Galdós's *La de Bringas*', *Romance Quarterly* vol. 40.1 (1993), 35–47. Poststructuralist analysis of the representation of female desire and sexuality in the novel.

Willem, Linda M., 'The Narrative Voice Presentation of Rosalía de Bringas in Two Galdosian Novels', *Crítica Hispánica* vol. 12.1–2 (1990), 75–87. Shows how adverse reaction to Rosalía stems mainly from her presentation in *Torment*.

Wright, Chad C., 'Images of Light and Dark in *La de Bringas*', *Anales Galdosianos* vol. 13 (1978), pp. 5–12. Interprets the historical and social significance of light imagery in the novel.

TEXT SUMMARY

Chapter 1
Description of the completed hair picture.

Chapter 2
Francisco Bringas decides to make the hair picture as a thank-you present for the Pez family.

Chapter 3
Francisco calculates costs and materials and sets to work on hair picture in March 1868. We learn of his prior appointment as a Palace official in February.

Chapter 4
The narrator and Manuel Pez go to visit the Bringas family but get lost in the labyrinthine Palace. They are rescued by Cándida, Condesa de García Grande.

Chapter 5
Description of Cándida's declining fortunes, and of the Bringas apartment.

Chapter 6
The narrator explains he first visited Francisco to seek protection from a threatened lawsuit. Comic description of Cándida and Colonel Minio.

Chapter 7
Description of Tula, widow of Colonel Minio, and of her sister Milagros, Marquesa de Tellería, and her children.

Chapter 8
People gather in the Palace to watch the Maundy Thursday celebration of the Paupers' Feast, served by the monarchs. Isabel Bringas subsequently has an attack of nightmares and vomiting.

Chapter 9
Explanation of Milagros's power over Rosalía, who has been seduced into a taste for luxury clothes by her wealthy relative Agustín Caballero's gifts.

Chapter 10
Rosalía and Milagros discuss fashions and work on an outfit. Rosalía is irresistibly attracted by a shawl in Sobrino Brothers.

Chapter 11
She buys on credit for the first time, and lies to Francisco about having been given the shawl by the Queen. In early May, she receives the bill and borrows from the moneylender Gonzalo Torres to pay it off. She is persuaded to lend Milagros some of the borrowed money, and decides to pay only half of her debt at Sobrino Brothers for the time being, meanwhile spending even more money on fripperies.

Chapter 12
Introduction to the attractive but hollow and pompous Manuel Pez.

Chapter 13
Francisco is now spending all his spare time on the hair work, and Pez begins to accompany Rosalía on their daily walks, during which he complains to her about his wife.

Chapter 14
Rosalía hypocritically complains about Milagros's spendthrift ways to Francisco, who has fallen asleep.

Chapter 15
Francisco discovers Rosalía working on all the new materials she has bought without his knowledge. She invents a lie to placate him, hoping that he will accept the offer of a provincial governorship and leave her in Madrid to her own devices.

Chapter 16
She prepares more elaborate lies so as to be able to wear the clothes she is making. In May, she starts going to the Retiro Park every morning with Isabel and Alfonso, accompanied by Manuel Pez, to whom she begins to complain of Francisco's meanness.

Chapter 17
Rosalía secretly wishes she were married to Pez and despises her husband's lack of ambition. Bringas makes good progress on the hair work but begins to notice eye problems. On 12 June, Torres reminds Rosalía his loan is due back in two days.

Chapter 18
Rosalía, in desperation, seeks out Cándida and Milagros, both of whom owe her money. Milagros is in church all day, but when they meet it transpires she has even greater debts to pay than Rosalía.

Chapter 19
Cándida appears, pretending to have money, but only as a ruse to borrow money herself. Milagros leaves and a loud crash is heard.

Chapter 20
Francisco has gone blind. Cándida goes for the doctor.

Chapter 21
Rosalía realises that since Francisco cannot see, she can pawn the silver candlesticks and her diamond earrings to pay off Torres and Sobrino Brothers.

Chapter 22
Francisco begins improving slowly and renews his tyrannical hold over the family budget. He lifts his black eye-bandage and sees Rosalía wearing a new silk robe.

Chapter 23
Rosalía rushes out to change into old clothes. Milagros, who had temporarily solved her own financial problems via a mysterious short-term loan, is once again in need.

Chapter 24
Milagros begs Rosalía to ask Francisco for a loan.

Chapter 25
Manuel Pez keeps Francisco company by talking of politics and the possibility of a revolution. He flirst with Rosalía in private.

Chapter 26
Francisco lectures Rosalía on the need to economise. They receive a visit from a former poor relation, Refugio Sánchez Emperador, to whom Rosalía is initially rude until she notices the woman's elegant outfit.

Chapter 27
Rosalía and Francisco decide that Refugio's sister Amparo Sánchez Emperador must still be living in sin with their cousin Augustín Caballero. The narrator attends one of Tula's tea parties.

Chapter 28
Francisco temporarily regains his sight. Manuel Pez continues his flirtation with Rosalía.

Chapter 29
Rosalía worries about how to replace the objects she pawned before Francisco notices their absence.

Chapter 30
Milagros's financial needs become more pressing by 7 July. The generals conspiring against the Queen are arrested. Manuel offers to lend Rosalía money. The famed Dr Golfín is brought in to treat Francisco's eyes.

Chapter 31
Rosalía reflects on her marriage. Francisco hands over his savings box to her to administer. Milagros asks her for a loan.

Chapter 32
Rosalía lends five thousand reals to Milagros. Francisco begins to worry about the bill from Dr Golfín.

Chapter 33
Francisco becomes increasingly authoritarian. Rosalía secretly insults him and plans how to emancipate herself. Francisco asks for his saving box but does not count the missing notes.

Chapter 34
Rosalía makes imitation bank notes to deceive Francisco. Isabel has another attack of nightmares.

Chapter 35
In mid-July, Francisco's sight is pronounced cured. Milagros pays half of what she owes Rosalía. Pez tries unsuccessfully to seduce Rosalía.

Chapter 36
Rosalía's resistance analysed. Pez describes how he and others defy the Customs laws when crossing the border between France and Spain. Milagros leaves on holiday without paying the remainder of her debt to Rosalía.

Chapter 37
Rosalía seeks out the infamous moneylender Torquemada to borrow enough to replace what she has taken from the savings box. Golfín sends them an eight-thousand real bill for his services.

Chapter 38
Description of the family bathing excursions to the Manzanares river and of the heat and boredom in Madrid in August.

Chapter 39
Rosalía and Francisco receive an invitation to spend a free holiday in Arcachon with Amparo Sánchez Emperador and Agustín Caballero,

and debate whether they can accept. Francisco decides they should not
go and Rosalía is secretly resentful.

Chapter 40
Description of Alfonso's love of moving things and Isabel's mania for
collecting.

Chapter 41
August is drawing to a close and Rosalía must pay Torquemada. She
wonders why she had not accepted money from admirers in the past.

Chapter 42
Rosalía succeeds in delaying payment of her loan until 9 September.
She waits anxiously for Pez to return.

Chapter 43
Pez returns from his summer holiday but treats her coolly. Rosalía
manages to arrange a secret rendezvous with him.

Chapter 44
Rosalía reflects bitterly that she has given herself to Pez for free; he
writes the following day refusing her request for money.

Chapter 45
Rosalía visits Refugio to ask for money. Description of Refugio's
apartment.

Chapter 46
Refugio admits she has money but claims she cannot spare it. Lectures
Rosalía on high-society hypocrisy.

Chapter 47
Rosalía helps dress Refugio.

Chapter 48
Refugio gives her the money but reveals Milagros's betrayal. Rosalía
pays off Torquemada and resolves only to aim for the wealthiest lovers
in future.

Chapter 49
Revolution breaks out. The Bringas family wait with bated breath for
the Palace to be sacked by the mob, but nothing happens.

Chapter 50
The revolution is effected peacefully. The narrator becomes the custo-
dian of the former Royal Palace. The Bringas family moves out. The
narrator reveals his former relationship with Rosalía.